William Sydney Thayer

Lectures on the malarial fevers

William Sydney Thayer

Lectures on the malarial fevers

ISBN/EAN: 9783337414467

Printed in Europe, USA, Canada, Australia, Japan

Cover: Foto ©Lupo / pixelio.de

More available books at **www.hansebooks.com**

LECTURES ON THE
MALARIAL FEVERS

BY

WILLIAM SYDNEY THAYER, M. D.

ASSOCIATE PROFESSOR OF MEDICINE IN THE
JOHNS HOPKINS UNIVERSITY

NEW YORK
D. APPLETON AND COMPANY
1897

TO

WILLIAM OSLER

THESE PAGES ARE GRATEFULLY

AND AFFECTIONATELY

DEDICATED.

CONTENTS.

LECTURE I.
Introductory remarks.—A brief history of the development of our knowledge concerning the pathogenic agent of the malarial fevers ... 1

LECTURE II.
Methods of examination of the blood.—Description of the hæmocytozoa of malaria ... 34

LECTURE III.
Description of the hæmocytozoa of malaria (*continued*).—General conditions under which the malarial fevers prevail ... 70

LECTURE IV.
Clinical description of the malarial fevers.—Types of fever.—Period of incubation.—1. The regularly intermittent fevers: (*a*) tertian fever; (*b*) quartan fever. 2. Æstivo-autumnal fevers ... 97

LECTURE V.
Clinical description of the malarial fevers (*continued*).—Pernicious fevers.—Fevers with long intervals.—Combined infections.—Masked malarial infections.—The urine in malarial fever ... 145

LECTURE VI.
Sequelæ and complications ... 183

LECTURE VII.
Morbid anatomy.—Anatomical changes occurring in acute malarial infections.—Anatomical changes following repeated or chronic infections.—Cirrhotic processes and malaria.—Malarial pigment ... 211

LECTURE VIII.

General pathology.—General pathology of the main symptoms of malarial fever.—Infection with multiple groups of parasites.—Mechanism of defence.—Phagocytosis.—Spontaneous recovery . 245

LECTURE IX.

Diagnosis.—Prognosis.—Treatment.—Prophylaxis 272

LIST OF ILLUSTRATIVE CHARTS.

CHART	PAGE
I.—Tertian Fever—Single Infection	110
II.—Quotidian Fever—Double Tertian Infection	114, 115
III.—Tertian and Quotidian Fever—Double Tertian Infection	Facing 116
IV.—Quotidian Fever—Double Tertian Infection	117
V.—Quotidian Fever—Double Tertian Infection	118
VI.—Continued Fever due to Infection with Tertian Parasites	120, 121
VII.—Quartan Fever	123
VIII.—Double Quartan Fever	126
IX.—Quotidian Fever—Triple Quartan Infection	128
X.—Æstivo-autumnal Fever—Quotidian Paroxysms	131
XI.—Æstivo-autumnal Fever	133
XII.—Æstivo-autumnal Fever	135
XIII.—Æstivo-autumnal Fever	137
XIV.—Æstivo-autumnal Fever	138, 139
XV.—Æstivo-autumnal Infection—Remittent Fever	142, 143
XVI.—Æstivo-autumnal Fever—Remittent Fever—"Subcontinua Typhoidea"	Facing 144
XVII.—Quotidian and Tertian Fever—Double Tertian Infection	Facing 171
XVIII.—Intermittent Fever—Gonorrhœal Endocarditis	273
XIX.—Influenza	275

PLATE	
I.—The Parasite of Tertian Fever	Facing 313
II.—The Parasite of Quartan Fever	Facing 314
III.—The Parasite of Æstivo-autumnal Fever	Facing 314

" Sono già molti anni ch' io porto opinione che le febbri intermittenti vengono prodotte da parasiti che ne rinnovano l'accesso all' atto della loro riproduzione, la quale succede più o meno presto secondo le diverse loro specie."

Rasori *(1766-1837); conversation with Bassi.*

LECTURES ON THE MALARIAL FEVERS.

LECTURE I.

Introductory remarks.—A brief history of the development of our knowledge concerning the pathogenic agent of the malarial fevers.

In the following lectures I shall endeavor to place before you a summary of the present status of our knowledge concerning the malarial fevers. There are few diseases toward the comprehension of which greater advances have been made within the last fifteen or sixteen years, and yet it is surprising how slow the general medical public has been in appreciating the true significance and value of the results which have followed Laveran's discovery of the malarial parasite.

Much of the work of recent years has gone to confirm the accurate observations of such men as Morton, Sydenham, Lancisi, and Torti. But since the clear descriptions of some of these early observers the term "malaria" has come to be applied in so loose a manner to so great a variety of different pathological conditions that it has been difficult for many physicians to realize that malarial fever is in fact a disease as sharply defined and as easily recognizable as pneumonia, pulmonary tuberculosis, or diphtheria.

It is high time, however, that these facts should be understood and appreciated by all intelligent medical men, and I trust that in the following remarks I may succeed in convincing you of the satisfactory basis on which these assertions are made.

The malarial fevers have been described from the earliest times. They were, however, throughout the older writings, included without distinction among various other febrile processes, more especially typhus, typhoid, and relapsing fevers, and the different septic infections. It was not until some years after the introduction of quinine that Torti * succeeded in distinguishing among these fevers a special class which yielded to this drug. To the fevers yielding to quinine—fevers mainly characterized by their intermittence and more or less regular periodicity—the term "malarial" came to be applied.

The anatomical distinction between malarial and typhoid fevers in particular—two diseases which are so frequently confounded—became definitely established early in this century through the discovery of the intestinal lesions in typhoid, and by the recognition of the association of melanosis of the organs with malarial fever.

Clinically, the distinction of the malarial fevers from those of other nature by the so-called therapeutic test is, as we shall see from further consideration of the process, in the main reliable.

To-day, however, in the light of our present knowledge, we are able to distinguish the malarial infections from other febrile processes, however similar their clinical manifestations may be, not only by their behavior under treatment with quinine, but also by the presence in the blood of the specific parasites discovered in 1880 by Laveran.

---

* Therapeut. spec., etc., 4to, Mutinæ, 1712.

Despite this fact, it is a melancholy truth that a large body of medical men in this country have scarcely passed beyond the limits reached by Hippocrates in their clinical appreciation of the continued fevers. The term "malaria" is used very commonly to describe any continued or irregular fever the nature of which is not wholly clear. And the term is applied indiscriminately not only to fevers but also to a variety of non-febrile conditions, most of which have no relation to true malarial infection.

This fact has greatly impaired the value of our statistics with regard to the continued fevers. A glance at the vital statistics of a few of the larger Eastern cities reveals a state of affairs which is little less than appalling.

Thus in New York city during the six years ending in 1890 the statistics show:

Deaths from malarial fever 2,060, or 24·62 per 100,000 of average population.

Deaths from typhoid fever 2,031, or 24·27 per 100,000 of average population.

In Brooklyn for the same period of time there were:

Deaths from malarial fever 1,413, or 32·62 per 100,000 of average population.

Deaths from typhoid fever 1,002, or 23·13 per 100,000 of average population.

During the same years there were reported in Baltimore:

Deaths from malarial fever 934, or 41·51 per 100,000 of average population.

Deaths from typhoid fever 904, or 40·17 per 100,000 of average population.

It may be stated with certainty that these statistics are almost absolutely incorrect.

Let us consider for a moment the condition of affairs in Baltimore. During a period of somewhat over seven years since the opening of the Johns Hopkins Hospital, two of the years being included among those during which the above-named census statistics were compiled, there were:

Deaths from typhoid fever, 48.
Deaths from malarial fever, 3.

In other words, there was, in the hospital, a proportion of sixteen deaths from typhoid to every one of malarial fever, while outside the deaths reported from malarial fever were in excess, the proportion being as 1·01 is to 1. It is probably safe to say that 90 per cent at least of these deaths reported as from malarial fever were due to some other cause—in most instances, probably, typhoid. If this be true of Baltimore, which is situated in a malarious region where relatively severe infections are not altogether uncommon, what must we think of the condition of things in Brooklyn, for example, where only the milder forms of malaria prevail, the few fatal cases representing probably the occasional instances of pernicious fever brought from Panama and the tropics by incoming steamers?

The term "malaria," as it is now used, is unscientific and inexact, and leads to much confusion. Used, however, properly, and better in a qualifying sense (as "the malarial fevers"), it distinguishes a class of fevers due to a specific micro-organism, fevers which yield, always, to treatment by quinine; to this class of diseases alone may the term be properly applied.

We have in this country been lamentably backward in fully appreciating the clinical value of the advances in our knowledge concerning this disease, which have followed Laveran's discovery of the parasite sixteen years ago.

THE PATHOGENIC AGENT OF THE MALARIAL FEVERS.

The idea that the malarial fevers are of parasitic origin is very old. Varro (B. C. 118-29)* says: "Advertendum etiam si qua erunt loca palustria et propter easdem causas, et quod arescunt, crescunt animalia quædam minuta, quæ non possunt oculi consequi, et per aëra intus in corpus per os, ac nares perveniunt, atque efficiunt difficiles morbos." Morton,† in the seventeenth century, maintained that the disease was engendered by marsh air. This air, charged with heterogeneous poisonous particles, and the autumn season with cold mornings and evenings, were, according to him, the causes of the malarial infection.

This theory was accepted in 1716 by Lancisi,‡ and afterward by Rasori and a number of other observers.

Lancisi believed that the disease was due to animalcula arising from putrefactive processes in the vegetable matter of swampy districts; these were inhaled and capable of entering the blood and multiplying there, thus giving rise to the pathological symptoms. This theory had many adherents; indeed, at the beginning of this century the idea had become so generally implanted in the public mind that the supposititious animalcula had become known in Italy by the definite name of "serafici."

Bassi # reports that Rasori in a conversation expressed, himself as follows: "For many years I have held the opinion that the intermittent fevers are produced by parasites which

---

* De Rê Rustica, lib. i, cap. 12.
† Pyretologia opera medica, 4to, Genevæ, 1696.
‡ De noxiis paludum effluviis, lib. ii, Roma, 1717.
# Discorsi sulla Natura e Cura della Pellagra, etc., Milano, tip. chiusi, 1846. Referred to by S. Calandruccio, "Agostino Bassi di Lodi, il fondatore della teoria parasitaria, etc.," Catania, 1892, 70.

renew the paroxysm by the act of their reproduction, which occurs more or less rapidly according to the variety of their species."

Virey believed the disease to be due to infection with infusoria. Boudin * believed that the fever was caused by the inhalation of poisonous volatile principles given off by certain plants which grow in the marshes.

In 1849 J. K. Mitchell,† of Philadelphia, suggested that the disease was due to spores which were found in large numbers in marshy districts. The same idea was held by Muehry.‡

Lemaire # studied the vapor collected just above the surface of the marshes in Sologne, a malarious district. Finding that the air here contained a marked excess of micro-organisms of various sorts as compared with that in a neighboring healthy district, he inclined to the view that these lower organisms had a close causal connection with malarial fever.

Bouchardat∥ believed that the process resulted from the inhalation of poisons produced by microscopical animalcula which flourished in the swamps.

Later, in 1866, Salisbury ▲ described small vegetable cells of the family of *Palmella*, which he asserted he found in the urine and sweat of patients with malarial fever. These he believed to be the pathogenic agent. His communications excited considerable interest and attention; indeed, there are

---

* Traité des fièvres intermittentes, etc., Paris, 1842.
† On the Cryptogamous Origin of Malarious and Epidemic Fevers, Philadelphia, 1849.
‡ Die geographischen Verhältnisse der Krankheiten, etc., Leipzig and Heidelberg; 1856, pp. 124 *et seq.*
# Compt. rend. de l'Acad. des sc., sé. du 17 août, 1864, xlix, p. 317.
∥ Annuaire de thérapeutique, 1866, p. 299.
▲ Amer. Jour. Med. Sci., January, 1866.

observers to-day who with singular blindness still cling to the wholly groundless supposition of Salisbury. His views were satisfactorily controverted by Wood * in 1868.

Binz,† in 1867, noted that the efficacy in malarial fever of quinine which he had shown to be an active protoplasmic poison, pointed to the possibility that the disease was due to infection with lower organisms.

During the next ten years a considerable number of communications appeared in which various forms of vegetable life—mainly algæ—were regarded as the causal element of the malarial fevers.

Lanzi and Terrigi, in 1875, described bacteria which they believed to be the cause of the malarial infection.

It remained, however, for Klebs and Tomassi Crudeli,‡ in 1879, to first excite a world-wide interest and a really extensive belief in the bacterial origin of the malarial fevers. These observers found in the soil of malarious districts, certain bacilli which they cultivated and injected into animals, convincing themselves that they were able to reproduce the symptoms of malarial fever. Their researches were carried on with enthusiasm by Schiavuzzi and others, and despite the fact that practically all other careful observers have failed to demonstrate any conclusive connection between these bacilli and malarial fever, the general belief in the validity of the conclusions of Klebs and Tomassi Crudeli was so strong, that within twelve months of the time of writing, an editorial article appeared in one of the leading English medical journals referring to the connection between the bacillus of

---

* Amer. Jour. Med. Sci., 1868, vol. lvi, p. 333.

† (a) Centralbl. f. d. med. Wiss., Berlin, 1867, S. 308; (b) M. Schultze's Archiv f. mikr. Anat., Bd. iii, S. 383, 1867.

‡ Studien über die Ursache des Wechselfiebers und über die Natur der Malaria, Arch. f. exp. Path. u. Pharmak., 1879, xi, 311.

Klebs and Tomassi Crudeli and the malarial fevers as a settled fact. Let it be enough, however, to say that repeated researches in this line have clearly demonstrated the fallacy of the original ideas of these observers.

The parasite which is now generally recognized as the cause of the malarial fevers is not a bacterium, but belongs to the protozoa, and more closely to the class of sporozoa. Its further classification is not definitely settled; some of the theories concerning this question will be referred to later. These organisms live in the blood of the infected individual, attacking the red corpuscles, developing in their interior, accumulating dark pigment granules derived from the altered hæmoglobin, and eventually destroying the red elements, from the surrounding shell of which they burst at the time of their sporulation.

The parasites were discovered in 1880 by A. Laveran, a French army surgeon, who was pursuing a systematic study of the malarial fevers at his post at Constantine, in Algeria.

As is so frequently the case in scientific discoveries, these bodies had been frequently seen, and indeed described, years before they were recognized as parasites by Laveran. Thus, Meckel * in 1847, not only described pigment in the blood of a patient dead of malarial fever, but noted further that it was contained for the most part in round, ovoid, or spindle-shaped protoplasmic masses, which were, beyond a doubt, the malarial parasites.

In the following year Virchow † described and clearly pictured certain forms of the malarial organisms; it must be said, however, that the parasitic nature of these bodies appears never to have been suspected.

---

* Zeitschrift für Psychiatrie, 1847, 198.
† Virchow's Archiv, 1849, ii, 587.

It remained for Laveran to recognize the fact that these pigmented elements represented living parasites. This observer was stationed in 1879 in Algeria, where he took upon himself the task of investigating the malarial fevers. In November, 1880, while studying the blood of a patient suffering from malarial infection, his attention was attracted by one of these pigmented bodies from which there extended several actively motile filaments. The dancing of the pigment granules within and the active serpentine motion of the filaments were so striking as to convince the observer immediately that he was looking upon an animate object. In the same month a preliminary communication was made to the Academy of Medicine in Paris;* this was rapidly followed by a number of other communications.

In 1881 Laveran published a small monograph † in which he described his observations at length. The bodies which he had noted were small, colorless, pigment-containing elements varying in size from one sixth that of a red blood-corpuscle to nearly an equal volume. The smallest contained but one or two fine, dark bits of pigment, while the larger, which were at times nearly the size of a leucocyte, contained numerous actively motile granules. These bodies he believed to be attached to the red corpuscle, at the expense of which they grew and accumulated pigment.

He also noted larger bodies, crescentic or ovoid in form, eight or nine micromillimetres in length by three micromillimetres in diameter, which were quite transparent and colorless, excepting for a group of rounded pigment granules lying near the middle, or more rarely collected toward one end of the body. Sometimes the granules were arranged in

---

* Bull. de l'acad. de méd. de Paris, sé. du 23 Nov., 1880.
† Nature parasitaire des accidents de l'impaludisme, etc., 8vo, Paris, 1881.

the shape of a crown or wreath. At times the extremities of the crescentic bodies were connected by a pale curved line.

He noted, further, circular bodies about six micromillimetres in diameter with a collection of rounded pigment granules in the middle arranged in the form of a ring or wreath. At times these bodies might be seen to become extremely active, suddenly developing from three to four fine filaments with active serpentine motion, stretching out from the periphery. According to Laveran these pigmented bodies represent different stages in the existence of the parasite, the earlier forms being small cyst-like structures within which are contained the motile filaments which represent the organism at the stage of most perfect development.

These observations were confirmed by another French army surgeon, Richard,* studying at Philippeville, in Algeria. He went a little further than Laveran in that he recognized the youngest form of the parasite as a small, clear, non-pigmented spot in the corpuscle, and, moreover, in that he described round forms of the parasite in which the pigment had collected toward the middle into a single clump, from which delicate radial striations might be seen extending outward. In a second publication † he differed from Laveran in asserting that the parasite develops within rather than upon the red corpuscle.

During the first four years after Laveran's discovery the public remained almost entirely unconvinced, much more credence being given to the work of Klebs and Tomassi Crudeli, which has been referred to above.

In the meantime Marchiafava and Celli, studying in Italy,

---

* Compt. rend. des sć. de l'Acad. des sciences, 20 fév., 1882 ; also Gaz. méd. de Par., 1882, 6 s., iv. 252.

† Rev. scientifique, Par., 1883, 113.

had observed and pictured the parasites, believing them to represent areas of degeneration within the red cells; it is, moreover, interesting to note that, despite the fact that Laveran visited Rome and demonstrated the parasite to one of these observers, they remained unconvinced until they themselves began the study of fresh specimens.

In 1885, however, Marchiafava and Celli * began a series of most fruitful and valuable contributions upon this subject. They described with great accuracy the small, non-pigmented forms of the parasite. They noted that these forms, which were especially frequent in the more severe Roman fevers, were actively amœboid when observed in the fresh blood.

They proposed for the organism the unfortunately chosen term "plasmodium malariæ." Biologically, the term plasmodium has a perfectly well-recognized meaning; it is applied to large multinuclear masses of protoplasm. Such a structure is wholly different from the small hyaline amœba of malaria, and the use of the term as applied to the latter body is injudicious and misleading. It is most desirable that this term, which is not yet too deeply implanted in medical usage, should be eradicated.

Since 1885 all students who have had a proper opportunity to investigate malarial blood have confirmed the observations of Laveran in the main, and the diagnostic importance

---

* (a) Arch. per le sc. med., 1885, ix, No. 15; also, Fortschritte der Med., 1885, iii, No. 11, 14. (b) Fortschritte der Med., 1885, iii, No. 24, 787; also, Arch. per le sc. med., 1886; also, Arch. Ital. de Biol., 1887. (c) Bull. d. R. acc. med. d. Rom., 1887, 417. (d) Arch. per le sc. med., 1888, xii, 153: also, Arch. Ital. de Biol., 1888 A., ix, f. 3. (e) Fortschr. der Med., 1888, No. 16. (f) Arch. per le sc. med., 1890, xiv; also, Arch. Ital. de Biol., 1890, 302. (g) Bull. d. R. acc. med. d. Rom., anno xvi, 1890, 287. (h) Arch. per le sc. med., xiv, 1890, 449. (i) Bull. d. R. acc. med. d. Rom., 1889-'90, f. ii. (j) Festschrift z. R. Virchow's 70. Geburtstag, iii, 1891.

of the discovery of the parasite in the circulating blood is now generally recognized.

In this country the earliest observations confirming those of the French students were made by Councilman and Abbott,[*] Sternberg,[†] Osler,[‡] and James,[#] while valuable work has been done later by Dock,[||] and others.

In 1885, Golgi, of Pavia, made a great advance in the study of the malarial parasite by his investigations into the life history of the organisms observed in quartan fever.[▲] His studies led him to the conclusion that quartan fever depends upon a specific form of the parasite. The organism in its youngest stages is represented by a small, clear, hyaline body which lies *within*, and not, as Laveran had originally supposed, *upon* the red corpuscle. Within this corpuscle it grows, developing pigment granules at the expense of its host, which it gradually destroys.

At the end of the cycle of existence the pigment granules collect toward the centre into a little clump or block, while delicate radial striations extend from this toward the periphery, forming a figure exactly similar to that described by Richard in 1882. These radial lines are but indications of fissures which later on appear in the substance of the parasite, until finally the central pigment block is surrounded by from six to twelve delicate leaflets, forming a Marguerite-like figure.

---

[*] (a) Amer. Jour. Med. Sci., April, 1885, n. s., vol. lxxxix, 416. (b) Transact. of the Assoc. of Amer. Phys., 1886, i, 90. (c) Med. News, Phil., 1887, i, 59-63. (d) Fortschr. der Med., 1888, Nos. 12 and 13, 449, 500.

[†] Medical Record, N. Y., May 1 and 8, 1886, 489, 517.

[‡] (a) Phil. Med. Times, 1886; also, British Med. Journal, 1887, i, 556. (b) Medical News, Phil., April 13 and 20, 1889. (c) Johns Hopkins Hosp. Bull., 1889, i, 11.

[#] Medical Record, N. Y., March 10, 1888, 269.

[||] (a) Medical News, July 19, 1890, 59. (b) Fortschr. der Med., 1891, ix, 187. (c) Med. News, May 30 and June 6, 1891, 602, 628.

[▲] Arch. per le sc. med., x, 1886, 109; also, Arch. Ital. de Biol., viii, 1887.

Eventually these separate leaflets spring away from the central pigment collection and assume a round or ovoid shape, resembling in every way the small hyaline bodies which at the same time may be observed within other red cells.

Golgi thus confirmed a suspicion which had been previously expressed by Marchiafava and Celli that these Marguerite-like bodies represent parasites in the process of reproduction. These investigations demonstrated clearly that the quartan parasites present in the blood are aggregated into enormous groups, all the members of which are approximately at the same stage of development and pass through their cycle of existence simultaneously. The length of this cycle of existence is, in the quartan parasite, approximately seventy-two hours, so that in infections with a single group of organisms sporulation occurs every fourth day.

By carefully comparing the stage of existence of the organisms in the circulation with the clinical manifestations, Golgi discovered the remarkable fact that *the malarial paroxysm always coincides with the sporulation of a group of parasites.* Thus, in infections with a single group of the quartan organism a paroxysm occurs every fourth day.

In his first publication, however, Golgi pointed out the fact that a group of parasites must first attain a certain size before it is capable of producing a paroxysm, and in a similar manner the severity of the paroxysm depends within certain limits upon the number of parasites present in the blood.

It was also noted that often more than one group of the parasites may be present at the same time in the circulating blood. When this is the case the several groups reach maturity almost invariably on successive days; thus, if two groups be present, segmentation occurs on two successive days, with a day of intermission between; when three groups are present, segmentation occurs daily.

This observation was partially confirmed within a few months by Osler * in Philadelphia.

In his earliest communication upon the quartan parasite Golgi mentioned the fact that in several cases of tertian fever he had observed organisms with certain characteristic deviations from the type already described; this observation led him to suggest that possibly further study might show that tertian fever depended upon a different variety of parasite. He also noted that in none of these cases of quartan or tertian fever had he seen the crescentic bodies described by Laveran; they were present, however, in one case of more or less irregular fever.

This was shortly followed by an equally remarkable series of observations upon the blood in tertian fever,† resulting in the demonstration of a second variety of the parasite, morphologically and biologically distinctly separate from the quartan organism. This parasite also exists in the blood in enormous groups, all the members of which are nearly at the same stage of development; here, however, the cycle of existence lasts approximately forty-eight instead of seventy-two hours. In tertian as in quartan infections, more than one group of the organism may be present, though more than two groups are rarely seen. When two groups are present sporulation occurs daily.

These observations have been almost universally confirmed. Among the more important communications are

---

* Phil. Med. Times, 1886.

† (a) Boll. med.-chirurg. di Pavia, 1886; also, Gaz. d. osp., 1886, No. 53, 419. (b) Arch. per le sc. med., 1889, xiii, 173; also, Fortschritte der Med., 1889, vii, 81; also, Arch. ltal. de Biol., 1890, xiv, f. i, ii.

those of Grassi and Feletti * in Sicily; Antolisei,† Canalis,‡ Bastianelli and Bignami,# Patella,∥ Marchiafava and Celli,▲ Terni and Giardina, ◊ in Italy; of Mannaberg, ‡ in Austria; of Kamen, ‡ in Germany; of Sakharov, ‡ Titov,** Romanovsky, †† Korolko ‡‡ and Gotye,## in Russia; of Remouchamps, ∥∥ in Holland; of Jancsó and Rosenberger,▲▲ in Hungary; of Osler, ◊◊ Dock, ‡‡ Koplik, ‡‡ Hewetson, and the author, ‡‡ in this country.

Further studies, however, have revealed yet another dis-

---

* (a) Centralbl. f. Bakt., 1890, vii, 396, 430; also, Riforma medica, 1890, No. 11, 62, and No. 50, 296; also, Arch. Ital. de Biol., 1890, 287-293. (b) Centralbl. f. Bakt., 1891, ix, 403, 429, 461. (c) Centralbl. f. Bakt., 1891, x, No. 14, 448. (d) Arch. Ital. di clin. med., Milano, 1894, xxxiii, 207-265.

† (a) Riforma medica, 1890, Nos. 12 and 13, pp. 68, 74. (b) Riforma medica, 1890, Nos. 26 and 27, Feb. 1 and 3, 152, 158.

‡ Arch. per le sc. med., 1890, xiv, f. 1, No. 5, 73; also Fortschritte der Med., 1890, Nos. 8 and 9; also, Arch. Ital. de Biol., 1890, xiii, 262.

Riforma medica, 1890, Nos. 144-146, pp. 860, 866, 872.

∥ Atti e rendiconti della acc. med.-chirurg. di Perugia, ii, 1890, 85.

▲ Bull. d. R. acc. med. di Roma, xvi, May 4, 1890, 287.

◊ Arch. Ital. de Biol., 1891, 157.

‡ Die Malaria Parasiten, Wien, 1893, 8vo; also (English translation), The New Sydenham Society, vol. cl, London, 1894.

‡ (a) Beiträge z. path. Anat., etc., Jena, 1892, xi, H. 3, 375. (b) Beiträge z. path. Anat., etc., Jena, 1892, xii, 57-64.

‡ Acts of the Imp. Acad. of Med. of the Caucasus, Tiflis, 1890, No. 50 (Russian); (ref.) Centralbl. f. Bakt., etc., 1890, ix, 16.

** Cent. f. Bakt., 1891, ix, 284.

†† St. Petersburger med. Woch., 1891, Nos. 34 and 35.

‡‡ Vrach, 1891, No. 46 (Russian): ref. in Centr. f. Bakt., 1892, xi, 512.

O Parazitie Laveran'a, 8°, Moskva, 1896 (Russian).

∥∥ Weekblad van het med. Tijdschr. voor Geneesk., December 16, 1893, No. 24, 849.

▲▲ (a) Pest. med.-chir. Presse, 32. Jahr, March 1 and 8, 1896, Nos. 9 and 10. (b) Pest. med.-chir. Presse, 32. Jahr, No. 34, p. 794. (c) Deutsch. Arch. f. klin. Med., 1896, Bd. lvii, p. 449.

◊◊ Op. cit.

‡‡ Op. cit.

‡‡ New York Med. Jour., 1893., 315

‡‡ Johns Hopkins Hospital Reports, 1895, vol. v, p. 1.

tinct form of the malarial parasite. Golgi, in 1885,* called attention to the fact that in the blood of the one case of irregular fever which he examined there were found only the crescentic and ovoid bodies of Laveran, forms which were not present in any of his other cases. In view of this fact he suggested that these elements might represent a third type of the organism having a special cycle of existence differing from those already described. These organisms had also been described by both Laveran and Marchiafava and Celli, who found them with much greater frequency than did Golgi.

Marchiafava and Celli,† it will be remembered, found many cases in which the blood showed only small amœboid hyaline bodies—their "plasmodia." Laveran and the Italian observers had, however, been working in districts where, at the height of the malarial season, a large proportion of the cases are of a very severe, more or less irregular or continuous type, while Golgi, in Pavia, met only with the milder, regularly intermittent forms of the disease.

Thus it gradually became evident that there was a class of cases where the blood contained only the small hyaline amœboid bodies with perhaps a few fine granules of pigment, associated, often, with the large ovoid and crescentic bodies of Laveran, while in some cases only the latter forms were to be found.

Councilman,‡ in 1887, was the first to hint at the practical diagnostic value of this fact. He says: "The character of these bodies varies in different forms of the disease. Although they seem in rare cases to run into one another, still, in general, we can say that where the plasmodia inside the red corpuscles # are seen the patient has intermittent fever,

---
* *Op. cit.* † *Op. cit.* ‡ *Op. cit.*
\# He refers here to the large pigmented, probably tertian forms.—W. S. T.

and where the crescentic and elongated masses are found he has either some form of remittent fever or malarial cachexia. . . . We are not only enabled to diagnosticate the disease as such, but in most cases the particular form."

In 1889, on the basis of observations of several cases with irregular symptoms, Golgi suggested the association of these parasites with fevers with long intervals between the paroxysms. He believed that the cycle of development began with small hyaline bodies and passed through the crescentic and ovoid stages; its duration was unusually long—lasting ten days or more. He was, however, unable to trace the entire life history of the parasite, having never seen sporulating forms, and advanced this idea merely as an hypothesis.

In the fall of the same year, however, Marchiafava and Celli * and Canalis † almost simultaneously published articles describing the life history of the organism found in the severe æstivo-autumnal fevers of Rome. These fevers differ materially from the regularly intermittent tertian and quartan ague which, prevailing in the milder malarial districts, formed a great majority of all the cases which came under Golgi's eye. The regularly intermittent fevers pursue a characteristic cyclical course, are never pernicious, and yield rapidly to quinine, while the more severe æstivo-autumnal fevers of Rome are much more acyclical in their manifestations, tend frequently to become pernicious, and are more resistant to quinine.

---

* *Op. cit.*
† (*a*) Arch. per le sc. med., 1890, xiv, f. 1, No. 5, 73; also, Fortschr. d. Med., 1890, Nos. 8 and 9; also, Arch. Ital. de Biol., 1890, xiii, 262. (*b*) Lo Spallanzani, 1890, 172. (*c*) Arch. per le sc. med., 1890, f. 3, 333. (*d*) Intorno a recenti lavori sui parassiti della malaria, 8vo, Roma, 1890.

Both Canalis and Marchiafava and Celli noted a special variety of the organism differing distinctly from the tertian and quartan parasites, a variety which was apparently definitely associated with these æstivo-autumnal fevers. In many respects their descriptions are quite similar, and unquestionably relate to the same type of organisms which Golgi believed to be associated with fevers with long intervals.

They both believed that the parasites exist in the blood in groups, just as in tertian and quartan fever. They note that the forms most frequently found in the blood are small hyaline amœboid bodies which often tend to assume the shape of a ring, and rarely contain more than one or two minute pigment granules. In most instances, indeed, these parasites are quite free from pigment. During the cycle of development a few small granules appear, which eventually collect into the middle of the parasite as a very small group and finally fuse into a block. The body then undergoes segmentation much as does the tertian or quartan organism. The parasite of æstivo-autumnal fever is, however, much smaller, often less than half the size of the red corpuscle. Marchiafava and Celli in particular note the fact that many of the red corpuscles containing these small parasites become shrunken, crenated, and brassy colored.

Now in quartan fever all stages in the life history of the parasite are seen with equal frequency in the peripheral circulation, while in the majority of cases of tertian fever the same general rule holds, excepting that at the time of segmentation the bodies tend to accumulate in the internal organs. In infections with the æstivo-autumnal parasites, however, only the earlier stages of the cycle of existence of the organism are to be found in the peripheral vessels, while segmenting forms are rarely seen excepting in the blood of internal organs, the spleen, liver, bone marrow, brain.

Both these observers noted, in this type of fever, the presence of the crescentic and ovoid bodies originally described by Laveran, and recognized the fact that they develop from the small hyaline forms, both asserting that they do not appear until the clinical symptoms have lasted for some days or weeks. The interpretation of the significance of these bodies offered by Canalis and Marchiafava and Celli differs considerably.

Thus Canalis distinguishes two distinct cycles in the life history of the parasite:

(1) A more rapid cycle similar to that above described, and lasting, he believes, not less than two days on the average, though it may be as short as twenty-four hours.

(2) A slower cycle associated with the development of crescentic bodies, in which he believes he has made out segmenting forms; an observation which, however, few succeeding students have been able to confirm. This cycle lasts a much longer time, varying, he believes, in different cases. The period elapsing from the beginning of the amoeboid stage to the appearance of the crescents is not less than three or four days.

Marchiafava and Celli, on the other hand, considered that the cycle of existence of the parasite from the youngest forms to the segmenting bodies lasted a varying length of time between twenty-four and thirty-six hours. In some instances, with very rapid development, the parasite undergoes early segmentation before the accumulation of any pigment. They have never observed evidences of segmentation in the crescentic bodies.

A large number of confirmatory observations have been

made, the more important communications coming from Antolisei and Angelini,* Patella,† Terni and Giardina,‡ Bastianelli and Bignami,# Sanfelici,∥ in Italy; Grassi and Feletti,△ in Sicily; Sakharov,◊ Korolko,‡ Titov,‡ and Gotye,‡ in Russia; Mannaberg,** in Austria; Plehn †† and Kamen,‡‡ in Germany; Dock,## Koplik,∥∥ Hewetson, and myself,△△ in the United States.

The main point of difference has been in the interpretation of the crescentic and ovoid bodies. It is generally acknowledged that these arise for the most part in the internal organs, particularly in the spleen and bone marrow, and may appear in the blood from the fifth day on, but usually not before the end of the first or the beginning of the second week. It has been noted that while all other forms of the organism disappear rapidly under treatment by quinine, the crescents alone are very resistant, remaining in the circulation in some instances for months.

Antolisei and Angelini, Terni,◊◊ Grassi and Feletti, and Sakharov agree with Canalis in believing these bodies capable of segmentation, the latter two observers classifying them as a special variety of the parasite. The majority, however, assert that the crescents are incapable of proliferation by sporulation, and suspect that they are sterile bodies, some holding that they constitute a more resistant form of the

---

* (a) Arch. Ital. d. clin. med., 1890, 1. (b) Riforma medica, 1890, 320, 326, 332.
† Op. cit. ‡ Op. cit.
# Riforma medica, 1890, 1334, 1340.
∥ Fortschr. d. Med., 1891, ix, 499, 541, 581. △ Op. cit.
◊ (a) Op. cit. (b) Ann. de l'institute Pasteur, 1891, 445–449.
‡ Op. cit. ‡ Op. cit. ‡ Op. cit.
** Op. cit. †† Virch. Archiv, 1892, cxxix, 285. ‡‡ Op. cit.
Op. cit. ∥∥ Op. cit. △△ Op. cit.
◊◊ Gaz. d. osp., Milano, 1896, xvi, 3.

organism capable, perhaps, of further development outside of the body.

Marchiafava and Bignami * have gone further, distinguishing two varieties of the æstivo-autumnal parasite, one with a shorter cycle of existence, lasting about twenty-four hours, and another with a longer cycle, lasting about forty-eight hours. The general characteristics of the parasites are very similar; the main differences consist in the larger size of the tertian parasite, its slightly greater activity, and the fact that the number of segments is more abundant than in the quotidian organism. Both organisms develop crescentic forms after a certain length of time.

Golgi, in 1893,† studied the æstivo-autumnal parasites in Baccelli's clinic at Rome, and, while recognizing distinctly the association of a third variety of the organism with the more irregular æstivo-autumnal fevers, he believes that there are many points yet to be settled in relation to its life history, and that we are at present by no means justified in distinguishing two separate varieties.

It was early noted by Marchiafava and Celli and Canalis, as well as by subsequent observers, that only the early stages of the cycle of existence of the æstivo-autumnal parasite are found in the peripheral circulation; the later stages, and particularly the segmenting forms, are observed only in the internal organs.

Golgi goes further than this, asserting that in æstivo-autumnal fever the forms found in the peripheral circulation are practically accidental; that the main seat of the infection

---

* Bull. d. R. acc. med. d. Roma, xviii, f. v, 297: also (English translation, with notes and appendices by the authors), The New Sydenham Society, vol. cl, London, 1894.

† Arch. Ital. de Biol., 1893, xx, 288.

is in the internal organs. He advances the interesting theory that in the internal organs, more particularly in the spleen and bone marrow, the parasites may develop within the bodies of phagocytes. The youngest forms often cause a rapid necrosis of the red blood-corpuscle, which becomes brassy colored and shrunken, and is engulfed by the phagocyte; within this the parasite continues to develop, destroying eventually both its hosts, and escaping again after segmentation. A few of these young forms reach the general circulation in much the same manner as nucleated red corpuscles appear during active blood regeneration. They are an index, almost constant though "*non necessarie*," of the infection.

Golgi also hesitates to believe that the parasites of æstivo-autumnal fever are, with any regularity, arranged in groups; he maintains that organisms in all stages of development are usually present at one time.

Gotye also recognises but one variety of the æstivo-autumnal parasite, an organism possessing a cycle of development lasting about forty-eight hours.

Thus the majority of observers have distinguished sharply three main forms of the parasite:

(*a*) The parasite of tertian fever.

(*b*) The parasite of quartan fever.

(*c*) The parasite associated with the more irregular æstivo-autumnal fevers.

This third variety has been subdivided by numerous observers. Grassi and Feletti distinguish three separate parasites in this group:

(1) The *Hæmamœba præcox*, giving rise to quotidian fever with a tendency to anticipation.

(2) The *Hæmamœba immaculata*, which is similar to this

except that it runs its course more rapidly without the development of pigment.

(3) The *Laverania malariæ*. (The crescentic and ovoid forms.)

Sakharov distinguishes—

(1) The *Hæmamœba præcox* (Grassi).
(2) The *Laverania* (Grassi). These he believes to be separate organisms.

Marchiafava and Bignami distinguish—

(1) The quotidian parasite.
(2) The malignant tertian parasite.

Mannaberg subdivides this group into—

(1) The pigmented quotidian parasite.
(2) The unpigmented quotidian parasite.
(3) The malignant tertian parasite.

Hewetson and I have been inclined to regard all the æstivo-autumnal organisms as a single variety of the parasite, an organism whose cycle of development varies between twenty-four hours or less and forty-eight hours or more, according to various circumstances, depending partly on the organism, partly on the affected individual.

In a following lecture I shall enter more minutely into the characteristics of the forms of the parasite observed in this country.

While the great majority of observers have recognized the existence of these different types of parasites and their association each with special types of fever, it remains yet a wholly unsettled question whether they are varieties of one parasite, types which may be modified, perhaps, by external surroundings, or whether they represent separate and distinct species of closely allied organisms.

From our observations I can only say that while there are

facts which might suggest that the types of the organism are interchangeable, I have never seen the slightest actual evidence of such change.

It should be stated that Laveran is a vigorous opponent of the idea of the existence of more than one actual species of parasite; still more than this, he hesitates to accept the *regular* association of certain types of the organism with certain forms of fever, although in a recent paper * he says, "I do not dispute that this or that form of parasite is found more often in one clinical type than in another."

The Finer Structure of the Parasite.—Numerous researches concerning the staining reactions and the intimate structure of the malarial parasites have been made, but the results are, unfortunately, as yet rather indefinite.

Celli and Guarnieri,† who first studied the subject in specimens colored with methylene-blue dissolved in ascitic fluid, distinguished a deeper colored ectoplasm and a pale endoplasm. In the endoplasm they were able to make out a palely stained body, or sometimes one or more sharply staining points which they believed to represent the nucleus.

Grassi and Feletti ‡ described the clear, more palely staining area as a large vesicular nucleus which contains a deeper colored nucleolar mass situated more or less excentrically.

Romanovsky * also believes that the small spot which is noted generally toward the periphery of the ovoid or round clear area in the stained parasite, represents the chromatic part of the nucleus. Both he and Grassi and Feletti describe

---

* L'étiologie du paludisme, Proceedings of the Congress of Hygiene at Buda-Pesth, Revue scientif., October 13, 1894.

† Arch. per le sc. med., xiii, 1889, 307; also, Fortschr. d. Med., 1889, vii, No. 14, 521.

‡ *Op. cit.*

* (a) Vrach, 1890, No. 52 (Russian). (b) *Op. cit.*

the breaking up and division of this small deeply staining body at the time of segmentation, the former believing that he sees evidences of karyokinesis. Romanovsky's observations were made upon the tertian parasite, while Grassi and Feletti studied the quartan organism.

Communications apparently confirming Romanovsky's observations have recently been made by Geppener (Heppener)* (Russian) and Ziemann † and Gotye.‡

Sakharov # also interprets the pale area and the more deeply staining spot in the same manner.

Mannaberg ‖ describes the behavior of the nucleus in the tertian parasite at considerable length. The deeper staining dot in the pale area he believes to be the nucleolus. The nucleolus, he says, grows with the parasite, and, just before segmentation, disappears, passing out apparently into the substance of the organism. With segmentation there begin to appear within the nuclear substance small deeply staining dots which represent nucleoli, about which new spores eventually appear.

Bastianelli and Bignami,▲ studying the æstivo-autumnal parasite, conclude that one can not recognize in this variety of organism any body which has the various constituents of a true nucleus. The granular bodies of chromatin which form part of the cytoplasm and become dissolved in it when the body is ready for reproduction represent that part of the parasite which performs the function of the nucleus.

---

* Meditzinsk. Pribav., etc., St. Petersburg, 1896.
† Centr. f. Bakt., 1896, Nos. 18, 19.
‡ Op. cit.
# (a) Op. cit. (b) Amœbæ malariæ hominis, etc., 8vo, Tiflis, 1892.
‖ Cent. f. klin. Med., 1891, No. 27; also, op. cit.
▲ Bull. d. R. acc. med. di Roma, 1893-'94, xx, 151.

It may be said, then, in summary that the parasite consists of a more or less deeply staining substance containing pigment granules. At some point within the body, usually near the periphery, there is a round or ovoid pale, non-staining area, containing a small, more deeply colorable body situated usually at one side on the border line between this area and the colored substance of the parasite. The colorless area is generally interpreted as a bladder-like nucleus, the colored body within representing the chromatin substance or nucleolus.

Bastianelli and Bignami have been unable to distinguish in the æstivo-autumnal parasite any body which has all the characteristics of a nucleus. Romanovsky, Geppener, and Ziemann assert that they have been able to observe actual karyokinetic figures.

Attempts to cultivate the Parasites—Inoculation Experiments.—The question of the permanence of these different varieties of parasites has occupied considerable attention. Some observers assume that they represent distinct and separate organisms, while others believe that they are different varieties of one polymorphous parasite. It is undoubtedly true, as proven by numerous inoculation experiments, that each of these three types of parasites is associated with a definite type of fever.

Unfortunately, all attempts to cultivate the parasite outside of the body have been without result. Numerous attempts to inoculate lower animals with the blood of infected human beings, by Richard,[*] Guarnieri,[†] Fischer,[‡] Laveran,[#]

---

[*] *Op. cit.*
[†] Arch. per le sc. med., xii, 1887, p. 175.
[‡] Verhandl. Internat. Cong. f. Hyg. und Demog , Wien, 1887, H. xxxvi, 99.
[#] *Op. cit.*

Celli and Sanfelice,* Bein,† Angelini,‡ and Di Mattei,# have likewise failed.

Sakharov ∥ and Rosenbach △ believe that they have been able to keep the organisms alive for several days in the bodies of leeches. Rosenbach, experimenting with the tertian organism, thought that he could distinguish evidences of development during forty-eight hours, but his researches have not been confirmed. Sakharov ◊ placed the leeches upon ice, and found amœboid organisms within red corpuscles as much as seven days after the beginning of the experiment. Inoculating himself with blood from one of these leeches on the fourth day, he obtained a positive result, developing fever with similar parasites in his blood on the twelfth day.

These experiments have been in part repeated in this clinic by Dr. Blumer and Messrs. Hamburger and Mitchell. Dr. Blumer was able to distinguish the small hyaline bodies of æstivo-autumnal fever for over a week in the blood of a leech kept on ice. There was, however, no evidence of growth, and no amœboid movement was made out.

Mr. Hamburger took the blood from a case of æstivo-autumnal fever with quotidian paroxysms at a time when only small amœboid and ring-shaped, non-pigmented hyaline bodies were present. During the next several days he was able to distinguish a slight increase in size, with the accumulation in nearly every organism of a few small motile pigment granules. On the eighth day the organisms were distinctly visible, each with a small group of slightly motile granules in

---

* *Op. cit.* † Charité Annalen, 1891, 181.
‡ Riforma medica, 1891, v. 4, p. 758.
# (*a*) Riforma medica, 1891, 544. (*b*) L'Ufficiale Sanitario, No. 10, 1894.
∥ Vrach, 1890, 644; ref. in Baumgarten's Jahresbericht, 1890, 444.
△ Berliner klin. Woch., 1891, 839.
◊ Cent. f. Bakt., 1894, xv, 158.

the middle or at some point on the periphery of the parasite. The parasites, as in Dr. Blumer's case, showed no actual amœboid movement, though some slight change of shape could be at times made out. In both instances the parasite acquired after several days a peculiar refractive, glistening appearance.

Specimens stained on the eighth day showed characteristic ring-shaped bodies.

Mr. Mitchell placed a leech upon an individual suffering with a combined æstivo-autumnal and double tertian infection. The blood showed two groups of active tertian organisms and a few crescentic and ovoid forms.

In the body of the leech the tertian organisms were to be made out for ten days. The pigment was active for four days, but no amœboid movement was to be made out in the parasites. The crescentic and ovoid bodies remained unchanged; no flagellate forms were observed.

The experiment of Hamburger, which I was able to follow, furnishes the first demonstration of the actual growth of the parasite and the accumulation of pigment outside of the human body.

Coronado,* of Havana, alone believes that he has cultivated the parasite. His statements are, however, unconvincing, while attempts to repeat his experiments have been without result.

Gerhardt,† in 1880, first demonstrated that malarial infection might be transferred by the inoculation of infected blood into healthy individuals; at this time the parasite was not generally recognized.

---

* (a) Crónica med.-quir. de la Habana, xviii, No. 22. (b) Crón. med.-quir. de la Habana, 1893, 375.

† Zeit. für klin. Med., 1884, 375.

In 1884 Mariotti and Ciarrochi,* and Marchiafava and Celli † showed that the fever following such inoculations was associated with the appearance of parasites in the blood of the inoculated patient.

These experiments have been followed by a considerable number of observations by Gualdi and Antolisei,‡ Angelini,# Di Mattei,‖ Calandruccio,△ Bein,◊ Baccelli,‡ Sakharov,⟡ and Bastianelli and Bignami.⧺

These studies have shown that by intravenous or subcutaneous introduction of blood from an individual suffering from malarial fever into an healthy human being, the infection may be transferred. Furthermore, the type of fever and of the parasite in the inoculated individual are always the same as in the patient from whom the blood is taken.

In every instance, with the exception of the first two cases of Gualdi and Antolisei, the inoculation of one variety of organism has been followed by the development of a similar parasite, and by similar clinical manifestations. In the first two instances reported by Gualdi and Antolisei, where this was apparently not the case, later observation proved that the blood which had been injected was, in all probability, from a patient with a mixed infection.

The remarkable regularity with which the tertian and

---

* Lo Sperimentale, 1884, liv, 263.
† Arch. per le sc. med., 1885, ix ; also, Fortschr. d. Med., 1885, iii, Nos. 11 and 14.
‡ (a) Bull. d. R. acc. med. d. Roma, xv, 343. (b) Riforma medica, 1889. No. 264, 1580. (c) Riforma medica, 1889, No. 274, 1639.
# Riforma medica, 1889, Nos. 226, 227, 1352, 1358.
‖ (a) Riforma medica, 1891, No. 121, 544. (b) Archiv f. Hygiene, 1895, 191,
△ Cent. für Bakt., 1891, ix, 403, 429, 461.
◊ Op. cit.   ‡ Deutsch. med. Woch., 1892, 721.
⟡ Cent. f. Bakt., 1894, xv, 158.
⧺ Bull. d. R. acc. med. d. Roma, 1893-'94, anno xv, vol. xx, 151.

quartan parasites are to be seen during the early months of the year, and the æstivo-autumnal forms during the later summer and fall, has led many to believe that the organisms are varieties of one parasite, the morphology of which varies, depending upon the time of year and the conditions to which it is subjected. No direct confirmatory evidence has, however, been advanced in favor of this suspicion. I have never been able to trace the change in one individual from one variety of parasite to another.

Those cases which come to Baltimore during the spring and winter months from severe malarious districts (Cuba, Jamaica) preserve their original type notwithstanding the fact of its extreme rarity in this climate at that time of year. In one instance quoted in the Johns Hopkins Hospital Reports (vol. v, p. 99) we were able, in a case of mixed infection during the winter season, to follow distinctly the disappearance of the tertian parasites under quinine, and the reappearance of the more resistant æstivo-autumnal organisms, after two months' freedom from symptoms, at a time of year when cases of this variety are of extreme rarity.

Moreover, though such is not the rule, we have seen instances in which æstivo-autumnal infection occurring relatively early in the summer and disappearing under quinine, was followed at the height of the malarial season, at the time when æstivo-autumnal fever predominates, by a tertian infection. We have believed these cases to represent fresh infections.

It is, however, sufficient for all clinical purposes to recognize the fact that whether or not these varieties of parasites may change one into another, they are, when present, always associated with the characteristic variety of fever. From the clinical chart we may in many instances recognize the variety of parasite present; from the parasite invariably the variety of fever.

Inoculation experiments definitely proving Marchiafava and Bignami's division of the æstivo-autumnal parasite into a quotidian and tertian variety are as yet wanting.

Manner of Reproduction.—All observers agree that the parasite multiplies by segmentation. Laveran,* Danilevsky,† Mannaberg, ‡ Dock,# Coronado, ‖ and Manson,▲ however, cling to the idea that flagellation may represent another method of multiplication.

The fresh segments from the sporulating form resemble very closely the young individuals. They stain in the same manner, and differ only in that no one has ever observed any amœboid movement. What the significance of their lack of movement may be is not perfectly clear. There seems to be little doubt that they immediately attack other red corpuscles, and yet the actual process has never been noted. Whether they must undergo some change before they are capable of entering the blood-corpuscles—a change which, perhaps, is prevented from taking place by the abnormal influences to which they are subjected in the preparation of the specimen —or whether they represent already complete new organisms ("gymnospores"), is not determined.

Plehn ◊ believes that they possess small, almost invisible flagella, and in certain instances it must be acknowledged that they have a slight dancing movement, and change their

---

* Du paludisme et de son hématozoaire, Paris, 8°, 1891.
† Cent. f. Bakt., 1891, ix, 397.
‡ *Op. cit.*
# Med. News, July 19, 1890, 59.
‖ Crón. med.-quir. de la Habana, xviii, 1892, No. 22.
▲ Brit. Med. Journal, 1894, vol. ii, 1306.
◊ Aetiologische u. klinische Malaria Studien, Berlin, 80, 1890.

position in the field in a manner which might almost suggest the existence of organs of locomotion.

Classification of the Parasite.—Various names have been suggested for the malarial organism; the first, that of *Oscillaria malariæ*, advanced by Laveran in 1881, has since been generally abandoned.

Marchiafava and Celli in 1884 proposed the term *Plasmodium malariæ*, which, despite its inaptness, has been widely accepted.

The term *Hæmatomonas malariæ*, suggested by Osler, has not found general recognition.

To-day most observers have adopted Metchnikoff's * classification of the parasite among the Sporozoa. Recent writers have further generally accepted Mingazzini's new group of *Hæmosporidia*, which includes the organisms of man and the similar organisms found in birds. With this view Celli and Sanfelice and Mannaberg agree.

Kruse † has recently separated the Sporozoa into six orders:

Gregarinida.	Myxosporidia.
Coccidida.	Sarcosporidia.
Hæmosporidia (Hæmogregarinida).	Microsporidia.

The Hæmosporidia are separated into four genera:

Hæmogregarina (tortoise-lizard).	Hæmoproteus (birds).
Drepanidium (frog).	Plasmodium (man).

Grassi and Feletti ‡ separate the amœboid forms which they place among the Sarcodina, from the Drepanidium varieties which they place among the sporozoa.

---

* Cent. f. Bakt., i. 1887, 624.
† Flügge, Microorganismen, 8°, Leipsic, 1896, vol. ii, No. 637.
‡ Atti. accad. Gioien. sc. nat., Catania, 1892, 3.

They divide the Sarcodina into two genera:

1. *Laverania:*

L. ranarum.
L. Danilewskii (birds).
L. malariæ (man).

2. *Hæmamœba:*

H. relicta }
H. subpræcox } (birds).
H. subimmaculata }
H. malariæ (the quartan parasite) }
H. vivax (the tertian parasite) }
H. præcox) (the æstivo-autum- } (man).
H. immaculata) nal parasite) }

Labbé divides the blood parasites into two orders, both of which he includes among the sporozoa.

I. Hæmosporidia.
- 1. Drepanidium { princeps, monilis, avium } (frogs and birds).
- 2. Karyolysus lacertarum
- 3. Danilewskya { Stepanowi, Lacazei } (reptiles).
  { Krusei (frogs).

II. Gymnosporidia.
- 1. Halteridium Danilewskii } (birds).
- 2. Proteosoma Grassii }
- 3. Hæmamœba Laverani (man).
- 4. Dactylosoma splendens (frogs).
- 5. Cytamœba bacterifera (frogs).

LECTURE II.

Methods of examination of the blood.—Description of the hæmocytozoa of malaria.

METHODS OF EXAMINATION OF THE BLOOD.

It is impossible to make reliable examinations of the blood for malarial parasites without first being familiar with the ordinary appearances of normal blood and the more common pathological changes.

Large, pigmented, full-grown parasites are easily perceptible, but the distinction of small unpigmented hyaline forms from vacuoles and other changes in the red corpuscles requires an experienced eye. One can not learn to recognize all phases of the malarial parasite in two days or in two weeks. The lack of appreciation of this fact has led good observers in other fields of medicine to commit themselves in print to grievous errors. Thus an excellent foreign clinician within a few years published an article on the parasites in the malarial fevers of the city in which he lived, asserting that he found segmenting forms in every instance where he had examined the blood. This rather remarkable statement was shown on re-examination of his specimens to be based upon his misinterpretation of clumps of blood platelets which stained readily with methylene blue.

It is unfortunate that until recently very little attention has been paid in our institutions for medical instruction to the examination of the blood. There is no excuse, however, to-day, for any institution which allows a student to graduate without requiring a good passing familiarity with the ordinary appearances of human blood.

It is a mistake to attempt to study malarial blood without an oil-immersion lens. An oil-immersion lens is to-day a necessity in the outfit of a physician. Laveran, to be sure, discovered the parasite with a one-sixth dry lens. This achievement, however, while it reflects all the more credit on the observer, should not be used as an argument that good work is easy with such lenses, for this is not the case.

The best method of studying the malarial parasite is in the fresh untreated blood at the bedside or in the consulting room. The specimen is easily prepared, though certain precautions must be carried out with absolute accuracy. The cover glasses and slides must be carefully washed in alcohol, or alcohol and ether, in order to remove all fatty substances. They should be washed immediately before use. It is very easy for the physician to carry a small vial of alcohol in his instrument bag or in his pocket.

The blood may be taken from any part, Reinert[*] having shown that the results are the same no matter whence the specimen be obtained. The most convenient place, however, is the lobe of the ear, inasmuch as it is less sensitive and more readily approached than the finger tip, while a smaller puncture will draw more blood. It is often, also, important that the patient should not be able to observe the proceeding. This is particularly true in dealing with nervous patients and children.

The ear should first be thoroughly cleaned; the lobe is

---

[*] Die Zählung der Blutkörperchen, 8vo, Leipsic, 1891.

then punctured with a small knife or lancet. A needle or a pin may be used; they cause, however, much more pain, and are not as satisfactory. If one desire to be especially careful, the ear may first be washed with soap and water, and afterwards with alcohol and ether. In many instances, however, it is advisable to make the preparations as short as may be, and unless the ear or finger be extremely dirty one may proceed at once. Pigment or epithelium coming from the skin is readily recognized by the skilled eye.

An instrument with a sharp cutting edge, or, better, a very sharp spear-pointed lancet, is taken in the right hand, while the lobe of the ear is held firmly between the fingers of the left in such a way that the skin is held tense. If one proceed in this manner very slight pressure will cause an incision deep enough for all purposes, while the process is almost painless to the patient. I have in a number of instances obtained blood from a sleeping infant without its awakening. The first several drops of blood should be wiped away, while a freshly cleaned cover glass held in a pair of forceps is allowed to touch the tip of the minute drop of blood which next appears. This is then placed immediately upon a perfectly clean slide. It is well if a third person be present to allow the slide to be vigorously rubbed with a clean linen cloth just before the application of the cover glass. This proceeding considerably facilitates the spreading out of the drop of blood.

If the slide and cover be perfectly clean the drop of blood will immediately spread between them, so that, unless the amount be too great, the corpuscles may be seen lying side by side quite unaltered in their main characteristics. The drop of blood which is taken should be small unless the patient be very anæmic. It is important that the cover should touch only the tip of the drop of blood. If it be applied rudely and pressed, perhaps, against the ear, the blood is so spread out that drying may begin at the edge of the drop before the glass is laid upon the slide. If this be the case the immediate spreading out of the blood between the slide and the cover does not occur. It is an error to exert any pressure whatever upon the top cover; neither should the cover be pushed or allowed to slide. All of these proceedings damage the specimen.

A convenient and satisfactory modification of this procedure is the following: The drop of blood is taken from the ear upon a slide, which is immediately inverted and gently lowered until the tip of the pendant drop just touches a clean cover glass which lies upon the table or bed. It is then lifted, the cover, of course, adhering to it. The blood usually spreads evenly between the two glasses.

Such specimens will remain in good condition for a considerable length of time—an hour or more—long enough to be thoroughly examined. If it be desirable to preserve the specimen for a greater length of time, vaseline or paraffin may be placed about the edge of the glass.

The parasites may thus be examined while yet alive and in active motion. Degenerative and regenerative processes may be followed out, and the most exquisite examples of phagocytosis may be observed. Such a specimen surrounded by paraffin or vaseline may be carried by the physician from the patient's residence to his consulting room, though under such circumstances one generally relies upon dried and stained specimens.

Preparation of Stained Specimens.—The preparation of specimens for staining is easy, but, like all other clinical methods, it requires a little experience and practice—practice in observation, also, as well as in preparation. A small drop of blood from the lobe of the ear or the finger tip is collected upon a perfectly clean cover glass, which is immediately placed upon another glass. The drop of blood, if the two covers be perfectly clean, spreads out immediately between them. The cover glasses are then drawn apart; if neither glass be lifted or tilted during the process they will slide apart readily without sticking. If, however, they have remained together so long that they have begun to adhere one to the other, one may be sure that the specimen is no longer of value.

The covers should always be held in a forceps. The fingers, of course, may be used, but often the glass will stick to the finger and hinder the smooth performance of the act, while in other instances the slight moisture from the hand may deform and destroy the corpuscles. The glasses thus prepared are allowed to dry in the air, after which they may be preserved for an almost indefinite length of time.

An interesting accident which occurs not infrequently in summer time may be here alluded to. If the specimens be laid upon the table and left for any length of time, one often finds the previously regular layer of blood dotted with a number of clear round spots, while sometimes the blood may have almost disappeared from the slide. One may be at a loss to account for this change until the discovery of the fly *in flagrante delicto* reveals the true nature of the process.

To prepare the glasses for staining various methods may be used. They may be heated upon a copper bar or in a thermostat at a temperature of from 100°· to 120° C. for two hours, according to the method of Ehrlich ; or they may be placed in absolute alcohol and ether, equal quantities (Nikiforov's method), for from an half to eight hours, according to the stain; while in other instances, with certain stains, a good result may be obtained after leaving the specimens for as short a time as ten minutes in absolute alcohol.

The malarial parasite is well stained by most of the basic nuclear dyes. Loeffler's methylene blue is an excellent agent. This may be prepared as follows:

Concentrated alcoholic solution of methylene blue...... 30 c.c.
Solution of caustic potash 1–10,000 .... 100 "

A simple aqueous solution of methylene blue may also give good results. In either instance the specimen, heated or hardened at least one half hour in absolute alcohol and ether, should be stained from thirty seconds to a minute, washed in water, dried between filter paper, and mounted in oil or balsam. The red corpuscles here remain unstained, while the nuclei of the leucocytes and the parasites are of a clear blue color.

Good results may be obtained by adding a few drops of a saturated alcoholic solution of methylene blue to two or three cubic centimetres of water, and staining for a similar length of time. Here, however, the red corpuscles take a slight bluish tinge.

A good contrast stain may be obtained by the following method: The cover-glass specimen is fixed in absolute alcohol and ether for from four to twenty-four hours. It is then placed for a few seconds (thirty seconds to five minutes) in a 0·5-per-cent solution of eosin in sixty-per-cent alcohol, washed in water, dried between filter paper, and placed for from thirty seconds to two minutes in a concentrated aqueous solution of methylene blue, or in Loeffler's methylene blue. It is then washed in water, dried between filter paper, and mounted in Canada balsam. The red corpuscles and eosinophilic granules are stained by the eosin, while the nuclei of the leucocytes and the parasites take on a blue color.

Perhaps the most satisfactory stain is that of Romanovsky.* Two solutions are necessary—a saturated aqueous solution of methylene blue and a one-per-cent watery solution of eosin. The older the methylene-blue solution the better the results. The staining mixture should be made just before it is used. About two parts of the eosin are added to one part of the filtered methylene-blue solution. The mixture is carefully stirred with a glass rod and poured into a watch glass. Do not filter after making the mixture. The cover glasses, fixed according to the methods above described, or by hardening in alcohol for from ten minutes upwards,† are allowed to float upon the top of this fluid. The specimens are then covered by another inverted glass, and the whole by an inverted cylinder, which is moistened on the inside. In from half an hour to three hours—best in two or three hours—good specimens are obtained. This method gives the clearest and best results that we have ever seen. The one objection is its unreliability. An abundant sediment is formed which may obscure the specimen. An excellent method of procedure is the following:

Equal quantities of an one-half-per-cent solution of eosin and a saturated solution of methylene blue diluted one half with distilled water are mixed in a watch glass. Upon this the specimens are floated, and the subsequent procedure is just as above described. The specimens should remain in this mixture twenty-four hours. There is no danger of overstaining.

---

* *Op. cit.*

† Excellent results may also be obtained with specimens hardened in absolute alcohol and ether for half an hour.

Geppener (Heppener)* has recently proposed a slight modification in the preparation of the specimens. A little filtered methylene-blue solution is poured into a fifty-cubic-centimetre graduate, and to this the one-per-cent eosin solution is added gradually, while the mixture is stirred or shaken, until a well-marked precipitate becomes evident upon the side of the glass. The fluid is then poured into a watch glass and staining carried out as before described. It is well sometimes to test the staining power of such a fluid by observing its immediate influence upon the nuclei of leucocytes in test specimens. If such a fluid be successful it may be kept and used during several days. Specimens sufficiently good to justify a diagnosis may be obtained in ten or fifteen minutes, though good specimens demand longer exposure. If the preparation has been stained twenty-four hours or more it may be hastily decolorized in absolute alcohol, then washed in water and mounted. The specimens may be prepared for staining by heating, immersion in alcohol and ether, or by immersion in absolute alcohol for ten minutes. Contrast stains with eosin and hæmatoxylin also give good results.

To bring out most clearly the small hyaline bodies of æstivo-autumnal fever, which with ordinary stains appear as very pale rings, stronger stains, such as gentian violet, may be used. With gentian violet the small rings with the deeper staining dot at one side are brought out with great distinctness, though the appearance of the specimen as a whole is usually rather unsatisfactory.

For quick work in the consulting room a simple stain with methylene blue is satisfactory, and not infrequently the experienced observer may obtain good results sufficient to jus-

---

* Med. Pribav. k. Morsk. Sbornik., 1895, 1, 67.

tify a diagnosis by rapid heating of the cover glass over the flame and immediate staining. Such results, however, are rather uncertain.

DESCRIPTION OF THE HÆMOCYTOZOA OF MALARIA.

Our observations have led us to distinguish three types of the malarial parasite:

(1) The parasite of tertian fever (*Hæmamœba vivax*, Grassi).

(2) The parasite of quartan fever (*Hæmamœba malariæ*, Grassi).

(3) The parasite of æstivo-autumnal fever (*Hæmatozoon falciparum*, Welch); (*Hæmamœba præcox*, Grassi; *Hæmamœba immaculata*, Grassi; *Laverania malariæ*, Grassi).

(1) *The Parasite of Tertian Fever* (*Hæmamœba vivax*, Grassi).—The malarial organism most commonly observed in this country is the parasite of tertian fever. This is a body whose complete cycle of development from the earliest stages to sporulation and the reproduction of a new group of young parasites, lasts approximately forty-eight hours.

On examining the blood from a case of tertian infection one notes the interesting characteristic that the organisms present are all at approximately the same stage of development—that is, the blood contains a group of parasites, which pursues a cycle of existence lasting about forty-eight hours, all the members arriving at maturity, undergoing sporulation, and again passing through their cycle of existence in unison.

At times there may be two groups of organisms in different stages of development; rarely perhaps more. Almost invariably, however, the fact may be noted that the parasites are present in *distinct groups*. It is extremely rare in tertian infections to find more than two groups of organisms present.

The first stage in the life history of the parasite within the red corpuscle is represented by a small, round, colorless, disk-shaped body. This body is usually actively amœboid, showing undulating movements at the periphery, or again changing its shape rapidly from the original disk-like appearance to that of a cross or a star, forming at times most irregular and bizarre figures. (Plate I, Figs. 2, 3, 4.) Sometimes the parasite takes the appearance of a refractive ring with a more shaded, apparently thinner central portion. There may be an apparent fusion of two pseudopodia including a bit of red corpuscle within, thus forming a true ring. (Plate I, Fig. 5.)

Some observers believe that such a portion of the corpuscle included within two pseudopodia is gradually digested by the parasite. Geppener, who has recently studied the growth of the organism in stained preparations, asserts that he can, in many instances, trace the formation of such a ring and the gradual concentric growth of the parasite. That such a process is, however, a rule in the development of the organism, our observations would lead us to doubt. No evidence of a nucleus is to be made out in the fresh specimen. Sometimes several hyaline bodies may exist within one red corpuscle.

As the parasite grows, minute yellowish-brown granules begin to appear; these are usually distributed toward the extremities of the pseudopodia of the amœboid organism. The granules are generally in active dancing motion, so marked that it has been ascribed by most observers to undulatory waves of the protoplasm of the parasite, rather than to simple Brownian movements. The parasite at this stage of development is very amœboid. So delicate is its structure, and so little does its index of refraction differ from that of the including corpuscle, that in this stage it is often extremely difficult in fresh specimens to determine the outlines of the body; the unskilled observer in many instances discovers only the pigment granules which appear to him to lie scattered within the substance of a red corpuscle. (Plate I, Figs. 5, 6, 7.)

The parasites appear distinctly to lie *within* rather than *upon* the corpuscles. Of this fact there is good evidence:

(1) The outline of the parasite is extremely pale and indistinct, and the skilled observer readily notes that he is looking at the organism through a layer of red corpuscular substance.*

(2) On carefully focusing one may readily satisfy himself that the parasite lies below the upper surface of the corpuscle.

(3) Observe as long as one will, the protrusion of a pseudopod beyond the outline of the red corpuscle is never to be seen.

(4) An excellent proof of the intra-corpuscular nature of the body is afforded by the observation of the escape of a parasite from its host. While studying one of these parasites under the microscope we may see a sudden explosion, as it were, of the corpuscle. From a small point in the periphery of the red cell the parasite suddenly slips out into the field, while at the same time the color of the corpuscle may be seen to flow out at this same point, leaving the disk a pale, almost indistinguishable shadow, very soon to disappear entirely from view. (Plate I, Figs. 5 and 21).

---

* On one occasion I demonstrated a specimen of fresh malarial blood to an artist who, though familiar with the microscope, knew nothing of the malarial parasite. He immediately turned to me and said that the parasites were not white, as they were represented in a plate which lay before him. "They have a distinctly yellowish tinge. They lie *within* the corpuscles, and not *upon* them."

The parasite which has escaped may show amœboid movements for a short time, though usually it becomes motionless, and often deformed and misshapen. Not infrequently it becomes fragmented, breaking into several minute round pigmented bodies, which are often connected by delicate thread-like processes in which pigment granules may lie. The outlines of these extra-cellular forms become very pale and indistinct, so that often they appear simply as collections of scattered pigment granules.

As the parasite grows the red corpuscle which contains it becomes somewhat expanded and loses its color. After twenty-four hours' growth the body occupies somewhat less than half of the area of the red corpuscle, which by this time shows a distinct pallor, and is larger than its unaffected neighbors. The amœboid movements of the organism begin to be a trifle less active ; the amount of pigment is increased, while the granules are distinctly coarser and of a darker color. After about forty hours of development the body has reached nearly its full growth. It is then almost as large as a normal red corpuscle, while the element in which it has developed is represented by a pale shell, which is often difficult to distinguish. This decolorized remnant of a red corpuscle may be half again as large as the normal red cell. (Plate I, Fig. 9.)

Shortly after this certain changes begin to be apparent within the parasite, which are indicative of the onset of sporulation. (Plate I, Figs. 10–14.) The pigment first shows a tendency to become collected toward some one point, usually near the centre of the body. This proceeds until finally the granules gather into one small clump, or indeed are fused into a single block. This block may lie exactly in the middle, or at times more toward the periphery of the parasite. The surrounding red corpuscle has by this time become almost indistinguishable; it is, however, a question whether, in the earlier stages of segmentation, the shell of the corpuscle ever entirely disappears. If one look very carefully he may almost always distinguish the pale surrounding rim; in many instances where, in the fresh specimen, it is difficult to make this out, well-marked evidences of its existence are brought out by staining.

Shortly before and with the collection of the pigment at one point in the parasite certain changes become evident in the protoplasm of the body. This begins to have a slightly opaque appearance, as if it were more dense, while a number of small slightly refractive points appear about the periphery of the organism, and sometimes also within its substance. Soon after this there appear evidences of radial striations, coming in from the periphery, while a slight crenation of the outer margin of the body may be seen, until finally a figure like that in Fig. 12 of the plate is to be made out; a central pigment clump surrounded by from twelve to twenty or thirty leaflets.

Usually, however, these striations do not extend actually to the pigment mass. Other small refractive points appear within the substance of the body, while gradually lines of separation develop about them until at length each minute refractive point lies within a small separate segment. At last, at a given moment, if we are lucky enough to observe the body at this instant, there is a sudden movement suggesting strongly the rupture of a capsule, while the fifteen to twenty little separate segments burst from about the central pigment which they now surround like a bunch of grapes. The separation of these segments may not occur all at once. At one point on the periphery several of these bodies may suddenly escape from the group, the others remaining longer about the central pigment mass.

These small hyaline bodies may sometimes be followed for some little distance from the original segmenting form. Under these circumstances they may show a slight dancing to-and-fro movement which suggests the possible existence of flagella. Usually they are quite motionless.

Sometimes all the pigment may not collect at one point, but separate single granules or collections of granules may be scattered throughout the segmenting organism, while rarely a fresh segment may contain a single granule at the time of its origin. This I have distinctly observed on one occasion.

These small, clear hyaline segments resemble the young amœboid intra-corpuscular forms very closely, as well in appearance and size as in staining characteristics; the latter appear in the red blood-corpuscles simultaneously with or shortly after the appearance of the sporulating bodies. It is generally acknowledged that the segments represent spores or actual young organisms. Whether they are gymnospores (Grassi and Feletti), complete young parasites, or whether the spores must undergo some slight change before they are able to attack the red corpuscles, is a question.

Certainly we have never observed the actual invasion of a red corpuscle by a fresh segment, nor have we ever been able to make out distinct amœboid movements of these bodies. On the other hand, the staining reactions are the same as in the case of the young intra-cellular parasites, while we never have been able to distinguish evidences of a membrane about the spore. The chain of evidence is so strong that there can be little doubt that the fresh segments represent the new group of parasites, which appears almost immediately within the red corpuscles, starting again upon another cycle of forty-eight hours' development.

Not infrequently at a time when the group of organisms has reached nearly complete development bodies may be found which have reached the full size of a red corpuscle, while all evidences of their surrounding host has completely disappeared. These bodies may, indeed, be considerably larger than the normal red corpuscle. They are usually pale; their outlines are indistinct, while the pigment granules are in very active motion. (Plate I, Fig. 18.)

Studying these large extra-cellular forms we may observe one of several changes:

(1) After a certain length of time the organism, the pigment of which is usually extremely active, may put forth several bud-like protrusions which finally become cut off, the original parasite breaking into a number of smaller bodies. These become rapidly deformed and indistinct, just as do the half-grown parasites which escape from the red corpuscles. The motions of the pigment granules gradually cease, until finally there are left a number of small, irregularly shaped, indistinct masses with motionless pigment. (Plate I, Figs. 19, 20.)

(2) In other instances there appear a number of small round vacuoles of irregular size, the development of which is usually associated with a deformation of the body, while the movements of the pigment gradually cease. Sometimes an interesting phenomenon may be observed, an appearance which was interpreted originally by Golgi, probably incorrectly, as a method of sporulation. A single large vacuole develops, containing one or more hyaline masses, which are not dissimilar in appearance to the segments of the sporulating body. At the same time smaller vacuoles of irregular

size appear throughout the rest of the parasite; eventually the pigment becomes motionless and the body itself deformed and indistinct in outline. There is little doubt that this is a degenerative rather than a regenerative process. (Plate I, Figs. 23, 24.)

(3) The third and, in many ways, the most interesting change which occurs in these large, swollen bodies is the appearance of the flagella first described by Laveran. The pigment first becomes extremely active, dancing in a most tumultuous manner; often, in association with this, the periphery of the body is seen to undulate violently, suggesting, as Richard long ago remarked, an attempt on the part of some included body to escape. Finally, in an instant there appear from one or more points on the periphery of the organism small, thread-like, colorless, actively motile flagella, while at the same moment the pigment tends generally to collect rather toward the centre of the mother body; it never, however, gathers into a small mass, as in sporulation. (Plate I, Fig. 22.)

The flagella have a singularly regular outline, showing often a slightly clubbed extremity, and further, at times, small olive-shaped swellings in their course. Their length is usually not more than two or three times the diameter of the body from which they arise. Their motions are extremely active, the red corpuscles in the neighborhood being stirred about in a violent manner. The pigment is very lively. Occasionally one or more small granules may pass from the interior of the parasite out into one of the flagella. At this period the mother body, which is in active motion, often becomes extensively fragmented; one usually, however, gains the impression that these fragments have some delicate connection one with another.

After the body has existed for a longer or a shorter time, flagella may break loose from the mother organism, rushing off among the surrounding corpuscles, preserving the same active serpentine movements which they possessed before. Sometimes several free flagella may be seen in a single field. The activity of the flagella may last for a considerable time, certainly up to three-quarters of an hour. Gradually, however, the movements cease, and the filaments, becoming motionless, are quickly lost to the eye. At times there is an appearance as if they were withdrawn again into the body; often they seem to be folded about it. With the cessation of the movements of the flagella the pigment becomes usually quite motionless, and the central body remains a shrunken, deformed, motionless mass.

The significance of these large, extra-cellular forms is not entirely settled. Many observers believe them to be degenerative stages of the parasite, bodies which are overgrown and have failed to enter upon a reproductive stage—involution forms.

This would appear to be true in the case of the fragmenting and vacuolated forms.

The true significance, however, of the flagellate bodies is not entirely clear. Certain considerations speak in favor of their representing a degenerative stage of the parasite. The most important of these are perhaps the facts:

(1) That they are derived from the same bodies which give rise to fragmenting and vacuolating forms, in association with which they are usually found.

(2) That they are rarely found immediately after the formation of the specimen, but usually five, or ten, or fifteen minutes after a fresh specimen of blood has been made: that is, after exposure to abnormal and doubtless injurious condi-

tions. In bird's blood, where the change from the body temperature to that upon a slide is more marked, the development of the flagellate forms is rather quicker, and this change may be readily followed out in a number of organisms upon the fresh slide. Within five minutes after the preparation of such a specimen we may observe the rapid change of from five to ten organisms in a field into flagellate forms, which, after existing a certain length of time, become finally motionless and deformed.

(3) That the analogous forms in the æstivo-autumnal parasite, which will be discussed later, are derived from bodies which are incapable of further development, and are considered by some to be degenerate forms.

On the other hand, the surprising regularity in the shape of the flagella and their power of individual motion suggest strongly that they are preformed bodies, and permit us to sympathize to a certain extent with those observers who still believe that they represent an important stage in the development of the parasite, the true significance of which we do not yet know. The comparison of the flagella to the filaments which develop from red blood-corpuscles on exposure to heat, a comparison which has been made by good observers and recently repeated by Bignami,* is, it seems to me, extremely far-fetched. It is difficult to understand how any one who has observed the two processes can consider them analogous.

Now while all these different phases in the cycle of existence of the parasite are to be observed in a fresh specimen of the blood, Bastianelli and Bignami† pointed out some years ago that the different phases are observed with by no means

---

* Lancet, 1895, ii, pp. 1363, 1441. † *Op. cit.*

equal frequency. Thus in a given group of tertian parasites, while a very considerable number may be seen in the stage of fresh hyaline bodies, and again as half-grown and nearly full-grown forms, the segmenting forms are seen with much less frequency.

These excellent observers carried on careful systematic studies not only of the blood from the peripheral vessels, but also of that obtained by aspiration from the spleen. By this means they discovered that as the organism becomes full grown and segmentation begins, the parasites are found with much greater relative frequency in the blood of the spleen.

They suggest a very plausible explanation of this fact. The red corpuscles having been almost completely destroyed by the growth of the parasite, become practically foreign bodies, and as such tend to accumulate in the spleen. The reason that in quartan fever the organisms are so much more readily found in the peripheral circulation is simply because the changes produced in the red corpuscles are relatively slight.

Thus, in tertian infections with a single group of moderate dimensions it may be rather difficult to find organisms in the peripheral circulation just before or during the early stages of the paroxysm, while not infrequently the discovery of segmenting bodies may be almost impossible.

The Appearance of the Organisms in Dried and Stained Specimens.—Our best results have been obtained by staining with eosin and methylene blue according to Romanovsky's method.

In stained specimens the youngest forms of the parasite are represented by delicate blue rings. The central part of the ring is occupied by a colorless area, at one point on the periphery of which there is usually a small, deeper blue spot.

This pale area, it will be remembered, is what has been assumed by many observers to represent the nucleus, the smaller deeply staining spot representing the chromatic substance or nucleolus.

As the parasite grows, pigment granules begin to appear in the peripheral blue part of the organism, while the amœboid character of the parasite becomes evident by the excessively bizarre figures which the element assumes. When one studies the stained specimen of a half-grown tertian parasite it is easy to realize how in the fresh blood one might mistake a single organism for several separate bodies. At one point in these pigmented parasites, often at the end of a pseudopod, there is to be made out a clear, pale, non-staining area, inside of which is a round or ovoid body which takes on a blue color, though paler than that of the rest of the parasite. This area is to be distinguished from islands of red corpuscular substance which may be surrounded by confluent pseudopodia of the parasite. The clear, colorless area appears to be quite free from pigment, though at times there may be a single granule which looks as if it might lie accidentally upon rather than within the clear spot.

When the parasite has reached full development it is often impossible to make out any further evidences of this non-staining area, though frequently there may be a nonpigmented area which takes on a clear blue color like the rest of the parasite. With the agglomeration of the pigment granules and the beginning of the sporulation the parasite assumes a somewhat granular or mottled appearance, due to the development of small more deeply staining spots throughout the substance. Finally, it is possible to make out that these spots form part of a large number of small separate blue rings, each having exactly the same structure as the fresh intra-corpuscular bodies excepting that they are a little smaller. In the segmenting body, before separation of the segments, it is difficult to make out the structure of the separate spores, as they are crowded together and often overlap one another.

These appearances are readily to be observed; they correspond fairly well, as will be noted, to the observations of Mannaberg. In specimens prepared in the ordinary manner the deep lilac chromatic substance described by Romanovsky, Geppener, and Ziemann has not been apparent. It must be said, however, that our researches have been largely made upon fresh specimens, and we do not feel, as yet, in a position to dispute their results.*

In the large swollen extra-cellular forms there is no evidence of the clear area which is called by so many observers the nucleus, while the parasite also takes a very pale stain.

Attempts to stain flagellate bodies have always been unsuccessful, inasmuch as they are practically never to be found upon the freshly prepared slide. Sakharov alone believes that he has succeeded. He makes a fresh specimen of blood, and at the same time puts a number of covers, each with a small drop of blood upon it, into a moist chamber. As soon as flagellate bodies are observed in the fresh specimen under the microscope the covers are removed from the moist chamber and smear preparations made. In these preparations Sakharov believes that he is able to stain the flagellate forms with gentian violet. In later observations† he has stained these bodies with eosin and methylene blue, and convinced himself

---

* Gotye has recently asserted that he has been able to obtain these pictures only when using two special varieties of methylene blue, namely, C and BGN from the Badisch. Soda Anilin Fabrik.

† Centralbl. f. Bakt., 1895.

that the motile flagella represent the chromatic filaments of the nucleus which have, by a perversion of the process of karyokinesis, broken loose from the cell.

Other observers have not confirmed these results.

As has been mentioned above, Golgi in 1885 pointed out the remarkable connection which exists between the development of the parasites and the clinical symptoms. It is easy to confirm his assertions that the paroxysms which in tertian fever occur so regularly at intervals of forty-eight hours, are associated invariably with the segmentation of a group of malarial parasites. The first segmenting forms are discovered in the blood several hours before the onset of the paroxysm, while during and toward the end of the paroxysm the appearance of a new group of bodies, as shown by the fresh hyaline forms within the red corpuscles, is to be made out. So regular is the association between the cycle of development of the parasites and the clinical manifestations of the case, that one may, within certain limits, prophesy the hour at which a paroxysm will occur.

Very commonly the blood shows evidence of an infection with two groups of parasites. These groups are almost invariably so arranged that they reach maturity on alternate days. As might be expected, in this case the clinical manifestations are those of quotidian fever.

As has been already stated, the parasite at the time of its sporulation has almost entirely destroyed the red corpuscle. In certain instances, however, sporulating forms may be found within corpuscles which are no larger than the normal red cell, and which are but little decolorized. Bastianelli and Bignami* are inclined to believe that such bodies are more

---

* *Op. cit.*

common in cases of anticipating tertian fever—a fact suggesting, therefore, a definite connection between the anticipation in the segmentation of the parasite and the clinical manifestations of the case.

Our observations have not been sufficient to justify us in forming a definite opinion concerning this point. We have seen not infrequently the presence of occasional small sporulating bodies in association with larger forms in cases which showed no very marked anticipation.

Very rarely one finds evidences of infection with multiple groups of the parasites, or perhaps the presence of parasites in all stages of development. This is a discovery which is most unusual with the tertian organism.

In over one thousand cases of malaria, the majority of which have been infections with the tertian parasite, we have never observed a case in which two well-marked groups of tertian organisms segmented on the same day.

(2) *The Parasite of Quartan Fever* (*Hæmamœba malariæ*, Grassi).—The quartan parasite is relatively rare in this country. I have observed it in ten or fifteen instances in over one thousand cases at the Johns Hopkins Hospital. The blood in quartan fever, as in the case of tertian fever, shows the presence of parasites in great groups, all the members of which are at relatively the same stage of development. The cycle of development of the quartan parasite lasts approximately seventy-two hours. Thus in infections with one group of this organism, sporulation occurs every fourth day.

The earliest intra-corpuscular forms are similar to those of the tertian parasite; the small amœboid bodies, indeed, are practically indistinguishable. Soon, however, after pigment begins to appear within the body certain differences are to be noted. The pigment in the young quartan parasite is distinctly coarser than in the tertian organism, while it has also a darker, deeper brown color, possibly owing to the greater size of the granules. The youngest pigmented forms are still quite actively amœboid, and excepting for the size and color of the pigment, which also tends to collect toward the periphery of the organism, they are difficult to distinguish from the tertian forms. (Plate II, Figs. 3–5.)

As the body increases in size, however, and more pigment develops, the distinction between the two varieties is more readily made. The quartan parasite shows a much clearer and sharper outline than the tertian organism; it has a somewhat refractive appearance. The difference in refraction and distinctness of outline between the tertian and quartan parasite may be compared to the difference between a pale hyaline and a waxy cast in the urine. The movements of the quartan parasite are slow and lazy, while the pigment is very much less active. The organisms, as early as the second day, are usually represented by small, round, or ovoid bodies, which show but little amœboid movement. They are very distinct in outline, and contain relatively coarse, dark-brown pigment granules lying about the periphery, collected usually more at one side. (Plate II, Figs. 6, 7.)

The behavior of the red corpuscle which harbors the quartan organism is in marked contrast to that of the element in which a tertian parasite develops. In the latter case the corpuscle becomes expanded and decolorized. In the former there is rather a tendency toward retraction of the corpuscle about the body, while its color becomes, if anything, a little deeper, showing sometimes a somewhat greenish hue, like that of old unpolished brass.

As the organism increases in size the amœboid movements practically cease. The pigment becomes coarser and is extremely slow and lazy in its movements, while the contraction of the red cell about the body becomes more evident. On the third day the round or ovoid parasite is surrounded by but a very small rim of deeply colored corpuscular substance. (Plate II, Fig. 8.) Finally, after about sixty hours, the wholly motionless parasite is surrounded by an almost imperceptible rim of protoplasm. In fresh specimens the parasites very frequently have a somewhat elliptical shape. (Plate II, Figs. 9–11.)

Shortly after this the small rim of red corpuscle entirely loses its color, while the first evidences of the reproductive process set in. Such parasites usually impress one as being free in the blood, though in stained specimens the remains of the surrounding red corpuscle are always to be observed. The first evidences of segmentation are usually made out about ten hours before the paroxysm. The pigment, as in the tertian parasite, tends to collect toward the centre of the body; but during the process of collection it often assumes a radial arrangement, as though it flowed inward in distinct streams. (Plate II, Figs. 12, 13.)

Figures showing this starlike arrangement of the pigment are in my experience quite characteristic of the quartan parasite. I have never observed similar pictures in segmenting tertian organisms, and have more than once been led to recognize a quartan infection by coming upon one of these bodies under the microscope. At the same time the body begins to show the opaque, slightly granular, waxy look which was described in the tertian organism, and small refractive points appear about the periphery.

Here, however, the figures are usually much more regular than in the case of the tertian parasite. The radial striations which mark out the future divisions into segments reach completely to the central pigment clump, which eventually is surrounded by from six to twelve exquisitely symmetrical leaflets, the whole meriting well the term Marguerite or rosette form so freqently applied to them. This small number of segments, from six to twelve, is characteristic of the quartan organism. The process of separation of the segments is exactly similar to that in the tertian parasite. (Plate II, Figs. 14, 15.)

Often, though somewhat less frequently than in the case of the tertian parasite, large, pale, free, extra-cellular forms of the quartan organism may be observed. These forms show changes quite analogous to those in the similar forms of the tertian parasite. They become expanded and pale, while the pigment granules become most actively motile. They may further undergo deformation, fragmentation, and vacuolization, as in the case of the tertian organism, while occasionally also flagellate forms may be observed. These flagellate bodies, as in the case of the large, free, extra-cellular forms, are distinctly smaller than the corresponding tertian parasites. They are more similar to those observed in the æstivo-autumnal parasite. (Plate II, Figs. 16, 17, 18.)

The quartan parasite, then, is to be clearly distinguished, morphologically and biologically, from the tertian organism.

(1) It differs in size, being smaller throughout its course.

(2) It is more refractive, and has a more distinct outline than the tertian organism.

(3) The amœboid movements of the quartan parasite are relatively much less active.

(4) The pigment granules in the younger forms are coarser, darker, and tend much more to seek a peripheral arrangement.

(5) The activity of the pigment granules is much less, the

movements of the pigment in the quartan organism being extremely slight after the first twenty-four hours.

(6) The sporulating forms are much more regular, and show a smaller number of segments, from six to twelve, instead of upwards of fifteen. Furthermore, they are arranged as definite regular leaflets about the pigment clump. Never, apparently, in the quartan parasite, do we see the irregular breaking up of the organism into segments.

(7) The pigment as it collects into a single mass or block before segmentation, tends to flow in toward the centre in radial lines, forming a star-like picture not seen in the tertian bodies.

(8) The cycle of development lasts approximately seventy-two instead of forty-eight hours.

(9) Its effect upon the surrounding corpuscle differs from that of the tertian parasite in that, instead of becoming expanded and decolorized, the red element becomes rather retracted and deeper colored.

The staining reactions of the organism appear, from a limited number of observations, to be essentially the same as in the tertian organism.

Not infrequently we find more than one group of parasites, and, as in tertian infections, these groups almost invariably reach maturity on different days; thus we may have infections with two or three groups of quartan parasites. It may be that infections with more than three groups of quartan organisms occur. Such cases, however, I have never observed.

The same rules with regard to the clinical manifestations apply here as in tertian infections. Where one group of organisms is present paroxysms occur every fourth day; where two groups of organisms are present the paroxysms occur on successive days with a day of intermission between. Where three groups of organisms are present quotidian paroxysms result.

(3) *The Parasite of the Æstivo-autumnal Fever* (*Hæmatozoon falciparum*, Welch).—While of recent years many observers have given their special attention to the parasites associated with the irregular æstivo-autumnal fevers, we must acknowledge that the subject is yet far from being clearly understood. Infections with the æstivo-autumnal parasites differ in several respects from those with the organisms just described. It will be remembered that one of the most striking characteristics of the tertian and quartan parasites is their tendency to be aggregated in great groups, all the members of which are at approximately the same stage of development, passing through their cycle of existence, reaching maturity, and sporulating practically at the same time. Furthermore, the length of the cycle of existence is relatively constant in each variety of the organism, lasting about forty-eight hours in the one instance and seventy-two in the other; from this rule, variations, while they do occur, are but slight.

In the case of the æstivo-autumnal parasite, while we have been able to study all the stages of the existence of the organism morphologically, many questions with regard to its biology remain unsettled. Thus there is reason to doubt that the same constant aggregation in groups is the rule, while the length of the cycle of development of the parasites is by no means as yet clearly determined and is very probably open to extensive variations.

Again, in tertian and quartan infections, particularly in the latter, it will be remembered that we are able to observe all the stages in the life history of the parasite in the circulating blood, to follow out the development of the organism, and to prophesy with considerable accuracy, from the stage of development of the parasites present, the time at which the succeeding paroxysm will occur. In infections, however, with the æstivo-autumnal organism, only the earliest stages of its development are ordinarily to be found in the peripheral circulation, while occasionally, perhaps, in most severe infections prolonged examinations of the blood from the peripheral vessels reveal little or nothing. In the spleen and bone marrow, however, one may find all stages in the development of the parasite, while only certain of the youngest forms appear in the peripheral circulation.

It is thus easy to see why our knowledge concerning many points in the life history of the organism is much more imperfect than in the case of the preceding varieties, which may be so readily studied throughout their cycle of existence. By repeated examinations, however, of the peripheral blood, as well as of the blood obtained by punctures of the spleen, we have been able to trace, at least in part, the life history of the parasite.

Owing to the fact that we can not follow out all the phases of the growth of the parasite in the peripheral circulation, and because often we find organisms present in all stages of development in the spleen, there has been much difficulty in determining the length of the cycle of existence, and many different opinions are held. Thus, it will be remembered, Canalis believes that under ordinary circumstances the cycle lasts two or three days at least, while others believe the ordinary cycle to be as short as twenty-four hours. Marchiafava and Bignami believe that they can separate two distinct varieties of the parasite, one having a cycle of development lasting about twenty-four hours, and the other about forty-eight hours—parasites which they have termed the *quotidian* and *malignant tertian* organisms.

Golgi, however, who, it will be remembered, holds the interesting view that the main development of these parasites occurs in the internal organs within the bodies of macrophages, insists that as yet our knowledge of the duration of the cycle of existence is quite incomplete, and leans toward the view that the cycle may vary greatly in length, in some instances being considerably longer than that of any other known form of the organism.

Our studies of the organism have not as yet enabled us to settle these much-disputed questions. From a number of simultaneous observations of peripheral and splenic blood we are inclined to believe that in most cases, at the beginning of the infections at least, the organisms are arranged in groups, just as in tertian and quartan fevers. We have not, however, been able to convince ourselves of the existence of the two distinct varieties of the parasite which Marchiafava and Bignami and Mannaberg describe. The differences between the two varieties of the organism as described by these observers are so slight that we are inclined to believe they result simply from the fact that the organisms grow larger and accumulate more pigment in those instances where the cycle of development is longer.

We further believe that while in some instances groups of parasites of this variety pursue a cycle of development lasting but twenty-four hours, or possibly even less, in others, probably, the duration of the cycle is longer, lasting, perhaps, forty-eight hours, or even more. To these ideas we have been led especially by the study of cases early in their course, when they show a more or less regularly intermittent character, while the parasites appear to be arranged in groups. Later on, in the course of such cases, examination of the splenic blood may show organisms in all stages of development, and it is practically impossible to determine whether or not actual groups are present; the clinical symptoms usually suggest either the presence of multiple groups or the complete absence of such arrangement. We have been unable to convince ourselves of the existence of two distinct varieties of the parasite.

It will be remembered that while the tertian parasite pursues a cycle of existence lasting about forty-eight hours, and the quartan parasite a cycle lasting about seventy-two hours, these figures are, however, not absolute, and cases not infrequently occur in which the length of the cycle varies considerably from the mean. This is particularly true of the tertian parasite, where anticipation and retardation of several hours is not at all uncommon.

Now our observations suggest to us that the parasites associated with the æstivo-autumnal fevers, without showing constant differences justifying their separation into two groups, yet possess a cycle of development which is subject to variations similar to those occurring in the case of the tertian organism, but so much greater that its duration may in some instances be at least forty-eight hours, in others as short as twenty-four hours. Transitional stages between these parasites with longer and shorter cycles appear to occur.

So, then, we must regard the æstivo-autumnal parasite as an organism whose definite arrangement in groups is certainly less constant than in the case of the other varieties; the length of whose cycle of existence is as yet undetermined, and is probably very variable; whose life history is to be followed out for the most part in the internal organs; whose morphology alone has been fairly well traced.

The youngest forms of the æstivo-autumnal parasite are similar to those of the tertian and quartan organisms, and yet certain rather characteristic points of difference may often be made out. In the first place the youngest forms are smaller than similar stages of the parasites of the regularly intermittent fevers.

They often appear as very small, round, refractive bodies with a central darker point, which at first gives one the impression that he is looking upon a complete ring; on focusing, however, it would appear rather to be indicative of a biconcavity of the parasite. This point is commonly not exactly at the centre of the body, but a little to one side, so that the appearance is not unlike that of a seal ring.

Many have believed that these forms represent true rings. That this is not the case the skilled observer may readily convince himself, not only by focusing but also by observing the changes which take place in such a body. If one of these forms be watched for a short time certain striking changes may generally be made out. The small, ring-like, refractive body which may at first have been quite motionless, suddenly loses much of its refractiveness, becomes a trifle expanded, and shows marked undulatory waves about the periphery. With this change the central spot, which looked like the lumen of a ring, suddenly disappears. Such a pale, amœboid, hyaline disk is not to be distinguished from a tertian or quartan organism. Its movements are active and irregular, and every conceivable picture may result. At any moment, however, such a form may suddenly cease to be amœboid, change into a pale disk, and from that quickly again into a smaller refractive ring-like form. (Plate III, Figs. 1–6.)

As the bodies increase slightly in size, at a period differing in different cases, pigment granules begin to appear. The pigment, however, is very scanty. In the small ring-like or disk-like body, which may be no larger than a fifth the diameter of the red corpuscle, one or two extremely minute dark-brown pigment granules may be observed lying usually upon the periphery of the parasite, or sometimes about the border of the central lumen-like depression. The first granules are so minute that only the skilled eye detects them. They are usually motionless, though sometimes they may be seen to dance actively. (Plate III, Figs. 8-12.)

One of the most striking features connected with the growth of the parasite is the behavior of the red corpuscle which contains it. It will be remembered that during the growth of the tertian organism the red corpuscle becomes pale and expanded, and finally entirely decolorized, while during the growth of the quartan parasite the red corpuscle tends rather to retract about the organism, assuming sometimes a deeper, somewhat brassy color.

In infections, however, with the æstivo-autumnal parasite the corpuscles often show more marked degenerative changes. While in tertian and quartan infections the disks containing the very youngest forms of the parasite show almost no points of difference from the normal red corpuscle, in æstivo-autumnal fever the changes may come on very early. Not infrequently in the presence of the smallest ring-shaped forms we may notice that the surrounding corpuscle has become wrinkled and crenated or spiculated and of a very distinct greenish brassy color (*globuli rossi ottonati*). In other instances the hæmoglobin may retract from the periphery of the red disk about the small parasite, leaving the pale rim of the corpuscle still visible upon one side. The colored part of the corpuscle in these instances is almost always of a somewhat brassy hue. These changes are probably to be interpreted as necrobiotic. (Plate III, Figs. 7, 13, 16, 22, 23, 29.)

According to Golgi, it is to these changes that the great accumulation of parasites in the spleen and certain internal organs is due, the necrotic red corpuscles being readily engulfed by macrophages.

As the parasite continues to develop the few pigment granules gradually increase, though often at the end of development they are scanty in number. The parasite itself often reaches its complete development before it has acquired half the diameter of a normal red corpuscle, though in some instances forms may be found which are nearly as large as the red cell.

As the full development of the parasite is approached, the pigment begins to gather toward a single point, usually near the centre of the body, at first in a small clump, and later usually as a definite minute block. In some instances the pigment before being fused into a block, may show more or less active movement. Never in this stage of the æstivo-autumnal parasite do we see bodies with diffusely scattered pigment. The older the form of the parasite the more frequently does the containing corpuscle show degenerative changes in the forms of crenation, spiculation, or partial decolorization, though not infrequently full-grown forms may be seen in quite unaltered corpuscles. (Plate III, Figs. 13–24.)

In the full-grown bodies with central pigment blocks, bodies which may be anywhere from one fifth the diameter to nearly the actual diameter of a red blood-corpuscle, segmentation takes place in a manner quite similar to that described in the tertian parasite. The organism takes on the slightly opaque, waxy look; there is the same appearance of small glistening dots, the same gradual development of radial striation, the same gradual separation into minute segments. The parasite here, as shown in the plate (Plate III, Figs. 25-28) breaks up, as does the tertian organism, throughout its entire substance, and not always with the perfect symmetry of the organism of quartan fever.

It may be remembered that in tertian and quartan fever, when segmentation actually occurs, the red corpuscle is usually completely decolorized. This rule does not appear to hold in the case of the æstivo-autumnal organisms, as Marchiafava and Bignami described characteristic segmenting bodies occurring within yet unchanged red-blood corpuscles. Sometimes such forms may be seen in shrunken or brassy corpuscles, or in corpuscles whose coloring matter has retracted about the parasite. Usually, however, according to our observations, the surrounding corpuscle has entirely lost its color at the time of segmentation.

The great point of difference, however, between the parasite of æstivo-autumnal fever and those of the regular tertian and quartan fevers consists in the fact that only the youngest forms in the development of the organism are to be observed in the peripheral circulation. Thus while small, hyaline, ring-shaped, and amœboid forms are common, and also forms with one or two peripherally arranged pigment granules, the forms with central pigment clumps and blocks are unusual. These are most frequently seen during or just before the paroxysm.

If, at the same time, we aspirate the spleen, we find enormous numbers of these more developed bodies, and, not infrequently, segmenting forms. It is a very striking point, however, that the great majority of the more developed forms in the spleen are to be found within shrunken and brassy-colored corpuscles, which in turn are not infrequently within the bodies of macrophages—an observation which lends some plausibility to Golgi's idea that an actual development of the parasites may occur within macrophages.

Actual segmenting bodies are very rarely observed in the peripheral circulation, though most of the Roman observers agree in stating that under rare circumstances an occasional example may be found, while Sakharov asserts that in Tiflis he has found them with greater frequency. At the medical clinic of the Johns Hopkins Hospital we have observed actual segmenting bodies in the peripheral circulation in only two instances.

As I have said above, the length of this cycle is uncertain. We believe that it may last from twenty-four to forty-eight hours, and possibly even more.

LECTURE III.

Description of the hæmocytozoa of malaria *(continued).*—General conditions under which the malarial fevers prevail.

Crescentic and Ovoid Bodies.—After the fever has lasted for a week or more, other forms of the parasite, which are characteristic of this type of fever, occurring here alone, begin to appear in the peripheral circulation. They may be made out in the internal organs at times as early as the fifth day. These are large ovoid and crescentic bodies, the crescents being sometimes considerably longer than the normal red corpuscles, the ovoid bodies almost as large as the ordinary red cells. The protoplasm of these elements is highly refractive, so much so that they appear often to have a double outline, which many observers have interpreted as a membrane. The periphery, however, often shows a slight yellowish rim; in stained specimens there is good proof that this represents a coating derived from the red corpuscle in which the parasite has developed.

On the concave side of the crescentic or at one side of the ovoid body we may observe a slight convex bib-like attachment; this reaches in some specimens from tip to tip of the crescent, though in most it covers only the depth of the concavity. This bib often shows distinctly a pale yellowish color, indicating clearly that it represents the remains of the red corpuscle; it may have more color and show a crenated border.

There has been much discussion among different observers as to the origin and significance of these crescentic and ovoid bodies. Grassi and Feletti,* for instance, believe that they are a separate species of the parasite (*Laverania malariæ*). This view is, however, probably incorrect, as their origin from the smaller forms belonging to the ordinary cycle of development may be traced with considerable distinctness. It seems probable that after the infection has lasted for from a week or ten days, certain of the full-grown parasites instead of undergoing segmentation, continue to develop in size and to accumulate pigment, destroying gradually the red corpuscle as they grow. Every stage of transition may be made out between the small bodies and the larger crescentic and ovoid forms.

At first the small bodies begin to show coarser, more rod-like pigment granules, while the parasite assumes usually a fusiform shape. The fusiform bodies grow, stretching the red corpuscle as they lengthen. The corpuscle sometimes becomes crenated; usually paler. Generally by the time the body reaches about the length of the normal diameter of the red cell it begins to mould itself along one side of the corpuscle and to assume a crescentic shape. The pigment is scattered throughout the substance of the parasite in the younger forms; in the older it is collected in a more or less compact clump or ring toward the middle. The granules and rods of pigment become gradually coarser. Sometimes we may trace the progressive decolorization of the body of the red cell, the coloring matter retracting closely about the crescent and forming the glistening contour.

The relation of these bodies to the red corpuscle is quite

---

* *Loc. cit.*

clear. Developing within it, and destroying it until nothing is left but a pale shell, the crescent, which has more body than the decolorized corpuscle, becomes enveloped by the shell as with a moist veil. The shell of the corpuscle thus clinging to the body, furnishes it with the outer coat which to so many has suggested a membrane, while the remains hang from the concavity as a bib.

The crescentic and the ovoid bodies are readily interchangeable. One may observe upon a single specimen the transition of one form into the other.

We have never been able to observe reproductive changes in these crescentic and ovoid forms, and we are convinced that they do not occur. This idea is, however, disputed by certain observers, Canalis,* Antolisci and Angelini,† Grassi and Feletti,‡ and later Terni,# asserting that segmentation does take place.

Certain other changes, however, we have repeatedly followed out. Not infrequently crescents or ovoid bodies may be seen to change into symmetrical round forms somewhat smaller than the normal red corpuscles. To these the remains of the red corpuscles may be attached, though in some instances no evidence of the red cell is to be made out, while the sharp, glistening, membrane-like rim is lost. In these round forms the pigment often has a marked tendency to collect in the shape of a ring. Wherever such forms are to be found we may expect to see the development of *flagellate* bodies.

The process of the development of the flagellate form is much the same here as in the other types of malaria. The central pigment first becomes extremely active; there are marked undulatory movements of the periphery of the body,

---

* *Op. cit.* † *Op. cit.* ‡ *Op. cit.* # *Op. cit.*

and finally delicate flagella, similar to those observed in the tertian and quartan organisms, break out from the periphery. The flagellate forms in æstivo-autumnal fever are not materially different from those observed in tertian and quartan fever, excepting for the fact that they are a trifle smaller than the tertian bodies. They bear a strong resemblance to the quartan flagellate forms.

Vacuolization of the crescentic, ovoid, or round bodies is not very uncommon. This is usually associated with a diminution in the refractiveness of the parasite and often with a loss of its regular outline. The vacuoles are small, but may vary considerably in size, sometimes becoming confluent and larger. Such a form is shown in No. 37 of Plate II. The process is evidently degenerative.

Further, we may observe in certain instances the protrusion of small, delicate, bud-like bodies which are cut off from the cell; this probably represents a *fragmentative*, degenerative process (pseudo-gemmation).

Under quinine the forms of the ordinary cycle of development disappear rapidly from the peripheral circulation, just as in the case of the tertian and quartan parasites. The crescentic and ovoid bodies may, however, remain for a much longer time, sometimes even for months. In many instances, however, the presence of these bodies appears to have no influence whatever upon the general condition of the patient who has apparently entirely recovered.

What is the significance of these bodies? This is a question which has been much disputed. Canalis[*] and his followers, Terni[†] and Giardina,[‡] as well as Antolisei and Angelini[#] believe that they represent forms having a longer

---

[*] *Op. cit.* [†] *Op. cit.* [‡] *Op. cit.* [#] *Op. cit.*

cycle of development, asserting that they have been able to find undoubted reproductive forms.

Grassi and Feletti * and Sakharov † believe that they are capable of reproduction, although in the opinion of these authors they represent a distinct and separate variety of parasite.

Mannaberg ‡ holds a view which differs distinctly from other observers, a view which is as yet unconfirmed, and seems, on the whole, improbable. He believes that the crescents result from a pseudo-conjugation of two smaller forms existing in the same corpuscle. He also believes that they are in some way or other capable of reproduction.

Sakharov,# who has advanced the remarkable view that the æstivo-autumnal parasites develop in nucleated red corpuscles, believes that the crescents represent forms which enter the corpuscle at a particularly young stage, before the development in the cell of any large amount of hæmoglobin. They obtain their nourishment from the nucleus, about which they grow, thus taking their characteristic shape.

Marchiafava,‖ Bignami,▲ Celli,◊ and Bastianelli believe, on the other hand, that the crescents represent deviate and sterile forms of the organism, which are quite incapable of reproduction. More recently Bignami and Bastianelli have given utterance to the interesting hypothesis that these organisms may represent some more resistant form of the parasite, which is sterile as long as it remains within the human being, but which is perhaps capable of further development on transmission to some other medium. Bastianelli and Big-

---

* *Op. cit.*
† *Op. cit.*
‡ *Op. cit.*
\# Cent. f. Bakt., 1896, xix, 268.

‖ *Op. cit.*
▲ *Op. cit.*
◊ *Op. cit.*

nami * call attention to the fact that in certain other allied sporozoa, after the parasite has passed through its ordinary cycle of existence a certain number of times, there appear other forms, usually encysted, which are stationary as long as they remain within their original host, but are destined to preserve the organism for further development outside the body.

We have ourselves never been able to observe segmenting forms which we believed to be derived from crescentic, ovoid, or round bodies, nor have we been able in any way to confirm Mannaberg's ideas. Everything suggests that the crescents themselves are incapable of further development within the body of the individual, and there is much which renders the hypothesis of Bignami extremely plausible.

Essentially the same ideas with regard to the nature of the crescent have been independently advanced by Manson.†

With the object in view of testing some of these hypotheses, I have made several incomplete though not uninteresting experiments.

In the first instance it was desired to test the capability of the crescentic forms to transfer an infection on inoculation.

In all previous instances where inoculations with crescentic bodies have been made there is good reason to believe that hyaline amœboid forms were also present, though perhaps in small number. In this instance an hypodermic syringe full of blood showing only ovoid and crescentic bodies was injected into the median basilic vein of an healthy man who voluntarily offered himself for the experiment. The patient from whom the blood was taken was convalescent from his first attack. He had had quinine for four days, during

---

* Bull. d. R. acc. med. d. Rom , xx, 1894, 220.   † *Op. cit.*

which time no bodies excepting crescentic and ovoid forms were to be found in the peripheral circulation.

The inoculated individual was carefully observed for five weeks. There was never any fever, nor did parasites appear in the blood. The inoculation was made in the month of August. This observation would tend to uphold the views of Marchiafava and his students, that the crescents are sterile forms and unable to produce fever.

The other experiments were made with a view to determine whether by preserving crescents outside of the body changes might not take place which would enable them or their remains to give rise to an infection on reintroduction into the human organism. In these instances the blood was taken from an individual with an acute infection who had not taken any treatment. The blood, containing numerous young amœboid forms as well as crescentic and ovoid bodies, was taken in sterile Petri dishes, dried in a desiccator, and pulverized. In the fine brick-red powder which resulted, masses of pigment were to be made out as well as occasional distinct remains of crescentic bodies. These latter looked somewhat granular, and had lost their refractive appearance and sharp outline; they were, however, readily recognizable as undoubted crescents. With this powder two experiments were made upon voluntary subjects.

(1) A small quantity of the powder was mixed with sterile salt solution and injected into the median basilic vein of a patient with a progressive myopathy.

(2) The dry powder was placed in an insufflator and inhaled by a patient with multiple sclerosis.

Neither patient had ever been the subject of malarial infection.

The results were negative in both instances. There was

no constitutional disturbance of any sort, nor did parasites appear in the blood. Both patients are yet under observation nearly a year after the experiment.

The Staining Reactions of the Æstivo-autumnal Parasite.—Our studies, as has been before stated, have been largely carried on with fresh specimens, so that for particulars upon this point I must refer you to the excellent work of Bastianelli and Bignami,* and that of Gotye.† As far as our studies have gone—and they have been limited mainly to the youngest amœboid forms and the crescentic and ovoid bodies—they agree entirely with the results of the Italian observers.

The youngest forms are represented by extremely delicate blue rings, each of which has a small deeper staining spot at one point on the periphery. In the more advanced bodies with central pigment block (pre-segmenting forms), the protoplasm, according to Bastianelli and Bignami, stains diffusely blue, the deeper staining spot having entirely disappeared. Later it is noted that the parasite stains more markedly at its periphery, and finally individual deeper colored spots begin to appear, which eventually become the more deeply staining chromatin granules of the fresh rings.

The crescents stain more palely than the other parasites. The poles take a pale bluish color, while in the centre of the parasite, in the region where the pigment granules are usually collected, there is a colorless space. There is, however, as a rule, no deeper staining chromatin spot to be made out. The color of the parasite itself in specimens stained with eosin and methylene blue is often not a pure blue, but of a somewhat lilac tint.

---

* Bull. d. R. accad. med. d. Roma, xx, 1893–'94, p. 151.   † *Op. cit.*

The crescent is always surrounded by a slightly reddish border, which may be clearly distinguished as the remains of the red blood-corpuscle in which it has developed. It is doubtless in part this membrane which gives the crescent its peculiarly refractive double outline.

For a more minute description I must refer you again to Bastianelli and Bignami.

Concerning the Nature of the Flagellate Bodies.—Many views have been held concerning the nature of the flagellate bodies which are observed in all forms of malarial fever.

Laveran,* the discoverer of the parasite, believes that they represent the final and most perfect stage of development of the organism. He calls attention to the remarkable regularity in the shape of the flagella, to their extraordinary activity, to the power of individual motion which they possess when separated from the central body. He believes that the flagella are preformed elements which have developed within a cyst, represented by the growing parasite.

The same view is held by Danilevsky † concerning similar bodies observed in birds.

Dock ‡ likewise considers them "resting states of the organism, capable of existing independently, perhaps even of reproducing themselves, but also capable under favorable circumstances of reproducing the typical growth of the parasite."

Mannaberg # also believes that the flagella represent "organs which permit the parasite to enter into a saprophytic existence." "I suspect," says he, "that the flagellate bodies enter upon the first steps of a cycle of existence outside the

---

* *Op. cit.*
† Cent. f. Bakt., 1891, ix, 397.
‡ *Op. cit.*
# *Op. cit.*

human body, and that as a result of the unfitting culture medium the death of the young spores occurs."

Golgi * considers the flagellate bodies to be a passing phase in the development of the crescents. He appears to suggest that they are degenerate forms.

Antolisei was strongly of the opinion that flagellation is a degenerative process. He noted particularly that in the tertian parasite the flagellate bodies develop only from the large, swollen extra-cellular forms of the organism. These forms, he asserts, never segment, but undergo only degenerative changes—fragmentation, vacuolization, and flagellation. He believes the flagella to be sarcodic prolongations of the protoplasm. He asserts that he has seen vacuolization of the flagellate body itself.

Grassi and Feletti † believe also that they are purely degenerative forms, representing changes exactly similar to those occurring in the red corpuscles when subjected to high temperatures.

Marchiafava and Celli ‡ and their school are of a like opinion. They call attention to the fact that the flagellate bodies in tertian and quartan fever develop only from the large, full-grown extra-cellular forms. These large forms, they assert, as did Antolisei, never go on to segmentation, but show only degenerative changes—vacuolization, fragmentation.

In æstivo-autumnal fever the flagellate organisms develop only from the round bodies, which in turn come from the ovoid and crescentic forms. These bodies also, they say, are never observed to segment, and, with the exception of the flagellation, show only processes of vacuolization and pseudo-

---

* *Op. cit.*   † *Op. cit.*   ‡ *Op. cit.*

gemmation (fragmentation), which are degenerative in nature. The analogy, they assert, between these processes is so close that there can be no doubt that flagellation is a purely degenerative change.

Sakharov * has recently advanced a very ingenious hypothesis, which, however, needs confirmation. He believes that he has demonstrated that the flagella represent the chromatic filaments of the nucleus of the parasite; that the process of flagellation represents a perversion of karyokinesis, the chromatic filaments breaking loose from the body and appearing as the mobile flagella.

Manson † has recently reasserted the view that the flagella represent the forms in which the malarial parasite exists outside of the human body. This supposition he first made in 1894. He believes that the interesting observations of Ross form suggestive evidence in favor of this view. Ross placed mosquitoes upon individuals whose blood contained crescentic, ovoid and round bodies, and observed flagellation of these forms in blood taken later from the stomach of the mosquito. This interesting though insufficient evidence has led Manson to assume that the mosquito is a normal intermediate host in the life history of the malarial parasite.

Thus, with all the work that has been done, we can not as yet assume that the true nature of the flagellate bodies is entirely understood. The arguments of Marchiafava and Bignami in favor of the degenerative nature of the flagella are certainly strong. It is true that regenerative processes are probably never seen in those forms of the parasite from which flagellate bodies develop, the large extra-cellular bodies in tertian and quartan fever, and the crescentic forms in æsti-

---

* Cent. f. Bakt., xviii, 1895.   † Lancet, 1896, i, pp. 695, 751, 831.

vo-autumnal fever, while degenerative changes are common. Moreover, it is true that these bodies show no evidence, on staining, of the structure which many believe to be the nucleus.

Extremely suggestive that these changes are evidences of degeneration is the fact that the flagellate forms rarely, if ever, appear until after the specimen has been for some little time upon the cover glass. In human beings this is usually from five or ten to fifteen minutes.

In certain forms of parasites in the blood of birds it is extremely interesting to observe the formation of flagella. We have never seen these immediately after making a specimen of blood, but one may often observe the change to the flagellate state, within five minutes, of perhaps four or five parasites in one field. Such a picture certainly suggests that the change is due to deleterious external influences.

On the other hand, the regularity of the shape of the flagella, their extraordinary power of individual motion, the suddenness with which they break forth, apparently formed, from the full-grown body, make it really difficult to believe that they are not preformed elements, whatever the significance of the process may be.

As yet no one has confirmed Sakharov's assertions that they represent the chromatic filaments of the nucleus, while Manson's idea can scarcely be regarded as more than an interesting hypothesis.

GENERAL CONDITIONS UNDER WHICH THE MALARIAL FEVERS PREVAIL.

Distribution.—The malarial fevers occur in all parts of the world, but are more frequent in tropical and warmer temperate climates. While extensive epidemics and pandemics of malaria have been described, there are certain main foyers of the disease where it has been endemic from all time. These regions, where the most severe forms of malarial fever are seen, are for the most part in the tropics, the disease becoming less frequent as the temperate and cooler climates are approached. The exact geographical limits within which the malarial fevers exist are very hard to determine, all the more so in that the diagnoses on which the statistics are based are often unreliable. According to Celli,[*] cases have been observed at Irkutsk, in Siberia; Haparanda, on the Gulf of Bothnia (65·5° north latitude); Julianshaab, in southern Greenland; New Archangel, in Alaska (57·3° north latitude). To the south the disease has been reported as far as the isotherm +16°.[†]

The chief endemic seats of malaria lie along the banks and about the deltas of great rivers. In this continent the malarial fevers are frequent in the low regions along the coast south of New York, while of late the milder forms have not infrequently been observed in southern New England. In the Gulf States, and particularly along the Mississippi and its tributaries in the south and southwest, the most severe forms of the disease are met with. In certain regions about the

---

[*] Verhandl. d. X. Internat. med. Cong., Bd. v, Abth. xv, 68.
[†] This would pass through the southern part of the Argentine Republic, through Cape Town in Africa, and about through the most northern point of New Zealand and the southern part of Australia.

Great Lakes in this country and in Canada, as well as in some of the Middle States, the milder forms are not uncommon. On the Pacific coast malarial fevers occur, though they are less frequent.

In Mexico, Cuba, and Central America, as well as in the tropical parts of South America, the most severe forms of the disease are seen. This is particularly true of Guiana and Brazil, while the fatal Chagres fever of Panama is well known.

In Europe the disease is common in the lowlands about the coasts of Italy, Sicily, Greece, and on the borders of the Black and Caspian Seas. It is particularly common in the lowlands bordering on many of the great rivers; about the Tiber, Danube, Volga, and Po. In Spain, in certain regions about the coast, in several districts in France, Sologne, Les Landes, Le Forez, in Holland and Belgium, the milder forms of the disease are to be seen. About the mouth of the Elbe and on the Baltic coast of Prussia, in Silesia, on the plains of the river Mark, and in Pomerania, occasional mild forms of malaria occur. In Austria cases occur along the Danube and on the coast of Dalmatia.

In tropical Africa the malarial fevers are everywhere met with in their worst forms. In India, Ceylon, southern China, and the East Indies the disease is frequent. In Japan, on the other hand, malaria is rare, and in some of the South Sea islands, despite the climate and telluric conditions, the disease is infrequent. This is true of Australia and New Caledonia, while in the Sandwich Islands, Samoa, New Zealand, and Van Diemen's Land the disease is unknown.

Effect of Climate, Seasons, Time of Day.—From this general summary of the distribution of the malarial fevers it may be readily seen that warmth is important for the development of the disease. Thus in temperate climates malaria appears only during certain seasons of the year. In the tropics the disease is endemic throughout the year, but passing northward there is a diminution in the cases occurring during the winter months, until in temperate climates, as in Baltimore, they are almost entirely absent during the months of January and February, becoming gradually more frequent from this time on, until the maximal number of cases is seen during the months of August, September, and October. In the four years from January 1, 1890, to January 1, 1894, four hundred and ninety cases of malarial fever were observed at the Johns Hopkins Hospital. These cases were distributed through the seasons as follows:

January, 9; February, 8; March, 8; April, 17; May, 21; June, 18; July, 38; August, 66; September, 122; October, 120; November, 38; December, 25. Total, 490.

In like manner, the seasons have an influence on the type of the fevers which occur. In the more severe malarious districts all types of the parasites and of the fevers are to be seen throughout the season, but as we approach the temperate climates it is to be noted that the few infections occurring early in the malarial season are of the milder types—tertian and quartan. Moreover, the earlier the season of the year, the less is the likelihood to infection with multiple groups of parasites; single tertian and quartan infections are the rule. As the season advances double tertian and double and triple quartan infections become more common, and finally toward the height of a malarial season infections with the æstivo-autumnal parasite begin to appear. In Baltimore, æstivo-autumnal fever forms the majority of the cases occurring during September and October.

A few tables from a recent publication by Hewetson and

CONDITIONS UNDER WHICH MALARIA PREVAILS. 85

the author will illustrate this point. Out of five hundred and forty-two cases of malarial fever observed at the Johns Hopkins Hospital, there were in the first half year:

Tertian infection. { Single............................ 63
                    { Double........................... 49
                                                        — 112

Quartan infection. { Single........................... 1
                   { Double........................... 0
                   { Triple........................... 0
                                                        — 1

Æstivo-autumnal infection......................... 5
Combined infections............................... 3
                                                    — 8

Total.. 121

While in the second half year there were:

Tertian infection. { Single............................ 87
                   { Double........................... 139
                                                        — 226

Quartan infection. { Single........................... 1
                   { Double........................... 0
                   { Triple........................... 3
                                                        — 4

Æstivo-autumnal infection......................... 183
Combined infections............................... 8
                                                    — 191

Total.. 421

These tables show in an interesting manner how the severity of the type of infection increases as the summer and fall approach. Thus in the first half year there are more single than double tertian infections, while in the second half year, when malarial fever assumes a more severe type, there are nearly twice as many cases of double tertian as of single tertian infection. The increase in severity of the malarial fevers becomes more evident when we observe the course of the æstivo-autumnal cases. While in the first half year only five cases were noted—a little less than one twenty-fourth of the total number of cases observed—in the second half year we see one hundred and eighty-three cases, or nearly half of all the cases which occurred.

Thus it may be seen that with the earliest cases of malarial fever in the year the mildest types of infection are met with, the single tertian type predominating. As the season advances and the months approach which are richest in malaria the single tertian cases become less frequent and the double tertian infections more common; while at the height of the malarial season a majority of the cases are of the æstivo-autumnal, the most severe type in this climate.

It seems to be a well-established fact that the danger of malarial infection is greater by night than by day.

The Influence of Moisture.—A very important part in the development of malaria is apparently played by moisture. Almost all the regions where the malarial fevers are regularly endemic are low and marshy or situated about the banks of rivers or lakes. Mixed salt and fresh marshes appear to be particularly dangerous. Rainy seasons are, as a rule, more dangerous than others. Likewise regions where the atmospheric moisture is high are generally more malarious than arid districts.

Soil.—A damp, marshy region, with an impervious subsoil, is generally recognized as particularly dangerous. A region rich in organic matter, such, for instance, as is furnished by highly cultivated areas which have been allowed to fall into ruin and are covered with a rank, tropical vegetation, are especially to be feared. On the other hand, fevers may be observed in almost any district and upon sandy or even rocky strata. Marshy regions and districts where the surface of the ground is covered for a part of the time only with water are often rich in malaria.

CONDITIONS UNDER WHICH MALARIA PREVAILS. 87

Small islands are, as a rule, healthy. Malarial fevers never arise at sea. Those cases reported owe their infection, doubtless, to exposure before leaving land.

Altitude.—The more severely malarious districts are all in lowlands, while the higher regions are usually relatively exempt from the disease. In many malarious districts sanatoria have been established upon hills and mountains in the neighborhood. The exemption of these regions is not, however, an absolute rule. Parkes states that the malarial fevers have been observed in the Himalayas at an elevation of 6,400 feet, while Hertz * asserts that they have been found in the Tuscan Apennines at 1,100 feet, in the Pyrenees at 5,000, in Ceylon at 6,500, and in Peru at a height of from 10,000 to 11,000 feet. In connection with some of these statements one should, however, remember the looseness with which the diagnosis of malaria is often made. It is still common to see the so-called "mountain fevers" referred to as malarial. These fevers are undoubtedly, in great part at least, typhoid.

In a malarious district it has been shown that the dangers of infection are greater to one sleeping upon a lower floor of the house than to one living in an upper story.

In regions severely malarious, new-comers, inhabitants of temperate and non-affected regions, are particularly susceptible to the disease. Prolonged residence in malarious districts does not, however, give the white race the relative insusceptibility which the colored races generally possess. Frank, outspoken attacks are said to be somewhat less frequent in old residents, but when they do occur they are usually more severe and intractable.

Some observers believe that a sudden change of climate

---

* Ziemssen's Cyclopædia.

from a malarious to possibly a non-malarious district predisposes to a fresh outbreak of the disease. In certain instances outbreaks of the disease may occur in districts quite free from malarial fevers in individuals who have never previously suffered from the disease. This has led to the supposition that many individuals in malarious districts may actually be the subjects of completely latent infections. That the malarial parasite may exist for long periods of time in the organism without producing symptoms is abundantly proved by the relapses which occasionally occur after very long intervals in cases where a second infection has been practically impossible.

Bearing in mind the occurrence of these relapses after very long intervals, one must acknowledge that there is no reason, theoretically, why sometimes a relapse might not simulate a primary attack. An individual might well be the subject of an infection from which spontaneous recovery might occur before the parasites had reached a number sufficient to produce distinct subjective symptoms. A relapse from such a case as this would of course be considered as the original attack. There are facts which might lead us to suspect that cases of this nature occur. Most of the instances of malarial fever developing in individuals who have moved into healthy regions are, however, probably cases where the infection occurred shortly before leaving the affected district—cases where the symptoms would have appeared under any circumstances.

It has also been asserted that in expeditions in tropical Africa, attacks of pernicious malarial fever are particularly frequent at the end of long journeys after reaching the coast, while during the expedition, despite the exposure and exertion, the liability to such outbreaks is less. The reason for this fact —if fact it be—is not clear.

Winds.—There seems to be some reason to believe that the contagion of malarial fever may be carried by the wind. Thus, it is noticed that of the two banks of a stream in a malarious district, that side toward which the prevailing winds blow is often the more affected. It has been brought forward as a proof of this, that strips of forest land seem sometimes to interrupt the spread of the disease, as if some infectious substance were filtered out. Lancisi * believed that it was through the sacred groves, the removal of which was followed by a marked increase in the severity of malaria in the Roman Campagna, that this region had been protected. The winds blowing over the Pontine marshes and carrying the contagion of paludism were purified, he fancied, as by a filter, by passing through these trees.

Effects of interfering with the Soil in Malarious Districts; Cultivation; Drainage.—Most disastrous results have followed the denudation of forest lands in tropical and marshy regions, while, in the main, forest regions, however moist and hot they may be, are relatively salubrious. In the same manner, excavations and turning up of the soil may cause outbreaks of malaria in regions where the disease has not existed for years, or it may aggravate the manifestations in districts where it is permanently endemic. In Paris, in the years 1811 and 1840 during digging the Canal St. Martin and during the construction of the fortifications, outbreaks of intermittent fever occurred where the disease had been for a long time practically unknown. The disastrous effects of the excavations for the ill-fated Panama Canal are fresh in the minds of all.

On the other hand, cultivation and drainage may do much

---

* *Op. cit.*

toward purifying gravely malarious districts. The drainage, for instance, of the Roman Campagna has greatly improved its condition. The lowlands of Holland were at one time the seat of the most fatal malaria; to-day only the mildest forms of the disease occur. London used to be surrounded by a marshy district where paludism was not infrequent; now it is unknown.

Besides other measures to secure drainage, the planting of trees has often a good effect in rendering an infected region more salubrious. At one time the *Eucalyptus globulus* was thought to possess special virtues from a prophylactic point of view, though its particular efficacy is doubtful.

If, however, highly cultivated regions are allowed to fall into decay, the reappearance of malaria in its worst forms is not infrequent. An example of this was the condition into which the Roman Campagna fell after the Augustan era.

While the malarial fevers are especially common in tropical regions, becoming less frequent as one approaches the temperate climates, and while they occur especially in low, marshy districts about the borders of large rivers or lakes, there are yet remarkable exceptions to this rule. As has been stated, certain south Pacific islands, regions which possess every climatic and telluric characteristic of the most malarious districts, are absolutely free from the disease. This is no proof, however, that the disease, once introduced, might not become widespread and fatal. It is highly probable that, were the infectious agent once brought to these regions, this would be the case.

Drinking Water.—It has long been a widespread view that drinking water is a common source of malarial infection. Many statistics would tend to support this theory. Unfortunately, however, many of the so-called malarial infections

CONDITIONS UNDER WHICH MALARIA PREVAILS. 91

which become less frequent on purification of the drinking water are probably cases of typhoid fever, while, on the other hand, every experimental attempt to produce malarial fever from drinking water has failed.

Celli * allowed six individuals to drink large quantities of water from the Pontine marshes through a considerable time, wholly without effect, while Marino † had similar results from like experiments.

Zeri,‡ in Baccelli's clinic, experimented in thirty cases with the administration of water from most malarious sources without a single positive result. The water was taken by the patients in large quantities by the mouth, by enema, and as an inhalation.

Grassi and Feletti # allowed healthy individuals to drink dew collected from malarious regions without ill effects. They also caused healthy men to drink fresh blood from malarial patients, and fed birds of prey on infected birds, without obtaining any satisfactory results. This is, of course, no proof that the parasite in some form or other may not live and even multiply in water; it is, however, strong evidence that infection does not ordinarily take place in this manner.

It must be remembered in connection with all inoculation experiments that the individuals upon whom the inoculations are practiced, though in some instances they may be debilitated, have always been in hospitals or under conditions where they were receiving the best general care and nourishment. And one could not absolutely refute him who might suggest that the infection would have developed had the patient been

---

* Bull. d. Soc. Lanc. d. Roma, 1886, vi, f. i, 39.
† Riforma medica, 1890, No. 251, 1502.
‡ Bull. d. R. acc. med. d. Rom., 1889-'90, xvi, 244.
# *Op. cit.*

under poorer surroundings, or, perhaps, had previous lesions of the gastro-intestinal tract existed. It is interesting that nearly twelve per cent (11·9) of the cases of amœbic dysentery treated at the Johns Hopkins Hospital have suffered simultaneously with malarial infection.

Variations in the Distribution of the Malarial Fevers. Cycles of Severity.—The manner in which the malarial fevers pass from one region to another has long excited interest. Regions which have been malarious for a long period may become relatively healthy, while others, after years of almost complete immunity, may be visited by grave epidemics. Many of these changes in the localization of malaria are due to human activity, but others are as yet inexplicable. In like manner, regions where the disease is permanently endemic show remarkable cycles of years' duration in which the disease is more or less severe—cycles which often are quite inexplicable.

Race.—In general, the dark-skinned races who have inhabited southern countries for generations appear to possess a certain insusceptibility to the disease. In this country the negroes are certainly relatively less affected than the whites. From the cases analyzed by Hewetson and the author, the relative susceptibility of the negro would seem to be by nearly two thirds less than that of the white.

Age.—The influence which age bears upon the susceptibility to malarial infections depends wholly upon the extent to which it affects the likelihood of the individual to exposure. The very old and the very young are less affected, as they are more likely to remain in the house during the more dangerous parts of the day and during malarial seasons.

Sex.—In like manner, women are less frequently affected than men, because they are less frequently exposed.

Occupation.—The influence of occupation on the frequency of malaria depends also wholly on whether or not the individual be compelled to expose himself at dangerous seasons of the year or at dangerous times of the day in malarious districts. Soldiers and tramps who sleep upon the ground out of doors in malarial seasons are particularly liable to the disease. In this country, fishermen and oystermen who live about the bays and inlets on the southern coast are especially open to infection. This is also true of the farm hands in the same regions.

Manner of Infection.—Despite all recent studies upon the malarial parasite, we are in complete darkness as to the form in which it exists outside of the human body. In like manner our views as to the form in which it is introduced are wholly speculatory.

Infection has been supposed to take place through:

(1) The respiratory tract.

(2) The digestive tract.

(3) The skin (insect bites, etc.).

(1) Clinical observation would lead us strongly to believe that the most frequent method of infection is through the respiratory tract. No positive proof, however, of this fact has ever been obtained. Most attempts at inoculation which have been carried on in birds which possess a parasite closely similar to that of man have proven unsuccessful. The author has recently made an unsuccessful experiment in this line, which has been above referred to, namely, the inhalation of dried and powdered malarial blood. It is, however, in every way probable that the parasites were destroyed in the preparation of the powder.

(2) All attempts to introduce malarial infection by the digestive tract have been wholly without result.

(3) Inoculation experiments have given us positive proof

that infection may take place by subcutaneous injection of living malarial parasites, while the interesting results of Theobald Smith, who showed that the organism of Texas cattle fever (*Pyrosoma Bigeminum*) is conveyed from animal to animal by means of the cattle tick, are suggestive evidence of the possibility of some such method of transmission in the case of the similar parasite in man.

This question has recently been brought prominently forward in Manson's Gulstonian lectures. On the basis of the observation of flagellate bodies in the stomach of a mosquito which had been placed on an individual whose blood showed ovoid and crescentic forms, Manson suggests that the malarial parasite may pursue a regular extra-corporeal existence, the mosquito, as in the case of the *Filaria sanguinis hominis*, forming the intermediate host. The individual flagella are, according to him, forms intended to live outside of the human body. As an hypothesis, Manson's idea is interesting, though it must be acknowledged that it is seriously lacking in foundation.

Bignami,* in an excellent review of Manson's article, goes over the subject of the manner of infection in malaria in an highly interesting manner. He points out the fact that almost all the conditions which are known to be conducive to malarial infection are at the same time favorable to the presence of certain suctorial insects, more particularly mosquitoes—the absence of wind, the night, etc. He asserts that many of the precautions that experience has taught the natives in malarious districts to adopt—namely, to avoid going out at night, to avoid sleeping in the open air, to close the windows—are just such as would protect them from in-

---

* Lancet, 1896, ii, 1363, 1441.

CONDITIONS UNDER WHICH MALARIA PREVAILS. 95

sect bites. Emin Pasha never failed to take a mosquito net with him on his African journeys, and attributed the fact that he was spared a malarial attack to this precaution.

And yet such experiments as have been made have not been successful. Thus, on two occasions Bignami and Dionisi placed mosquitoes collected in malarial districts upon healthy individuals without positive results. Bignami believes that the most important point to study is not, as Manson has sought to do, to attempt to follow the parasite from the human body into the external world—for we do not know that this ever occurs—but to search for the port of entry, which must certainly exist.

On the whole, it must be said that we are absolutely ignorant of the form in which the malarial parasite exists outside of the human body, and equally ignorant of the manner in which it enters.

Congenital Malaria.—It has been a disputed point for years as to whether malaria can or can not be transmitted from the mother to the fœtus. The possibility of such an occurrence seems not wholly unreasonable, in view of what we know to exist in the case of certain bacterial infections. Many observers assume this to be the case, but positive proof is as yet wanting. Among a number of doubtful cases in literature, the most positive appears to be that of Duchek, reported by Griesinger.* In this instance the child born of a malarious mother died shortly after birth, presenting, on autopsy, an enlarged pigmented spleen, and showing, further, pigment in the portal vein.

Since the discovery of the parasite, however, no one has been able to bring positive evidence of the congenital pres-

---

* Traité des maladies infect., 2 édit. (French translation, 1877, p. 20).

ence of parasites in the blood of the newborn child, or of the development of true malarial fever in the infant where the possibility of *post-partum* infection was out of the question. On the other hand, a number of instances have been reported where, in abortions occurring during pernicious malarial infections, the fœtus was found quite free from parasites.

Bignami reported two cases of abortion during pernicious paroxysms, one at the third and the other at the sixth month. The mothers died, and while the organs of the parent in each instance presented the appearances usual in pernicious fever, in neither case did the fœtus show organisms or any sign of a previous infection.

Bastianelli also made an autopsy upon a woman dead of pernicious fever who had aborted at the sixth month. The mother's organs contained an abundance of parasites and pigment, while the child, upon careful examination, showed neither parasites, pigment, nor evidences of an antecurrent infection.

Within a few days I have had occasion to observe an interesting case of similar nature. A colored woman with triple quartan fever (*vide* Chart No. IX, page 128) gave birth during a paroxysm to an eight-months' child. The infection in the mother's case had lasted at least five months. While the blood of the parent showed three groups of the quartan parasite, the child's blood, upon repeated examination, was quite free from parasites or pigment. Examination of the placenta showed pigment and parasites upon the maternal side, while the fœtal side was quite negative.

While some of the cases reported are certainly somewhat suspicious, we must wait for more positive evidence before we can assume the possibility of the transmission of malaria from mother to child.

LECTURE IV.

CLINICAL DESCRIPTION OF THE MALARIAL FEVERS.

Types of fever.—Period of incubation.—1. The regularly intermittent fevers: (*a*) Tertian fever; (*b*) quartan fever.—2. Æstivo-autumnal fevers.

TYPES OF FEVER.—The malarial fevers may be divided into two main classes:

1. The regularly intermittent fevers: (*a*) Tertian fever; (*b*) quartan fever.

2. The more irregular fevers: Æstivo-autumnal fevers.

The regularly intermittent fevers are to be met with in all malarial districts, and form the majority of the cases occurring in temperate climates. The more irregular, so-called æstivo-autumnal fevers, on the other hand, are chiefly characteristic of intensely malarious districts, particularly those regions in the tropics where the pernicious fevers are common. As one passes toward the temperate climates æstivo-autumnal fever becomes rarer and is met with only at the height of the malarial season, until finally, in the more mildly malarious districts, it is very rarely to be seen.

In the warmer temperate countries the first cases of fever, those occurring during the spring and early summer months, are almost entirely of the regularly intermittent types, while in the later summer and early fall the more irregular forms begin to appear; hence the name "æstivo-autumnal fevers," given to them by the Roman observers. The relation of the different types of fever to the times of the year is well shown by the tables upon page 85.

PERIOD OF INCUBATION.—By the period of incubation we must understand the time elapsing between the reception into the organism of the infectious material and the first subjective symptoms. This represents, in other words, the time required for the malarial parasites to reach by multiplication that number necessary to produce the symptoms of the disease. As we are as yet quite ignorant of the form in which the malarial parasite exists outside of the body as well as of the port of entry and the exact conditions under which infection occurs, it is but natural that our knowledge of the period of incubation of the malarial fevers should be indefinite and uncertain.

In the acute contagious exanthemata, where we are equally ignorant as to the nature of the poison and the manner and port of infection, we are yet able in many instances to definitely fix upon the moment of exposure. In the case of the malarial fevers, however, this is in the majority of instances impossible. Careful clinical observations have, however, given us data which are of considerable accuracy and value.

It has been estimated by most observers that the period of incubation—i. e., the time passing between the supposed exposure and the first symptoms of the disease—lasts from six to twenty days. It has, however, been asserted that in some tropical regions where pernicious fevers are common the paroxysm may appear within a few hours of exposure. On the other hand, cases are reported where many weeks, and even months, have elapsed after exposure before the outbreak of the disease. Bloxall reports an instance where a man-of-war spent five days in the harbor of Port Louis. As a result, apparently, of

CLINICAL DESCRIPTION OF MALARIAL FEVER. 99

this exposure, two of the crew fell ill with quotidian intermittent fever at the end of respectively twelve and fourteen days. Two other cases of tertian fever, however, occurred forty-eight and one hundred and sixty-four days after embarkation.

Recent experimental inoculations have furnished interesting information with regard to some of these points. In these instances, where the blood of the patient is introduced hypodermically or intravenously into healthy individuals, the period of incubation ranges from two to eighteen days. Bastianelli and Bignami have recently published an admirable note upon the period of incubation of the experimental malarial fevers. They conclude that

"The period of incubation with one variety of parasites varies inversely to the quantity of material inoculated. . . .

"The period of incubation represents the time necessary for the inoculated parasites to reach, by multiplication, the quantity necessary to determine the fever. . . .

"The mean and minimum periods of incubation under similar conditions vary in the different groups of fevers; they are least in the æstival fevers, longer in the tertian, and still longer in the quartan. . . .

"The period of incubation in experimental malarial infection is not a constant quantity, but varies in the same group of fevers and in different groups of fever. In the same group of fevers it depends chiefly upon the quantity of the inoculated material. In different groups of fevers it varies with the rapidity of the cycle of development of the organism and with the special capacity for reproduction of the type of the parasite."

These authors prepared a table on the basis of their own observations and those of others, showing the variations in the period of incubation of the several types of malarial infection:

	Maximum (days).	Minimum (days).	Mean (days).
Quartan fever............................	15	11	13
Tertian fever............................	12	6	10
Æstivo-autumnal fever..................	5	2	3

It is interesting to note how closely the period of incubation in these experimental infections agrees with the time which clinical observation has shown to elapse between supposed infection and the outbreak of the disease. Particularly interesting is the demonstration that in æstivo-autumnal fever, from the inoculation of two cubic centimetres of blood, clinical symptoms may appear in as short a time as forty-eight hours.*

It is but natural to assume that with a given variety of parasites the period of incubation should vary greatly, not only according to the quantity of the infectious material absorbed by the individual, but also according to the time of the year, the conditions under which the infection takes place, the physical condition of the patient himself, and the special virulence of the parasite.

Are we justified, then, in assuming that in certain instances the period may be as short as several hours, and in others as long as one hundred and eighty-four days? Neither of these extreme estimates can be said to be proven. In the present state of our knowledge we can not deny the possibility of the

---

* Celli and Santori (Centralblatt f. Bakt., xxi, 1897, 49), in an experiment to determine the incubation period of malarial fever in individuals previously treated with the serum of animals immune against the disease, observed the development of fever with parasites in the blood *thirty* hours after the subcutaneous inoculation of 1·5 centimetres of blood from a case of æstivo-autumnal fever.

CLINICAL DESCRIPTION OF MALARIAL FEVER. 101

appearance of symptoms within twenty-four hours after infection. We know parasites whose entire cycle of existence lasts only twenty-four hours, or even less. It is not unreasonable to suppose an infection with so many and so virulent parasites that the very first period of sporulation might be accompanied by well-marked subjective symptoms. Indeed, one is almost tempted to assume this as a probability. The assertion, however, that the disease may appear within a few hours after the first exposure needs confirmation.

It is possible that the febrile attacks which occur sometimes immediately after exposure at night in damp, marshy, malarious districts may have some other cause than actual malarial infection. Thus, Plehn describes cases where, after exposure at night in very severely malarious districts in West Africa, there was an immediate paroxysm in every way similar to those of malaria, which, however, did not recur until the appearance, ten days later, of a true malarial fever, which doubtless dated its origin to the night of exposure. At the time of the first paroxysm the blood was negative; the parasites—æstivo-autumnal—appeared ten days later with the usual symptoms of the disease.

How are we to explain those cases where an excessively long period elapses between exposure and the manifestations of the disease? It is certainly improbable that this long time represents a true period of incubation. One can scarcely imagine that the parasites should exist in the circulation, passing through their regular cycle of existence for periods of months, without ever reaching a sufficient number to produce any clinical symptoms. It is probable that we must fall back upon another explanation, which, to be sure, is purely hypothetical. We must probably assume that in these cases spontaneous recovery from the infection occurs before the parasites have reached a sufficient quantity to give rise to symptoms. The germs, however, of the infection remain within the organism in some form which is as yet unknown to us, possibly, as Bignami suggests, as encapsulated spores within the bodies of phagocytes. In such an individual insults of various sorts—over-exertion, exposure, debility dependent upon any exhausting process—may be the exciting cause of an awakening of these slumbering germs, which, undergoing rapid multiplication, give rise to an outbreak of typical malarial fever at a period long after possible exposure.

In conclusion, then, we may assume that:

(1) The incubation period of malarial fever is very varied, depending (*a*) upon the type of the potential parasite absorbed at the moment of infection, upon its capacity for rapid multiplication, and upon the quantity of infectious material absorbed; (*b*) upon the conditions under which infection takes place, climate, season of the year, and hygienic surroundings; (*c*) upon the physical condition and surroundings (and race ?) of the infected individual.

(2) Clinical observation and experimental inoculations would tend to show that the period of incubation of the malarial fevers may vary from twenty-four hours, or even a little less, to several weeks. The period is shortest in æstivo-autumnal infection, longer in tertian, and longest in quartan fever.

(3) How short the period of incubation may be has not been ascertained. By analogy it is reasonable to suppose that in some instances it may be as short as twenty-four hours, or a little less.

(4) In cases where very long periods of time, months or years, expire between exposure and the first manifestations of the disease, we must probably assume that spontaneous recov-

ery has occurred with the survival of the parasite in some more resistant form as yet unknown to us—a process similar probably to that which occurs in cases of relapse after long periods of time.

1. THE REGULARLY INTERMITTENT FEVERS.—(*a*) TERTIAN FEVER.

Single Tertian Infections.—Tertian fever is by far the commonest variety of malarial infection in the temperate climates. It is the form of the disease most frequently met with on the eastern coast of the United States. In single tertian infections we have to do with the presence in the blood of one group of the tertian parasite, an organism which passes through its cycle of existence in about forty-eight hours.

As has been pointed out in the description of the parasite, tertain infections are characterized by the aggregation of the organisms into groups, all the members of which are at the same stage of development, and pass through their cycle of existence in unison. Thus, the periods at which successive generations of parasites reach maturity and undergo sporulation occur every other day at intervals approximately forty-eight hours apart. As will be remembered from what has been said in the description of the parasite, the sporulation of such a group of organisms is always followed by a paroxysm of fever, provided only that the number of parasites has reached by multiplication a quantity sufficient to produce clinical symptoms.

Thus, if the blood contain but one group of tertian parasites the clinical manifestations will be tertian intermittent febrile paroxysms.

Clinical Symptoms.—*Prodromata.*—For several days before the occurrence of an actual paroxysm the patient may complain of indefinite symptoms of headache, backache, anorexia, pains in the limbs—symptoms such as are common in any acute infection. Usually it may be noted that these symptoms occur on alternate days, and often in the morning; on the day between the patient may feel quite well. In examining the charts of patients in whom malarial fever has developed in an hospital ward, we may almost always trace slight febrile elevations occurring before the first actual paroxysm—elevations which had passed quite unnoticed.

On the other hand, the first paroxysm may come without warning upon an individual in apparently perfect health.

The Paroxysm.—The paroxysm may be divided into three characteristic stages:

(1) The chill.
(2) The fever.
(3) The defervescence or sweating stage.

The Chill.—Especially characteristic of the malarial paroxysm is its very sudden onset. Often the slight prodromata which have been mentioned may be quite absent, and the first symptom which the patient notices of his illness may be the onset of a sharp paroxysm. The actual chill is, however, usually preceded by some indefinite symptoms of *malaise*, headache, and slight feelings of general lassitude; often repeated yawning and stretching may be observed. Sometimes there is a little giddiness, and there may be at the very beginning, nausea and vomiting. Frequently at this period a slight rise in the body temperature has already set in.

These symptoms are usually followed rapidly by chilly sensations, beginning sometimes in the hands and feet, and running up and down the back. These chilly sensations, at first interrupted by slight flashes of heat, rapidly increase until the patient falls into a general rigor. The chill may be most severe; the patient begs for coverings and hot applications. The actual shaking may be so violent that it is noticeable in other rooms of the house.

The face is drawn and pinched; the extremities are cold and shrunken. The skin is usually cool and cyanotic, sometimes pale; it is often moist, while the hair follicles are erect, giving rise to the characteristic "goose-flesh." The pupils are usually dilated; the pulse is small and rapid, sometimes irregular, and often of rather high tension. The respiration is short and rapid; the voice is broken; nausea and vomiting are frequent; there may be diarrhœa. The patient usually suffers extremely from headache; there may be vertigo or tinnitus aurium, and sometimes troubles of vision; aching pains in the loins are common.

The duration of the chill may vary considerably, being at times as long as an hour, though usually it is shorter, from ten minutes to half an hour. Sometimes no actual shaking may occur, the patient complaining only of more or less severe chilly sensations, while at times, though rarely in this type of fever, the chill may be entirely absent.

Out of 332 cases occurring at the Johns Hopkins Hospital, chills or chilly sensations were present in 97·5 per cent. During the chill, despite the intense feeling of cold complained of by the patient and the somewhat cool feeling of the moist and cyanotic skin, the body temperature rapidly rises. The maximum point is usually reached within two hours after the onset of the paroxysm, and indeed sometimes in a much shorter time. The climax may occur at the very beginning of the second stage.

The Fever.—The intensity of the chill slowly diminishes. The chilly sensations become interrupted by occasional flushes of heat, which, becoming more frequent, finally wholly replace the rigor. Then begins the second or febrile stage of the paroxysm. The patient now complains of intense heat. The skin is flushed, hot, and dry; the conjunctivæ injected; the pulse becomes fuller, but remains rapid and is not infrequently dicrotic. The headache, vertigo, and tinnitus aurium often become more intense, the patient complaining bitterly also of general aching pains in the back and extremities. The bedclothes are thrown aside, while the patient suffers intense thirst; he is often very restless, tossing from one side of the bed to the other; there may be active delirium. On the other hand, the patient may be dull and drowsy, presenting an appearance not dissimilar to that in typhoid fever, while the only complaint may be of intense headache and general aching pains. Sometimes there may be marked somnolence, and in one instance deep coma has been reported. A slight cough is not infrequent, and vomiting and diarrhœa are common. Bleeding from the nose has occurred in a few of our instances.

On physical examination during this period the patient is usually flushed, the conjunctivæ are suffused and injected, the tongue dry and coated. There is often a slight sallow, dusky-yellowish color to the skin, a tint which is almost characteristic of malaria, and becomes after a while familiar to the skilled observer. If the fever has lasted for any length of time there is almost always a distinct anæmia, recognizable by the pallor of the lips and mucous membranes. This may be a point of considerable importance in diagnosis.

The heart sounds are usually clear, though there may be a soft systolic murmur. On examination of the lungs a few sonorous and sibilant râles may be heard. The abdomen presents no abnormalities on inspection. On percussion, however, a well-marked enlargement of the spleen is demonstrable, while the splenic border is to be felt in the great majority of instances. This has been possible in about seventy-five per cent of our cases. In fresh acute infections the border may be soft and round; where, however, numerous infections have occurred, the edge is usually hard and sharp. After repeated attacks the spleen may attain a very considerable size, extending as far as or even below the umbilicus. There is often, especially in acute cases, a well-marked tenderness on palpation over the region of the spleen.

Massuriany * noted the presence of a soft murmur over the splenic area which Bouchard has compared to the uterine bruit.

Sometimes well-marked cutaneous manifestations may appear during the paroxysm; these may begin in the stage of the chill, but are usually more marked during the febrile period. Various forms of rash have been observed. The commonest, however, is urticaria, which we have observed in a number of instances. In several of the author's cases this urticarial eruption has had a most interesting morbiliform character. The eruption usually disappears with the paroxysm. It should, however, be remembered that some of these cutaneous manifestations attributed to the malarial infection may not impossibly be due to the treatment by quinine.

Herpes upon the lips and nose is very common in malarial fever, and in certain of the more irregular forms is of value from a point of view of differential diagnosis.

The temperature during this period reaches its maximum point. It may be as high as 108° F. The duration of the

---

* St. Pet. med. Woch., 1884.

febrile period is usually four or five hours, though not infrequently it may be considerably longer.

The Sweating Stage.—After the stage of fever has existed for some hours—four or five, perhaps, on the average—the severity of the symptoms begins to abate; the mouth becomes less dry, the skin begins to become moist, and profuse sweating follows. This is associated with a relief from the distressing sensation of heat from which the patient has been suffering. The sweating is usually excessive; the bedclothes are often drenched. The temperature rapidly falls. With the fall of temperature the pulse likewise becomes slow and full, and the patient often sinks into a refreshing sleep. Within a relatively short time, rarely more than four hours, often as short as two, the temperature reaches the normal point. It does not, however, remain here, but becomes usually subnormal, and often remains so during the greater part of the intermission between the febrile paroxysms. The length of the entire paroxysm, from the time the temperature passes 99° F. until it again reaches this point, averaged in our cases about eleven hours. The paroxysms are more frequent during the day than during the night, and the hour of onset occurs usually perhaps during the morning hours, though paroxysms in the afternoon and at night are not uncommon.

The clinical manifestations in children may be very different from those observed in adults. Frequently both the chill and the sweating stage may be quite absent or only abortive; under these circumstances the first stage is generally represented by a slight restlessness; the face looks pinched, the eyes sunken, the finger tips and toes become cyanotic and cold, while the child yawns and stretches itself. Nausea and vomiting and diarrhœa are very common. These may be the only manifestations of the first stage. Often, however, these symptoms are followed by grave nervous phenomena. The chill in malaria, as in other acute diseases, is not infrequently represented in a young child by general convulsions. These may begin with a slight spasmodic twitching of the eyelids or extremities, the spasm soon becoming general. The febrile stage and the whole paroxysm are often shorter in the child than in the adult, while the sweating stage may be wholly absent. In many instances, besides a slight coldness of the hands and blueness of the finger tips, and a somewhat pinched expression of the face during the first stage, the first and third stages of the paroxysm may be entirely lacking.

The Intermission.—Following the sweating stage, the patient passes through an afebrile period lasting usually fully thirty-seven hours. Often, during the greater part of this time, the temperature is subnormal; it is almost invariably so during the hours following the paroxysm. After the immediate exhausting effects of the paroxysm have passed away, the patient very commonly feels perfectly well, so much so that he may leave his bed and go about his business. Indeed, many patients feel so well between paroxysms that they allow several to pass before seeking treatment, believing, after each paroxysm, that the fever is at an end.

Almost exactly forty-eight hours, however, after the onset of the first paroxysm a second similar attack follows, the febrile periods and intermissions continuing thus with great regularity. (*Vide* Charts No. I and XVII, pp. 110 and 171.)

While, as has been said, the cycle of existence of the tertian parasite is about forty-eight hours in duration, and the paroxysms are approximately forty-eight hours apart, it must not be forgotten that variations of several hours in the cycle of existence of the parasite are not uncommon. Thus, not

CHART I.

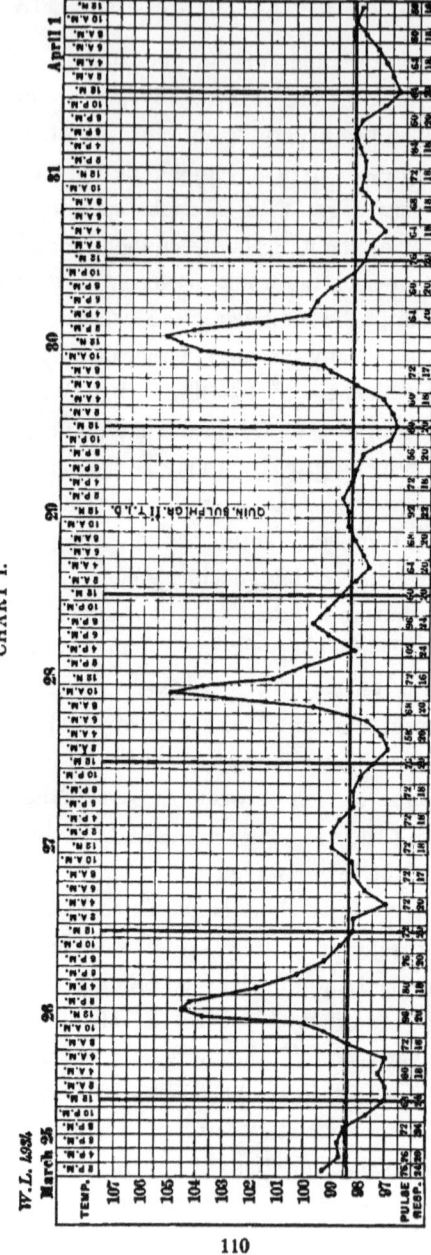

Tertian Fever—Single Infection.

CLINICAL DESCRIPTION OF MALARIAL FEVER. 111

infrequently, a group of tertian parasites may pass through their cycle in forty-five or perhaps forty-three hours instead of in forty-eight. This results in the *anticipation* of the paroxysms. In other instances, particularly during spontaneous recovery or after the taking of small doses of quinine, there may be a marked retardation.

The blood shows the presence of one group of tertian parasites. The cycle of existence of this organism may be usually well followed out in the peripheral circulation. During and after the paroxysm small actively amœboid, hyaline bodies may be made out within certain of the red corpuscles. Shortly after this, very minute brownish-yellow granules of pigment may be found to have appeared within the amœboid organisms. The activity of the parasite and the dancing of the pigment is, as will be remembered, much greater than in the case of the quartan parasite, while the surrounding corpuscle soon begins to show evidence of expansion and decolorization.

On the day between paroxysms the organisms are usually not quite half the size of an ordinary red corpuscle, and extremely amœboid and irregular in shape; the pigment is brown, very fine and actively dancing; the surrounding corpuscle is expanded and decolorized. On the day of the paroxysm, five or six hours before the onset, parasites may be observed which are nearly the size of a normal red corpuscle. The pigment is somewhat coarser and darker than it was in the beginning, and is usually somewhat less active. The amœboid movements of the parasite are almost lost. The surrounding corpuscle is scarcely visible.

Shortly after this the pigment collects at one point in the centre or nearer the periphery, in a single clump or block, and evidences of incipient segmentation are to be made out. The parasite, as will be remembered, breaks into more segments than the quartan organism, giving rise usually to from fifteen to twenty. At the same time with segmentation there are often to be observed large, swollen, apparently extra-cellular forms with actively dancing pigment granules, numerous fragmenting bodies, vacuolated and flagellate forms. All these forms arise apparently from full-grown parasites, which have not segmented. Toward the end of the paroxysm fresh hyaline bodies begin to make their appearance.

The discovery of segmenting organisms is much less frequent in tertian than in quartan infections for the reason, as has been stated above, that much of the segmentation goes on probably in the internal organs. Thus, just before or during the early part of a paroxysm in tertian fever, if the infection be a mild one, we may at times have to search very carefully before finding any organisms. It is very rare that one is able to follow in the peripheral blood the entire life history of a group of tertian parasites which is not large enough to produce well-marked clinical symptoms. We have never been able to do this.

As pointed out by Golgi, evidences of phagocytosis in the form of pigmented leucocytes may be made out in the regularly intermittent fevers at definite cyclical intervals. Thus, during and immediately following a paroxysm the appearance of a considerable number of phagocytes may be observed. These are both polymorphonuclear and mononuclear elements; the pigment may be in scattered granules, or in blocks similar to those seen in the segmenting forms. Often phagocytosis may be observed in the fresh specimen. It is interesting to note that while a very considerable number of large mononuclear pigment-containing cells are to be seen, actual phagocytosis is never to be observed upon the slide, excepting by polymorphonuclear neutrophilic leucocytes. Sometimes pigmented leucocytes and phagocytes are to be observed between paroxysms. At this period only extra-cellular bodies which have escaped from the red corpuscle are attacked. During the paroxysm we may see the engulfing not only of free pigment, but also of fragmented extra-cellular organisms, of flagellate bodies, and sometimes also of complete sporulating forms.

Beyond the presence of parasites the blood shows usually little that is remarkable. If the infection has lasted for any great length of time, the evidences of an acute anæmia become apparent—pallor of the corpuscles, marked difference in size of the individual elements, nucleated red corpuscles, and perhaps a little poikilocytosis.

The most striking feature is the fact that the number of leucocytes is almost always *subnormal*, while the large mononuclear forms are relatively increased at the expense of the polymorphonuclear varieties.

The whole subject will be discussed later in the remarks upon post-malarial anæmia.

Double Tertian Infections—Quotidian Intermittent Fever. —In this climate we more commonly meet with infections with two groups of the parasite—a double tertian infection. These groups reach maturity on alternate days, and give rise, therefore, to daily paroxysms—*quotidian intermittent fever.* The paroxysms differ in no way from those observed in single tertian infections, unless they be a trifle shorter, lasting on an average from ten to eleven hours, associated with regular stages of chill, fever, and sweating. The regularity in the recurrence of these paroxysms is not quite so great as in quartan infections.

The chills on alternate days often come at hours surpris-

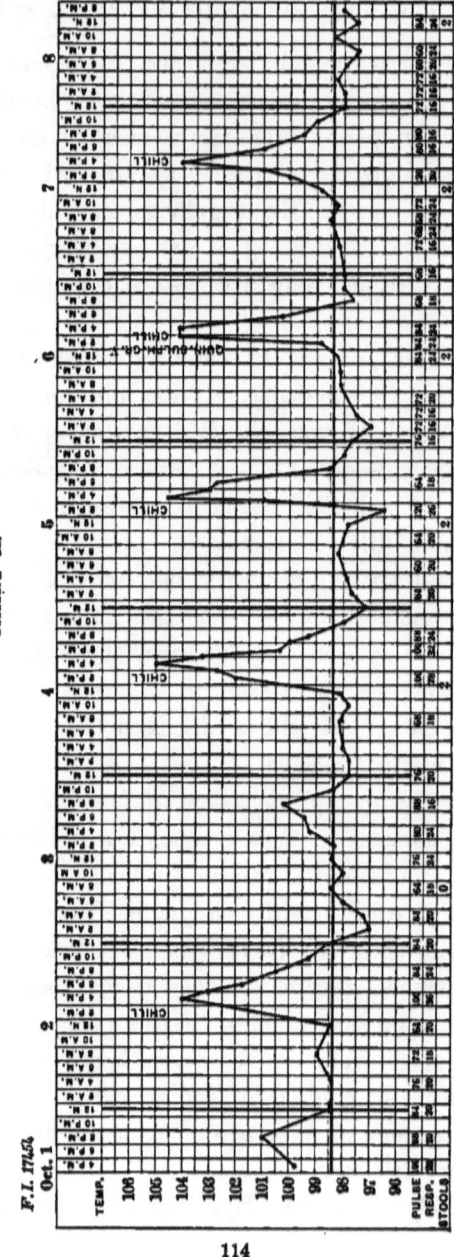

CHART II.

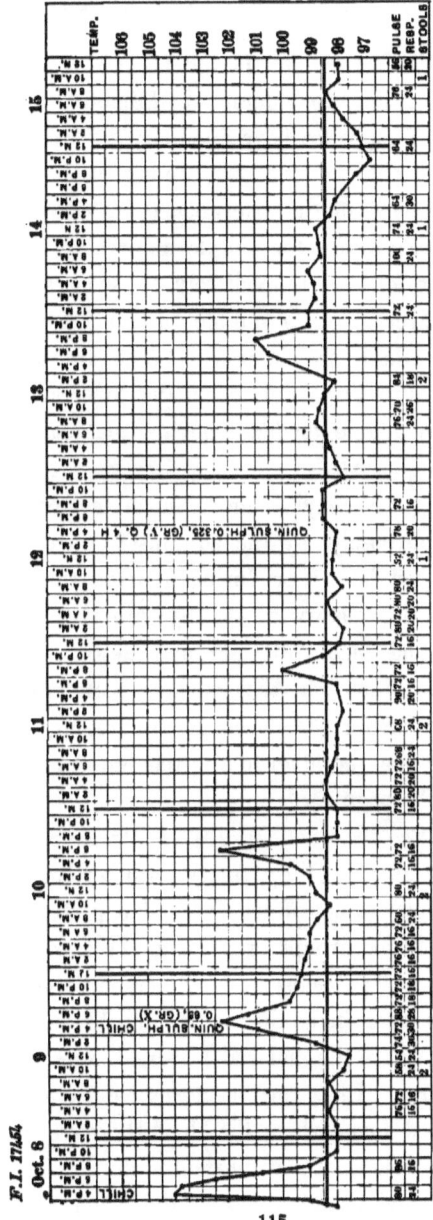

QUOTIDIAN FEVER—DOUBLE TERTIAN INFECTION.

The chart shows the gradual increase in the severity of the fever due to the originally weaker group of parasites. With convalescence the fever due to one group of parasites disappears first.

ingly similar (*vide* Charts Nos. II and III, pp. 114 and 116); the cause for this is hard to understand. Sometimes, however, the two groups of parasites have distinctly different hours of segmentation, the chill on one day coming in the morning, on the other, perhaps, in the afternoon (*vide* Chart No. IV, page 117). In such a case the simple observation of several paroxysms might lead us immediately to suspect the true nature of the fever—i. e., a double tertian infection. In other instances, where the hours of onset are nearly the same, it may be quite impossible from the fever curve alone to differentiate a double tertian from a triple quartan infection.

Often the diagnosis may be made in an interesting way, accidentally or purposely, by the administration of a single dose of quinine just before or during a paroxysm. It is at this stage in the life history of the parasite that quinine is most efficacious, and such treatment may destroy the single group of parasites which is at that moment segmenting without materially affecting the other group present, changing thus the chart from a quotidian to a tertian intermittent fever (*vide* Chart No. V, page 118).

Infections with Multiple Groups of Parasites—Irregular or Continued Fever.—Very rarely with tertian infection we may see irregular or continued fever, due probably to the infection with multiple groups of parasites or to the lack of arrangement of the parasites in well-marked large groups. This condition is rare in adults; it is probably more often seen in children, where the malarial infections pursue a much less regular course. In a few instances we have observed irregular continued fever where the blood showed only an occasional tertian parasite. In two instances the parasites were not found on several examinations of the blood, and it was

CHART III.

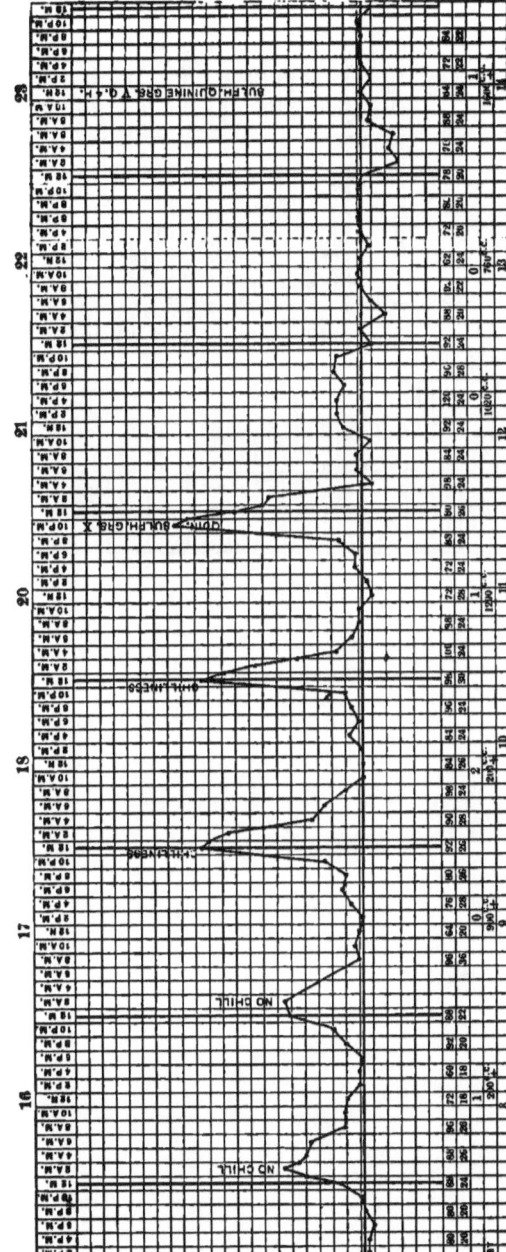

TERTIAN AND QUOTIDIAN FEVER—DOUBLE TERTIAN INFECTION.
quotidian from an originally tertian fever. The fever disappeared entirely following a single dose of quinine on the 19th.

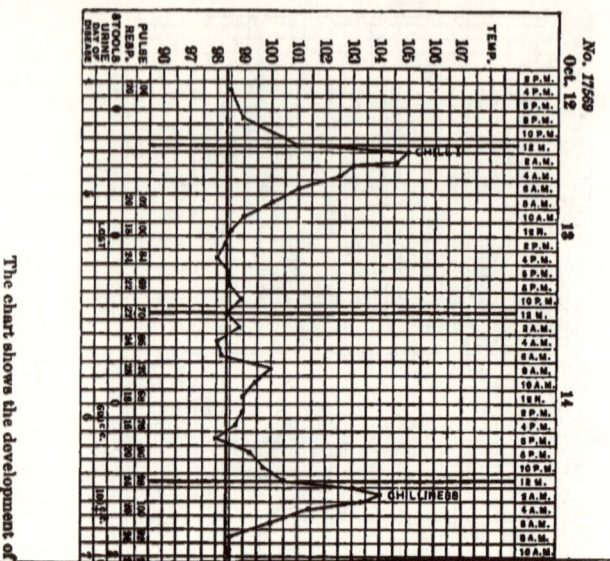

The chart shows the development of

CHART IV.

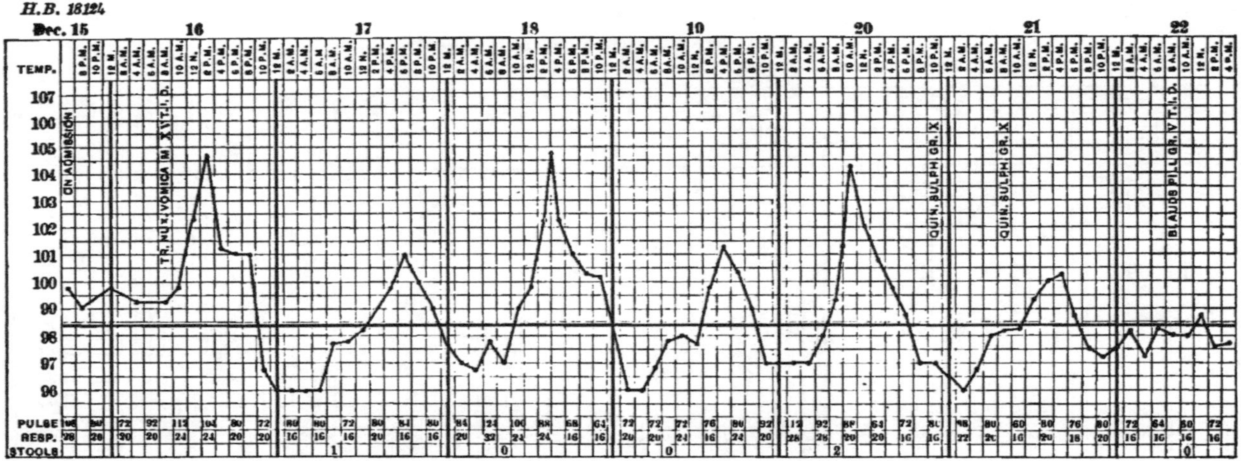

QUOTIDIAN FEVER—DOUBLE TERTIAN INFECTION.

The chart shows one severe and one mild set of paroxysms occurring at different hours on successive days.

CHART V.

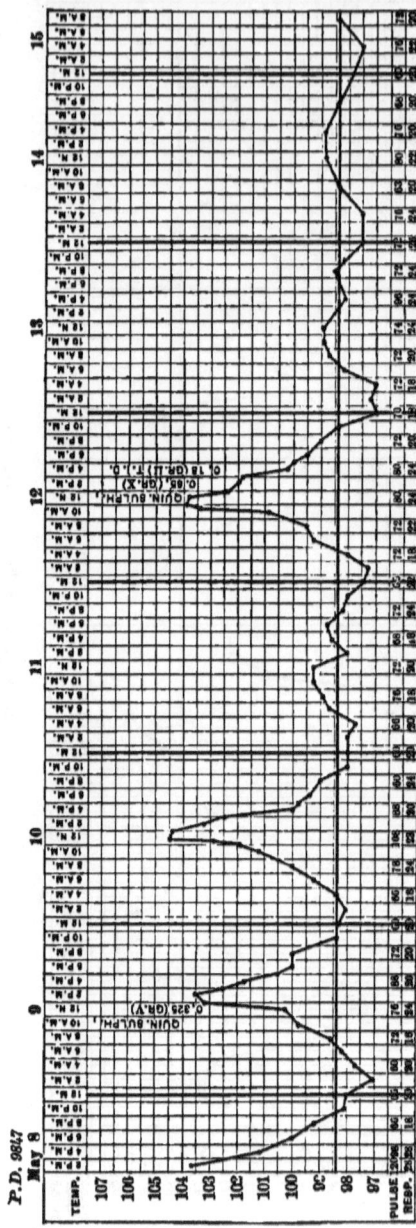

QUOTIDIAN FEVER—DOUBLE TERTIAN INFECTION.

Disappearance of one group of parasites following a single dose of quinine at the onset of a paroxysm with a consequent change in the chart from quotidian to tertian fever.

CLINICAL DESCRIPTION OF MALARIAL FEVER. 119

only after the fall of the temperature and the appearance of regular paroxysms that the organisms were found. These two marked instances suggest that at times the greater part of the cycle of development of the parasites may take place in the internal organs, while the irregularity in the manifestations suggests the presence of multiple groups (*vide* Chart No. VI, pp. 120 and 121).

(*b*) QUARTAN FEVER.

Single Quartan Infection.—Quartan fever, as has been said in the preceding chapter, depends upon infection with the quartan parasite (Golgi), an organism whose cycle of existence lasts about seventy-two hours. This parasite also possesses the remarkable characteristic of appearing in the blood in large groups, all the members of which are at approximately the same stage of development. The myriads of organisms forming such a group reach maturity and undergo sporulation all together within a period of a few hours. Thus, if the blood of the infected individual contain one group of quartan parasites which has acquired any considerable size, we may readily see that every fourth day a sporulation of this group takes place, and, as might be expected, the clinical manifestations are quartan, intermittent paroxysms.

Quartan fever is not common in the United States; indeed, it appears to be everywhere much less generally disseminated than tertian fever. In Italy there are special *foyers* where quartan fever is particularly frequent; such, for instance, are certain parts of Sicily and the neighborhood of Pavia in Italy. In this country we meet only with occasional cases. In Baltimore, out of one thousand six hundred and eighteen cases of malaria observed in the past seven years, there have been but fifteen instances of quartan fever.

CHART VI.

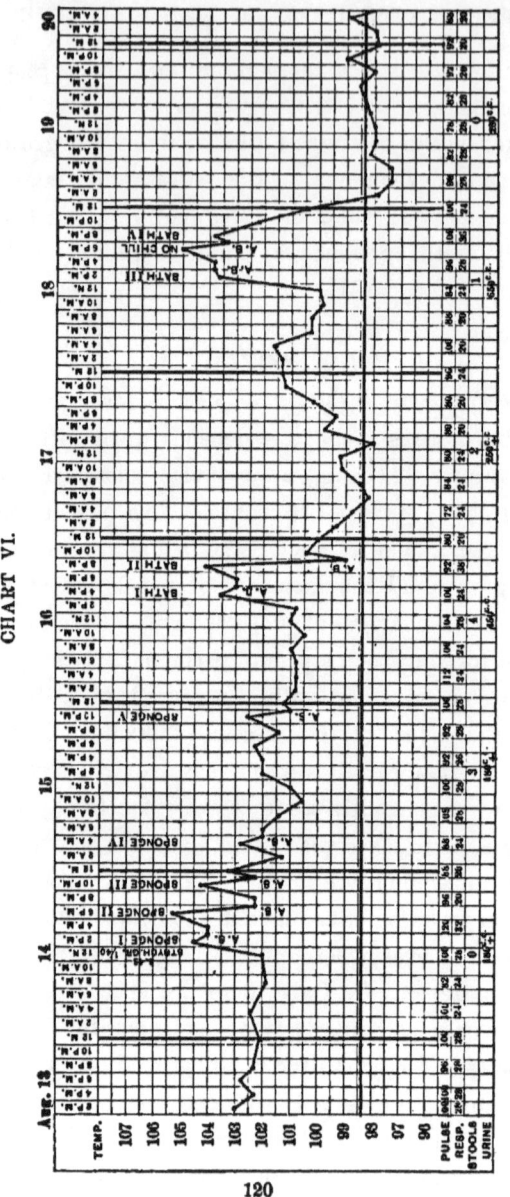

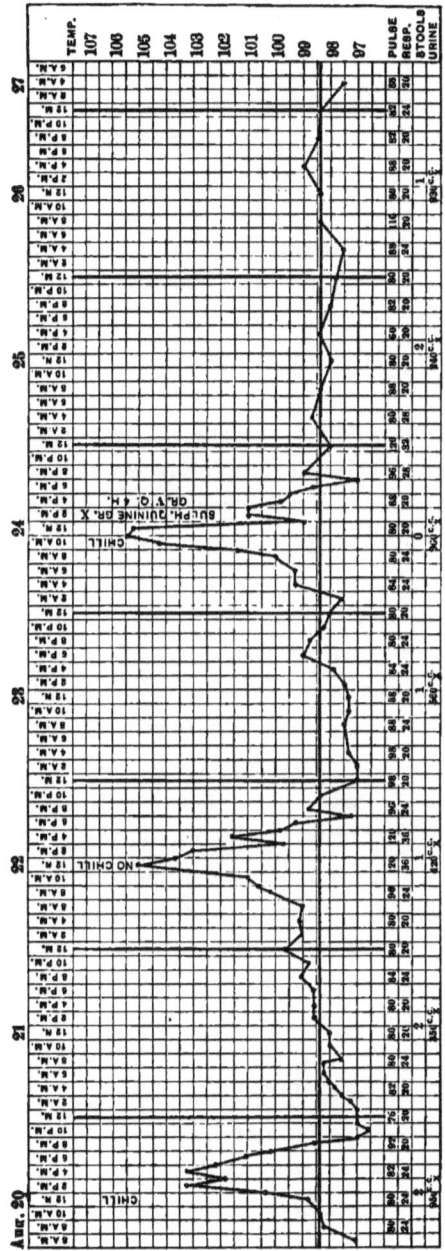

Continued Fever Due to Infection with Tertian Parasites.

Under treatment by cold baths the manifestations changed to those of ordinary tertian fever.

The interesting fact that in the same climate and with the same general telluric conditions certain regions are the seat of one type of fever, while other regions which may be in the near neighborhood show other forms, was pointed out very clearly some years ago by Trousseau. This keen observer,* when speaking of the different types of malarial fever, states: "The types seem to depend upon the nature of the miasm, and especially upon the locality which it infects, rather than upon conditions relative to the individual who is affected. Tours and Saumur, both situated on the left bank of the Loire, appear to me to present the same climacteric and telluric conditions; yet one observes at Tours only tertian fevers, while several cases of quartan fever which I have met with there were in individuals coming either from Saumur or Rochefort, or from other regions where they had contracted it. One of the examples which has most impressed me in connection with the subject is the following: Fourteen soldiers imprisoned at Saumur came to Tours to testify before a court-martial; they had been scarcely ten days in the last town when nine of them were compelled to enter the hospital, affected with quartan fever, the germ of which they had evidently contracted at Saumur, since all the fevers we observed with the inhabitants of Tours and the neighborhood were of the tertian type."

The paroxysms are quite similar to those of tertian fever. Their duration averages about the same length of time, while the defervescence is also followed by a period of subnormal temperature which may last until the onset of the succeding attacks (*vide* Chart No. VII, page 123).

Often for a considerable length of time the paroxysms may recur almost precisely at the same hour every fourth day, the

---

* Clinique médicale, 2d edition, 1865, vol. iii, p. 425.

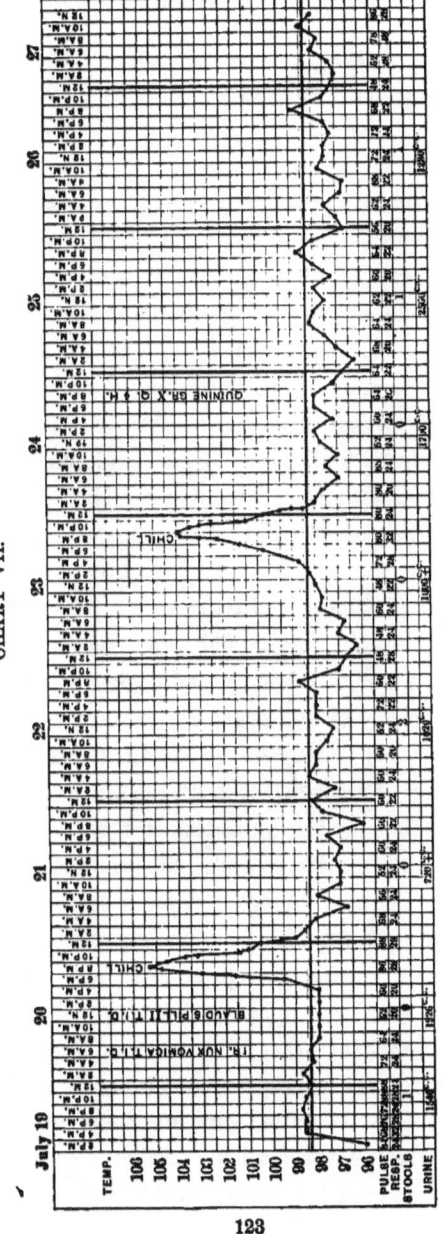

CHART VII. QUARTAN FEVER.

123

regularity in onset being very remarkable. Not infrequently, however, succeeding paroxysms occur at a period several hours in advance of or behind the hour of the appearance of the earlier attacks. Thus, one speaks of anticipating or retarding paroxysms. The anticipation or retardation in some instances of quartan fever may be well marked. This is, however, not very common, the paroxysms appearing, as a rule, at periods nearly seventy-two hours apart.

The blood shows the presence of a single group of the quartan parasites, and the diagnosis may therefore readily be made. This organism may be traced by examination on different days through all stages of its development. Shortly after the paroxysm the small hyaline amœboid intra-cellular bodies are to be found within the red corpuscles; in the course of a few hours a few dark, slightly motile pigment granules begin to appear. On the second day the parasites have grown somewhat larger and have become much less amœboid; the pigment is coarser and darker and tends to lie about the periphery of the organism, while the surrounding corpuscle is already usually somewhat smaller than it is normally, and often of a somewhat deeper color.

Upon the third day the parasites are a little larger, round or ovoid in shape, almost entirely non-amœboid. The pigment is lazy and slow in its movements; is coarser and darker, often arranged more particularly at the periphery of the parasite. The red corpuscle is represented by a small rim of deep yellowish-green protoplasm, often markedly darker and more brassy-colored than that of the surrounding corpuscles.

On the day of the paroxysm, sometimes as much as eight or ten hours before its onset, some of these large round or ovoid bodies, which now are a little smaller than a normal red corpuscle, may be seen apparently free in the blood current;

on very careful examination, however, they are usually seen to have a slight rim of now, perhaps, wholly decolorized protoplasm. At the same time, or a little later, the collection of pigment toward the centre in the characteristic star-shaped manner described in the section upon the parasite may be observed, while soon bodies with central pigment clumps or blocks and beginning radial striation may be made out.

Quartan fever affords an excellent opportunity for studying segmenting bodies. These bodies are found throughout the six or eight hours preceding the paroxysm, and are often associated at this time with large swollen forms with dancing pigment, vacuolating and fragmenting bodies, and flagellate forms. The sporulating bodies, as has been noted, contain usually from six to twelve segments. During the paroxysm fresh hyaline bodies begin to appear in the red corpuscles.

Phagocytosis is to be observed here just as in tertian fever, especially during and just following the paroxysms, while the same elements are attacked.

Double Quartan Infection.—Not infrequently the blood contains two groups of quartan parasites, which reach maturity on successive days. This naturally results in a temperature curve showing paroxysms on two successive days, followed by a day of complete intermission—*double quartan fever* (*vide* Chart No. VIII, page 126). Sometimes the paroxysms may occur in this manner when the case comes under observation; again, however, single quartan fever may, under observation, change into a double quartan. This is probably due to the fact that at the beginning of the infection two groups of parasites are present, one being considerably larger than the other, and reaching a size sufficient to produce paroxysms at a period earlier than in the case of the other

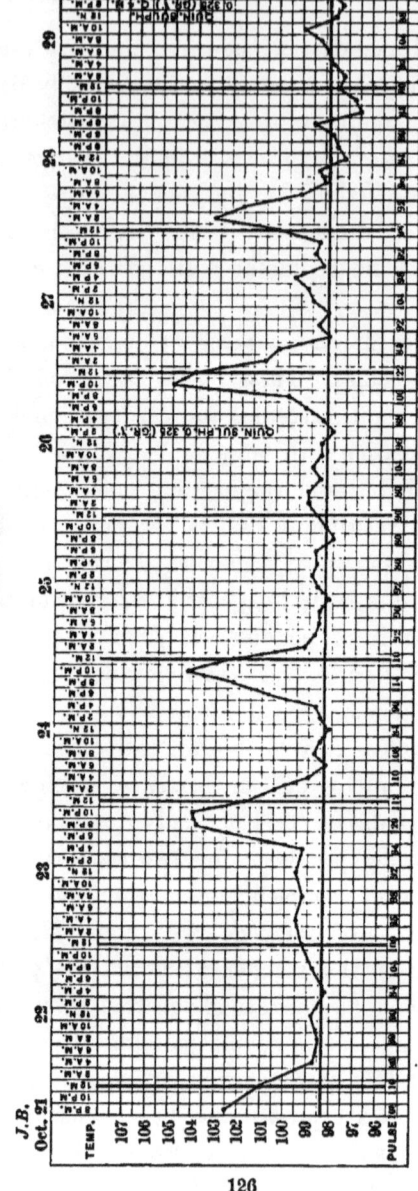

CHART VIII.

DOUBLE QUARTAN FEVER.

Slight retardation of the paroxysms due probably to two doses of quinine on the 25th.

126

CLINICAL DESCRIPTION OF MALARIAL FEVER. 127

group. The paroxysms in these instances are in every way similar to those in single quartan infections.

The *blood* shows the presence of two groups of the quartan parasite.

Triple Quartan Infection—Quotidian Intermittent Fever.—Again, we may have to do with cases showing infection with three sets of the quartan parasites, reaching maturity on successive days. Clinically, quotidian intermittent paroxysms are observed. These paroxysms may occur at almost exactly the same hour on successive days, though not infrequently there is a slight difference in the hours of onset. On study of such a chart we may sometimes make out that the time of onset of any given attack corresponds closely with the hour of onset of the paroxysm occurring upon the fourth day before or after. Thus, on Monday and Thursday the paroxysm may begin at nine; on Tuesday and Friday at eleven; on Wednesday and Saturday at eight. These differences, however, are usually very slight, and, owing to the possible anticipation or retardation of any one group, the definite diagnosis of a triple quartan infection would in most cases be difficult to make without an examination of the blood. The paroxysms are in every way similar to those occurring in single or double quartan infections, and each paroxysm is separated from the following one by a well-marked period of subnormal temperature (*vide* Chart No. IX, page 128).

The *blood* shows the presence of three groups of the quartan parasite. It is not at all infrequent to see cases of double and triple quartan infection where only one set of actual paroxysms occur, so that at first, from the observation of the clinical chart, we might suspect only a single quartan infection. In these instances, however, under further observation of the case, we very often may see the development

CHART IX.

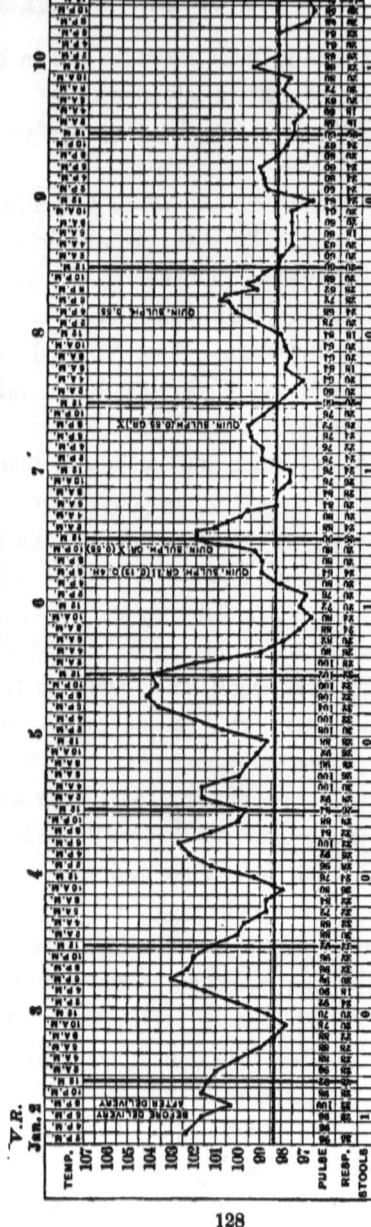

QUOTIDIAN FEVER—TRIPLE QUARTAN INFECTION.

Premature labor occurred during a paroxysm on January 2. The irregularity of the paroxysm beginning on the 4th may be due to puerperal complications.

CLINICAL DESCRIPTION OF MALARIAL FEVER. 129

on the intermediate days of abortive and finally well-marked paroxysms, owing to the multiplication of the other groups of parasites, which previously have been too small to produce well-marked clinical symptoms.

Again, in a double or a triple quartan fever it is not very infrequent to note the disappearance of the paroxysms due to one or two groups of the organism, owing possibly to treatment or to a spontaneous partial disappearance of one or more groups of parasites. The microscope will reveal the presence of a double or triple quartan infection.

The life history of a group of quartan parasites may be traced for weeks in the blood without its ever reaching a size sufficient to bring about more than a very slight abortive rise in temperature. This is due to the fact of the evenness of the distribution of the quartan parasite throughout the general circulation—a fact rendering a diagnosis of quartan fever easier than that of any of the other varieties of malarial infection.

We may see sometimes a triple quartan infection with single quartan paroxysms, where after treatment one set of organisms diminishes in virulence and another increases. This may result in the disappearance of the paroxysms due to the originally stronger group, and the appearance of manifestations due to one of the other groups of parasites which has previously been incapable of producing marked signs.

Very rarely we may see instances in which there are infections with multiple groups of the quartan parasite, resulting in an irregular temperature chart. These cases are, however, extremely unusual. We have never observed such an instance.

2. THE ÆSTIVO-AUTUMNAL FEVERS.

In temperate climates, where during the first half of the year the tertian and quartan fevers alone are observed, there begin to appear during the latter part of July, in August, and especially during the months of September and October, other infections which present certain characteristics sharply different from the regularly intermittent fevers which have just been described. These fevers are especially notable for the marked irregularity in their clinical manifestations. They depend upon the presence in the blood of the third variety of parasite which has been described above, the so-called æstivo-autumnal organism (*Hæmatozoon falciparum*, Welch).

This organism, as will be remembered, has not yet been as satisfactorily studied as the other two forms. Its life history and general biological characteristics are not as well understood. However, from the investigations which have been made, it appears that while at times the parasites may be present in groups undergoing sporulation with considerable regularity at periods varying from twenty-four to forty-eight hours, there are many instances in which the tendency toward arrangement in definite large groups is apparently lost. Here, probably, the segmentation of smaller groups of parasites occurs at frequent intervals, and, on examination of the splenic and peripheral blood, organisms in all stages of development are found at the same time. At the beginning of an infection the arrangement of the parasites in definite groups is frequently present, but after several cycles of existence this arrangement is often lost. When we consider the relation of the segmentation of masses of parasites to the clinical manifestations of malaria, it is easy to see why these fevers present such irregularities in their symptoms.

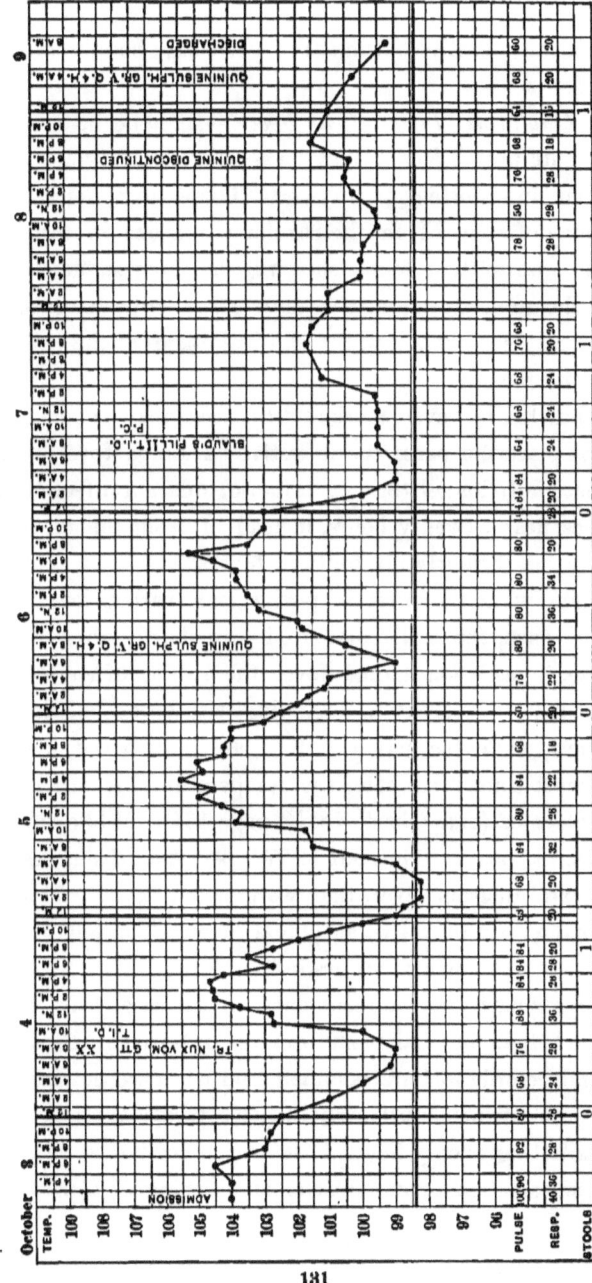

Æstivo-Autumnal Fever—Quotidian Paroxysms.

Clinically, æstivo-autumnal fever may be observed in many forms:

(a) *Quotidian Intermittent Fever.*—In some instances an æstivo-autumnal infection may be associated with well-marked quotidian intermittent paroxysms. These may, indeed, present few differences from the regular paroxysms of tertian or quartan intermittent fever, showing the same suddenness of onset, the same duration, the same rapid defervescence, the whole being separable into the classical stages of the chill, the fever, and the sweating.

Generally, however, marked differences may be noted. In the first place the paroxysm in æstivo-autumnal fever is usually materially longer than in tertian or quartan infections; it averages nearly twenty hours, instead of from ten to twelve hours in the regularly intermittent fevers.

Again, while the onset in tertian and quartan fever is extremely sharp, the chill coming on very shortly after the initial rise, in æstivo-autumnal fever the rise is often more or less gradual, the paroxysm beginning with headache and general pains, while the actual chill, if at all observed, may not occur until some time after the temperature has become already elevated (*vide* Chart No. X, page 131). While chills or chilly sensations were present in 97·2 per cent of our cases of tertian and quartan fever, they were noted in only 71·4 per cent of the cases of æstivo-autumnal fever. The fall in temperature is also much more gradual.

The regularity in the recurrence of the paroxysms is also much less than in tertian and quartan infections. Anticipation and retardation are common, and when we consider the short period which must of necessity separate quotidian paroxysms lasting twenty hours, it is easy to see how a relatively slight anticipation or an unusual lengthening of a paroxysm

CHART XI.

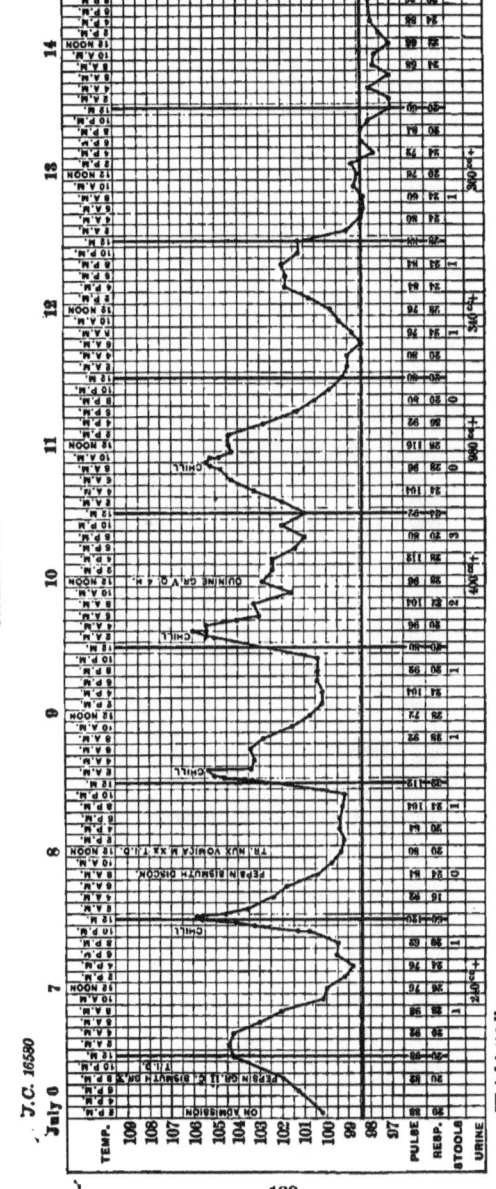

Æstivo-Autumnal Fever.
Quotidian paroxysms developing into subcutaneous fever.

might cause a subcontinuous fever, the temperature never actually reaching normal. Such an event is not at all uncommon, the originally intermittent temperature becoming after a few paroxysms subcontinuous (*vide* Chart No. XI, page 133).

(*b*) *Fever with Longer Intervals*—"*Æstival Tertian Fever.*"—Not at all infrequently in æstivo-autumnal fever the paroxysms occur at intervals of approximately forty-eight hours, a little less or a little more. Indeed, paroxysms may occur at intervals of all the way from twenty-four to forty-eight hours; yet it must be acknowledged that while retardation of quotidian paroxysms is not infrequent, and very marked anticipation of paroxysms occurring approximately at intervals of forty-eight hours may occur, still, the observation of the clinical charts alone would rather incline one in favor of the views advanced by Marchiafava and Bignami, who assert that there are two distinct types of æstivo-autumnal fever, the quotidian and the tertian, due, as they believe, to two definite subdivisions of the parasite. We have not been able to confirm their observations as to the parasites, and though we can not as yet accept the views of the Italian observers, still we must acknowledge the relative infrequency of intermediate stages between fevers with intervals of twenty-four and those of forty-eight hours. Such stages are, however, to be found (*vide* Chart No. XII, page 135).

The longer the interval between the intermittent paroxysms in æstivo-autumnal fever, the longer usually is the paroxysm itself; thus, in æstivo-autumnal intermittent fever, where the intervals between the time of onset of succeeding attacks is as much as forty-eight hours, the paroxysms themselves may be very long, lasting in some instances thirty-six hours, or even more. These prolonged paroxysms differ very markedly from those of the regularly intermittent fevers.

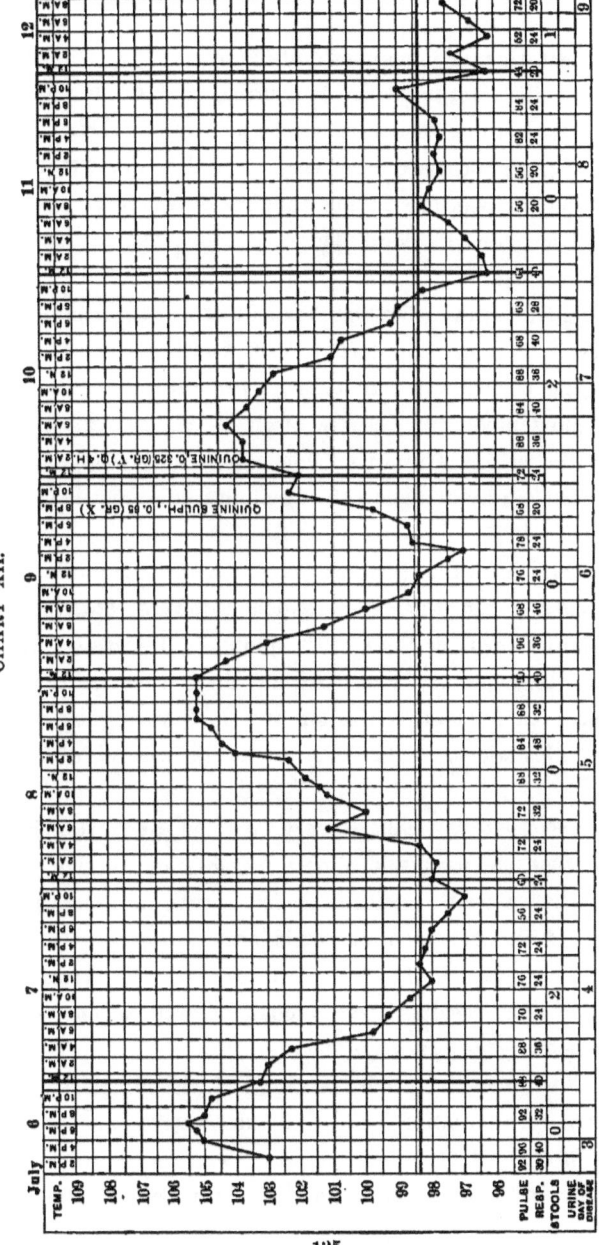

Æstivo–Autumnal Fever.
Paroxysms about thirty-eight hours apart.

Their onset, though sometimes quite rapid, is often very gradual; the chill is not infrequently wanting, and, when present, comes on sometimes relatively late in the course. During the period of fever there are often very marked oscillations in the curve, the temperature falling sometimes nearly to normal, only to rise again to a point higher, possibly, than it had previously reached.

Marchiafava and Bignami have described a typical curve for their æstivo-autumnal tertian fever, consisting of the chill, the febrile period, a pseudo-crisis, a pre-critical elevation in which the temperature reaches often its highest point, and, finally, the crisis. Curves of this nature may often be observed, but are by no means the absolute rule (*vide* Chart No. XIII, page 137).

It would seem that these paroxysms with longer intermissions show a much greater tendency toward anticipation and retardation than those with quotidian intervals. It is rare to observe more than two or three such paroxysms without a subsequent confusion and loss of regularity in the manifestations. This may occur in several different ways.

1. *Anticipation.* This is very common, and often is so marked that one paroxysm almost merges into another, producing thus a nearly continuous fever, with only occasional very brief intermissions or remissions—*malarial remittent fever.* Very frequently this anticipation may be actually so great that there results a continuous fever without any actual intermissions—*continued malarial fever.*

2. The same result may be obtained without marked anticipation or retardation if the individual paroxysms become greatly *prolonged.*

3. During a long paroxysm there may be oscillations in

CHART XIII.

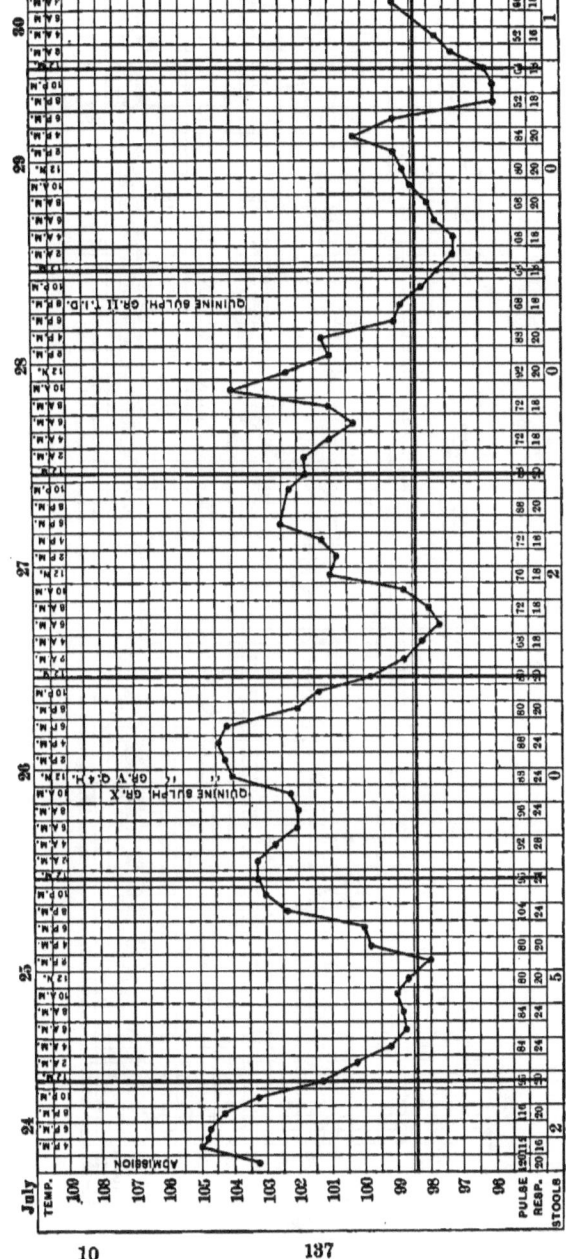

Æstivo–Autumnal Fever.

Tertian paroxysms showing the characteristic curve described by Marchiafava and Bignami.

CHART XIV.

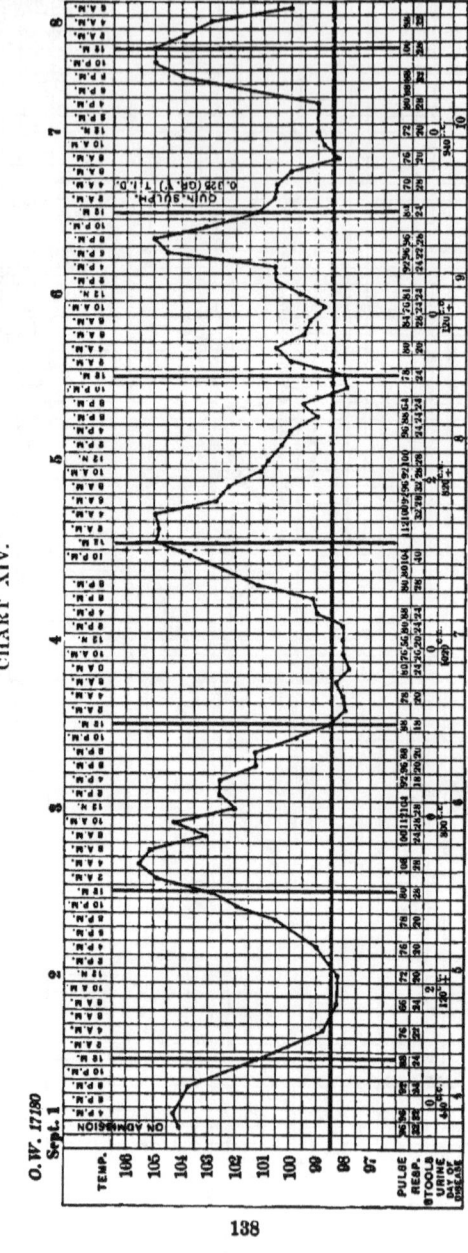

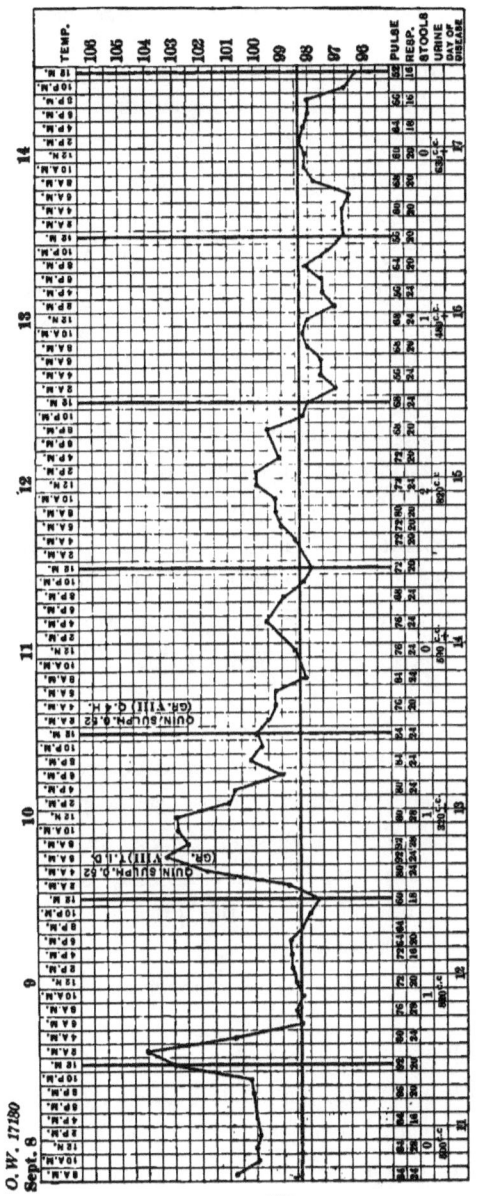

Æstivo-Autumnal Fever.

Paroxysms at first tertian, becoming quotidian.

temperature so marked as to mar the regularity of the fever curve and to render the chart quite incomprehensible.

4. The paroxysms may be markedly *retarded*, so that the intervals between their onset are considerably more than forty-eight hours. This is likely to occur only during a spontaneous recovery or a diminution in the malignancy of an infection. It may, however, be seen even in pernicious cases.

The clinical picture, then, in æstivo-autumnal fever may differ materially from that in the more regularly intermittent varieties. The frequent absence of regularity in the fever curve and the modification or absence of the three classical stages of the paroxysm remove two of the most characteristic symptoms of malarial infections. The patient when first observed is often in a distinctly typhoidal condition; he is dull and drowsy; the face is flushed; the conjunctivæ injected; the tongue dry and brown; the pulse often soft and dicrotic.

On examination of the *thorax* little is to be found, excepting, perhaps, evidences of a slight general bronchitis—sonorous and sibilant râles. The heart sounds are usually clear, though a soft, systolic souffle may be heard. The *abdomen* is negative, though there may be tenderness in the region of the spleen. In the great majority of instances the *spleen* is palpable: soft and round in fresh infections, hard and with a sharp margin in old, continued attacks.

The general picture is so similar to that of typhoid fever that confusion is sometimes inevitable without examination of the blood. In malarial fever, however, there is often a well-marked anæmia; this is the rule if the case has lasted for any length of time; generally, too, there is a distinct sallow, yel-

CLINICAL DESCRIPTION OF MALARIAL FEVER. 141

lowish-gray hue to the skin and conjunctivæ. Herpes upon the lips and nose are very common.

Subjectively, the patient complains bitterly of headache, intense aching pains in the back and extremities, often of giddiness, roaring in the ears, and vertigo. Delirium is common at the height of the attack; it may be of the mild, muttering variety, or, in some pernicious cases, violent and maniacal. Drowsiness increasing to actual coma may be observed. Nausea and vomiting are extremely common during the paroxysm, the patient sometimes being unable to retain any food. Diarrhœa, especially in children, is very frequent. The same cutaneous manifestations may be observed here as in the regularly intermittent fevers. Nosebleed is occasionally observed.

Certain of these cases may pursue a course quite similar to that of typhoid fever through some days, or even weeks. To these cases Baccelli has given the name of *Subcontinua typhoidea* (*vide* Charts XV and XVI, pp. 142 and 144).

Some cases of this nature have probably been included under the fallacious term "typho-malarial fever." This term is wholly incorrect and unscientific. Typhoid fever and malarial fever are two different processes. Certain of their manifestations are, however, somewhat similar, and may lead to confusion in diagnosis if proper steps be not taken. Instances of coexistence of the two infections in one individual are rare and should be readily recognized.

The regularly intermittent fevers, when left to themselves, pursue usually a favorable course, undergoing spontaneous recovery. This, to be sure, is often followed by relapses, which take in turn the same course. It is rare, however, for a regularly intermittent fever to prove of itself fatal; this

CHART XV.

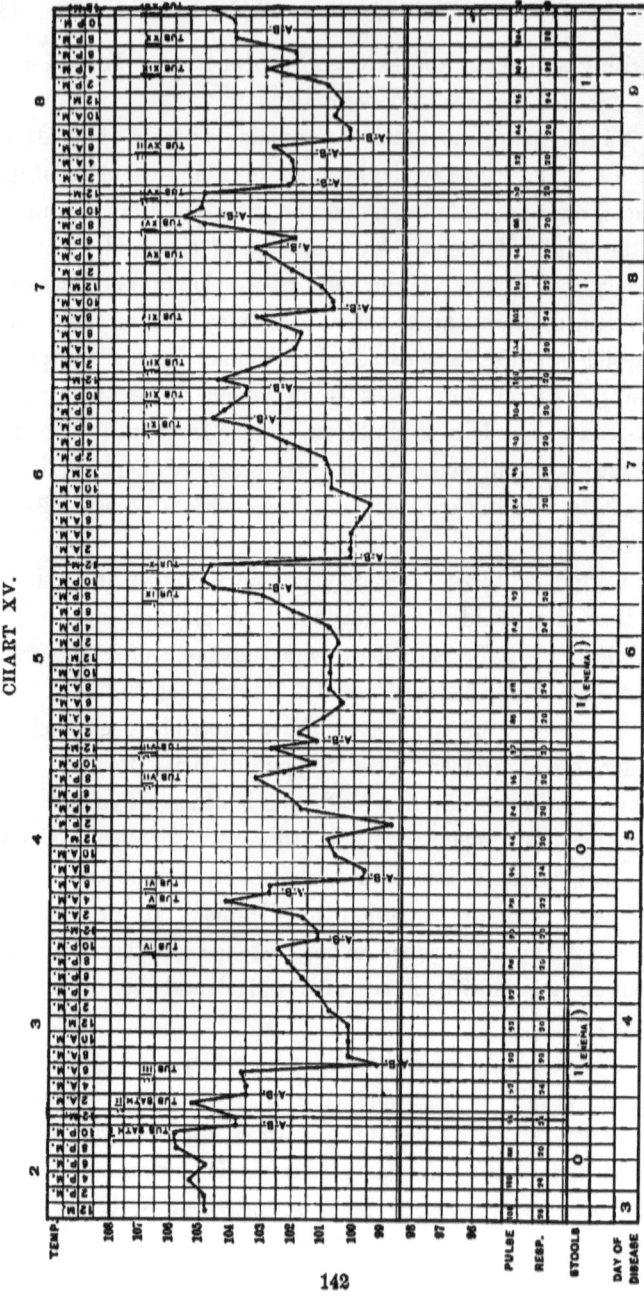

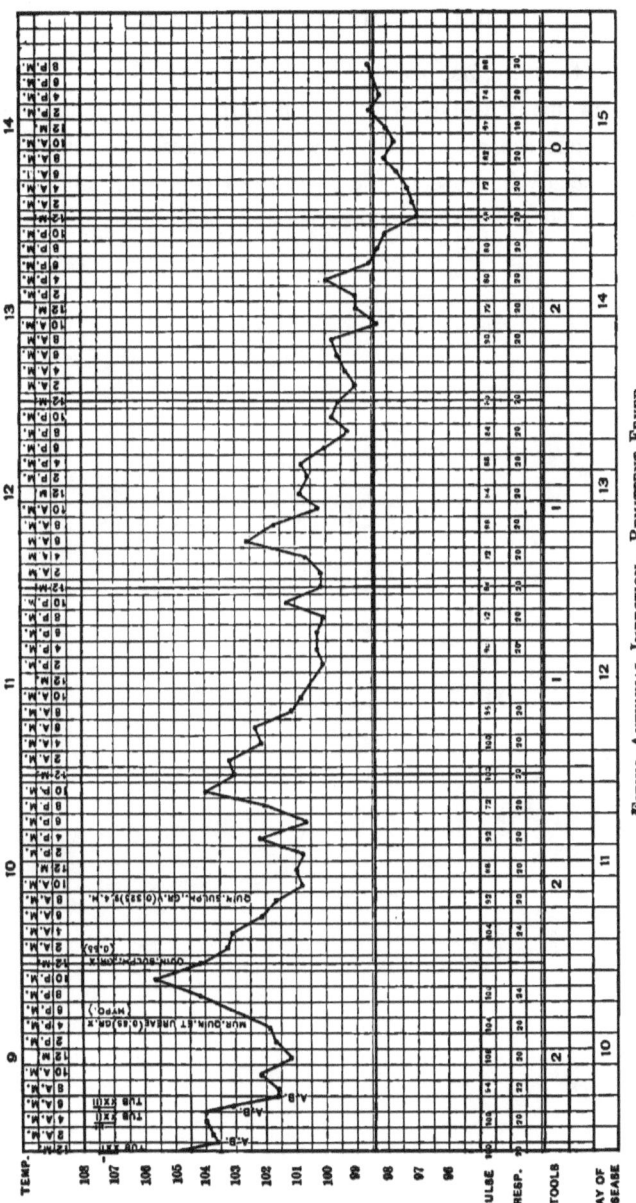

Æstivo-Autumnal Infection.—Remittent Fever.
The case was treated for a week as one of typhoid fever.

is, unfortunately, not true of æstivo-autumnal fever. Here, while in many instances untreated infections may undergo spontaneous recovery, with or without relapse, yet there is often a steady increase in the severity of the symptoms until the so-called pernicious manifestations appear.

Æstivo-Autumnal Fever.—Remittent Fever.—"Subcontinua Typhoidea." peared and the temperature had broken on the 31st. The fever after this was due to an acute parotitis.

TEMP.
105
104
103
102
101
100
99
98
97
96
PULSE
RESP.
TOOLS

LECTURE V.

CLINICAL DESCRIPTION OF THE MALARIAL FEVERS.—(*Continued.*)

Pernicious fevers.—Fevers with long intervals.—Combined infections — Masked malarial infections.—The urine in malarial fever.

"PERNICIOUS" is an adjective which has, through long usage, become definitely attached to the very malignant forms of malarial fever. The term pernicious has come into such general use that it should, I think, be retained, despite the attempt on the part of the English translators of Marchiafava and Bignami's work to introduce the more fitting appellation "malignant."

The pernicious forms of malarial fever are very rarely seen in temperate climates. They are common, on the other hand, in tropical countries and in the most severely malarious regions. They depend almost invariably upon infection with the æstivo-autumnal parasite, though we can not, I think, assert that this is the absolute rule. French,* of Washington, has recently reported a case of comatose malaria due to infection with ordinary tertian parasites, while the writer has on various occasions seen very grave cerebral symptoms in association with severe tertian infections. In the vast majority of instances, however, the pernicious fevers are due to the *Hæmatozoon falciparum.*

---

* N. Y. Med. Jour., 1896, lxiii, 674.

In a general way pernicious symptoms may be said to be due:

1. To the abundance of the parasites present and to their capacity for rapid multiplication. Thus Golgi long ago pointed out, as a regular rule, that the severity of the symptoms in malarial fever was to a certain extent in direct relation to the number of parasites present, and clinical experience has tended largely to support this view.

2. To the special involvement of certain vital organs. As has been noted in the description of the parasites, the æstivo-autumnal organism often undergoes the greater part of its development within certain special organs, and this localization of the parasite may differ materially in different cases. Thus, while in many cases the parasite may be found with equal frequency in all internal organs, in others certain special parts may be involved. In some instances the spleen, in others parts of the central nervous system, in others the gastro-intestinal tract, may be the main seat of the infection. In these cases, as one might naturally expect, the clinical symptoms often point directly to the seat of localization.

3. To the special malignancy of the parasite. Baccelli, in particular, has asserted that different groups of the malarial parasite may vary greatly in their malignancy; thus, in some instances a relatively small group of parasites may produce extremely grave, even pernicious, symptoms—symptoms such as under ordinary circumstances would be produced only by infection with enormous numbers of organisms. While from analogy as well as from clinical observation there is every reason to believe that a difference in the malignity of different cultures of the malarial parasite may exist, it is, however, probable that true pernicious symptoms are never seen without the presence of really a very considerable num-

ber of organisms in the system as a whole. There may be, it is true, very few in the peripheral circulation, but it may probably be safely said that pernicious symptoms never occur without the actual presence of a very large number of malarial parasites.

One can scarcely do better than to quote directly from the admirable article of Bastianelli and Bignami.

"The conditions through which a malarial infection becomes pernicious are:

"1. That the infection be produced by one of the varieties of the æstivo-autumnal parasite. On this condition all to-day are agreed, and we shall not insist further.*

"2. The second condition relates to the abundance of the parasites, and it may be stated as follows: In pernicious fevers, if one take into consideration not only the examination of the blood from the finger, but also the condition in the vessels of the various organs (Marchiafava, Celli, and Bignami), it is a striking point that however the distribution of the parasites may vary in individual cases, their total number is always considerable. As regards the distribution, one may make the following distinctions. There exist:

"1. Cases in which the number of parasites is most abundant—yes, enormous—while all the organs are uniformly invaded. These are the commonest forms of pernicious fever, and are usually accompanied by coma.

"There are some cases in this category in which the number of parasites in the blood of the finger, of the spleen, of the bone marrow, etc., is enormous. while the number in the brain is scanty. Clinically, the absence of cerebral phenomena is noted.

---

*¶ W. S. T.

"2. Cases in which the number of organisms is absolutely and relatively scanty in the bone marrow, in the spleen, in the liver, while they may be relatively few in the blood of the finger, and yet other organs are crowded with the parasites. Among these the following localizations are to be made out:

"(a) The brain and the meninges are filled with parasites either in sporulation or in all their stages of development; in such cases it is difficult to find not only sporulating forms, but even young parasites in the spleen. Clinically, there are cerebral phenomena.

"(b) The stomach and intestines are chiefly invaded. In these organs the mature forms of the parasite are usually found; these are the cases of pernicious fever which present clinically . . . intestinal phenomena."

The pernicious paroxysm, then, may vary greatly in its clinical character, its manner of onset, and the time in the course of the infection at which it appears. In rare instances, usually only in very malarious districts, the first paroxysm which is noted may show pernicious symptoms. This is, however, very unusual. It is most uncommon for the pernicious manifestations to appear without abundant warning in the shape of previous symptoms. Generally the patient has had a number of previous paroxysms, or perhaps a continued fever for some days, in the midst of which the symptoms suddenly assume a malignant nature.

The Comatose Type.—The commonest form of pernicious malarial fever is the comatose paroxysm. Such a paroxysm often begins with a period of excitement, possibly delirium; there is frequently nausea or vomiting. These symptoms are rapidly followed by drowsiness, somnolence, and finally by coma. The patient under these circumstances is usually en-

CLINICAL DESCRIPTION OF MALARIAL FEVER. 149

tirely unconscious. There may be restlessness and jactatation, but in other instances the patient may lie quite motionless. The respiration may be quiet, or loud and stertorous; it may assume the Cheyne-Stokes character. The pulse may be at first full and slow, but toward the end it becomes rapid and feeble. The skin is often extremely hot and dry; the pupils may be dilated or contracted, and in some instances irregular. The conjunctivæ are usually injected; the tongue is dry and coated. There is commonly a slight jaundice of the skin and conjunctivæ—a very important symptom. There are often evidences of a moderate anæmia. At times there are local spasms, which may, in some instances, point to a special localization in the central nervous system of changes due to the collection in these parts of a more abundant number of the parasites.

The examination of the lungs is usually negative, though sonorous râles may be present; with failure of the heart fine râles appear at the bases. The cardiac sounds are usually clear, though a soft systolic murmur may be present over the body of the heart.

The abdomen is, as a rule, negative, excepting for the palpable spleen. In a small proportion of the cases the spleen can not be felt. In such instances it may often be difficult to distinguish the case from sunstroke, and, as has been shown by Bastianelli and Bignami, such a confusion probably often occurs in the malarious districts of Italy.

In fatal cases the coma continues, the pulse is rapid, feeble, and irregular, becoming quite impalpable before the death of the patient. In more favorable instances the temperature, after remaining elevated for a certain length of time, begins to fall more or less rapidly, sometimes in association with sweating, while the patient gradually returns to consciousness. The local spasms which may have been present usually clear up entirely with the disappearance of the cerebral symptoms. Such an attack may last for hours.

Often there may be a temporary improvement in the symptoms, a fall in the temperature, associated with sweating and partial clearing of the sensorium, and improvement in the pulse, only to be followed in the course of a few hours by a fresh attack, which may result fatally.

Other Cerebral Manifestations.—Other cerebral manifestations are common in the pernicious fevers, sometimes preceding a comatose attack, sometimes unassociated with it. Thus the most violent maniacal *delirium* may occur, while active *hallucinations* and delusions are relatively common. In some instances tetanic *convulsions* have been observed, while *hemiplegia* has been reported. All these symptoms may clear up with the paroxysm.

A number of cases have been reported in which symptoms pointing to the involvement of the medulla oblongata have been observed; these cases may show symptoms of *bulbar paralysis*. In one such case the direct proof of the localization of the parasites in this region was furnished on post-mortem examination by Marchiafava.[*]

A special localization of the parasites in the cerebral cortex is not to be made out in every fatal case of comatose malaria. In many instances the organisms are to be found almost equally distributed throughout the general circulation, and we must not be too hasty in concluding that the coma in these pernicious cases is always definitely due to the cerebral localization of the parasites. It is readily conceivable that many of the cerebral symptoms might be due to a circulating

---

[*] Lav. del iii cong. della soc. Ital. di med. int., Roma, 1890, 142.

toxic substance, the presence of which we can not but acknowledge as highly probable.

The Algid Type.—In regions where the pernicious fevers are very common a train of symptoms not unlike those seen in the algid stage of Asiatic cholera may be observed. Here the patient, when he comes under observation, is often found to be in a condition of profound collapse. The eyes are sunken, the features drawn, the skin cold and blue and often bathed in a profuse sweat. The tongue is dry and tremulous and protruded with difficulty. Great prostration is a marked symptom, the patient being almost unable to raise his hand. The pulse may not be palpable at the wrist, while on auscultation the heart sounds are very rapid and feeble, the second sound being, perhaps, entirely absent. The temperature is often little, if at all, elevated. The mind is usually clear almost to the end, though the voice is often extremely weak and husky.

During the early stages of an algid paroxysm, owing to the quiet, listless condition of the patient, the severity of the case may fail to be appreciated. Thus, in one of our cases, a man walked into the out-patient department at eleven o'clock in the morning, and took his seat among the others waiting to be seen by the physician. Dr. Smith, noticing that he was somewhat blue and looked very ill, examined him and discovered that the pulse was impalpable at the wrist. The blood contained numerous æstivo-autumnal parasites. He was sent to the ward, and, despite hypodermic injections of quinine and all stimulation, he died an hour and a half from the time of admission.

Laveran * well remarks that in some such instances the

---

* Traité des fièvres palustres.

attention may be drawn to the case only by the discovery, perhaps accidental, that the patient is practically pulseless.

Choleriform Malaria.—The occasional manifestation of grave choleriform symptoms in malarial fever has long been recognized. Indeed, the sanitary commissioner for Bombay, in his report for 1884, makes the surprising statement: "In my opinion, cholera will in time be recognized as an intensified form of the malarial fevers common to the country." More recently the true nature of these choleriform paroxysms has been cleared up by the researches of Marchiafava,* who has shown them, as above mentioned, to depend upon the actual localization of the parasites in the gastro-intestinal mucosa.

Usually diarrhœa has accompanied the several paroxysms preceding the actual pernicious manifestations. Clinically these cases may show a picture closely resembling that of Asiatic cholera: sudden profuse watery diarrhœa, associated with intense prostration, the patient sinking into an algid condition similar to that described above. The attack often proves rapidly fatal, though in other instances a gradual remission in the symptoms occurs, which under proper treatment may be followed by complete recovery. Without treatment, however, choleriform malaria proves early and rapidly fatal.

The Hæmorrhagic Type.—A type of malaria has been described which is associated with profuse hæmoptysis, epistaxis, and often extensive cutaneous hæmorrhages; there may be hæmatemesis or melæna. Marchiafava and Laveran have reported such cases. It has never fallen to the writer to observe any cases of this nature, though in a number of instances a moderate epistaxis has been noted during a ma-

---

* Proc. XI Internat. Med. Cong., 1894; Centr. f. allg. Path. u. path. Anat., 1894, v, 418.

larial paroxysm, and in several instances a slight petechial eruption.

The Sudoriferous Type.—Some observers have described paroxysms in which the last stage, that of sweating, is so accentuated that the patient falls into a condition of profound prostration, from which he recovers only under the most active stimulation. These cases are also unusual.

The Bilious Type ("*Subcontinua biliosa*").—I have repeatedly emphasized the frequency in malaria of a slightly yellowish hue of the skin and conjunctiva. This jaundice is not one of pure obstruction but rather of overproduction of bile, with backing up in the ducts and reabsorption. It is associated with dark-colored stools and an increased quantity of urobilin in the urine.

There is a class of pernicious fevers where the polycholia and jaundice are among the more conspicuous of the manifestations. Here, in association usually with high fever, there is repeated vomiting of bile-stained fluid, while the dejecta contain an excess of bile. The urine is of a deep red color, and may be of a brownish or greenish hue, showing traces of the biliary coloring matters, as well as albumen. There may be obstinate epistaxis or hæmorrhages from other mucous membranes, while a grave anæmia rapidly develops. The temperature remains elevated. There is profound prostration. The patient is dull and apathetic, the face sunken and expressionless, the respirations feeble, the pulse almost impalpable. Delirium or coma may follow, and in the absence of energetic treatment death usually results.

Under quinine recovery may occur, the temperature falling usually by lysis and the symptoms gradually clearing up. There may be a more rapid fall in temperature with a critical sweat. The patient is, however, left in a very weak, exhausted, anæmic condition, from which recovery is slow.

Gastralgic and Cardialgic Type.—Very severe attacks of abdominal pain may be associated with a pernicious paroxysm. There is usually profuse vomiting and not infrequently hæmatemesis; intestinal symptoms may be quite absent. Laveran distinguishes a distinct gastralgic or cardialgic type of the pernicious paroxysm, describing well one case of this nature in his Traité des fièvres palustres (obs. xxxiii).

The Pneumonic Type.—Baccelli has described a type of paroxysm which suggests by its symptoms the existence of a pneumonia. This astute observer early recognized, however, that the condition was quite distinct from a true complicating pneumonia. There is usually a painful cough, great dyspnœa, and severe pain in the chest, while there may be moderate dullness over the affected lung. On auscultation, coarse, sonorous and sibilant râles, together sometimes with fine, moist sounds, may be heard. The sputum is mixed with dark fluid and clotted blood.

In other cases, however, despite the extreme dyspnœa, the physical examination may be negative.

The exact pathological basis for these paroxysms is not entirely settled, owing to the insufficient number of autopsy records. It is quite certain, however, that we are not dealing with a true pneumonia. It is more probably an active congestion of the pulmonary vessels, a condition not impossibly due to a special localization of the parasites in the capillaries of the lungs.

The Hæmoglobinuric Type—Malarial Hæmoglobinuria.—This condition is known by a number of other terms. The more important are, perhaps, malarial hæmaturia, ictero-hæmaturic fever, bilious hæmaturic fever (*Fièvre bilieuse hématurique*).

The association of hæmoglobinuria with malaria has long been recognized. The condition is often referred to as malarial hæmaturia, which may indeed exist, though in many instances actual blood-corpuscles are not to be found in the sediment of the urine, or, if they be found, are present in very small numbers; the condition is then due to the presence of a blood-coloring matter—a true hæmoglobinuria. The coloring matter is always present in the form of methæmoglobin.

Malarial hæmoglobinuria is very uncommon in temperate climates, and even in the more malarious tropical regions its distribution is rather remarkable. In some districts where severe malaria prevails and pernicious symptoms are not uncommon, as, for example, in Algeria, hæmoglobinuria is relatively rare, while in others, as in Sicily, in Greece, and upon the west coast of Africa, it is extremely common. In the United States it is unusual excepting in certain regions in the South, where it has been well described by Joseph Jones.*

Malarial hæmoglobinuria occurs probably only in æstivo-autumnal infections. Most instances studied by competent observers have shown the *Hæmatozoon falciparum*. Unfortunately the observations in the regions where this form of paroxysm is commonest have been made for the most part by individuals who were not entirely familiar with the various forms of the malarial organism. In a recent interesting article Plehn † describes figures which suggest strongly the æstivo-autumnal parasite, though he himself seems inclined to believe that it is a special form of the organism. More recently A. Plehn ‡ has recognized their identity. The process rarely,

---

* Medical and Surgical Memoirs.
† Deutsch. med. Woch., 1895, Nos. 25, 26, 27.
‡ Beiträge zur Kenntniss von Verlauf und Behandlung der tropischen Malaria in Kamerun, Berlin, Hirschwald, 1896.

if ever, occurs in infections with the tertian or quartan parasites.

Hæmoglobinæmia is a constant occurrence in paludism, owing to the extensive destruction of blood-corpuscles which takes place in every malarial infection. This destruction occurs in various ways:

(1) The red blood-corpuscles are slowly destroyed by the parasites, the hæmoglobin being transformed into the pigment melanin.

(2) A number of infected corpuscles, as we have seen, particularly in æstivo-autumnal infections, become early shrunken and brassy colored—a process which is generally believed to represent an early necrosis.

(3) We may frequently observe in a fresh specimen of the blood the rupture of a corpuscle which may be but little altered, associated with the escape of the parasite which it contains and the solution of the hæmoglobin in the surrounding serum. This may occur in corpuscles containing very young forms of the parasite. It is not at all impossible that such a process may take place frequently in the circulating blood. Moreover, it is probable that the corpuscle containing the full-grown parasite is by no means in every instance wholly free from hæmoglobin; a certain quantity of this substance escapes at the time of segmentation.

Thus it is probable that in any malarial paroxysm a considerable amount of hæmoglobin escapes and becomes diffused in the general circulation. Ponfick has estimated that up to one sixth of the total number of red blood-corpuscles may be destroyed within the circulation, and yet the hæmoglobin be disposed of in the economy without appearing as methæmoglobin in the urine. Though in every malarial process there is probably a more or less continuous escape of hæmo-

CLINICAL DESCRIPTION OF MALARIAL FEVER. 157

globin into the blood plasma, this does not under ordinary circumstances pass through the renal epithelium; it is in great part taken care of by the liver, by which it is transformed into the bile pigments. This results in the polycholia which is so characteristic of malaria and other conditions where there is extensive blood destruction (pernicious anæmia).

In severe æstivo-autumnal infections enormous numbers of red corpuscles, indeed as many as from one to two millions —a third of the entire number—may be destroyed in a single paroxysm and yet no hæmoglobinuria occur. It must, to be sure, be remembered that this destruction does not take place at one time, but during twenty-four or thirty-six hours, while many of the corpuscles have lost their hæmoglobin gradually through the action of the parasite in developing pigment.

That hæmoglobinuria should occur there must, however, be an enormous destruction of red blood-corpuscles—a destruction too great, probably, to be dependent wholly on the disintegration of parasitiferous elements. An infection so extensive that the decolorization of infected corpuscles alone is sufficient to account for an hæmoglobinuria probably never occurs.

We are compelled, in seeking an explanation of the occurrence of this process, to suppose the existence of some condition which renders the *uninfected* red blood-corpuscles unusually vulnerable, possibly some change in the blood serum by which its isotonicity is markedly disturbed. And, further, there must be a direct exciting cause—a cause which apparently varies under different circumstances.

In addition to the excessive destruction of red blood-corpuscles, it is probable that degenerative changes in certain of the internal organs, the liver and the kidneys in particular, may play an important rôle in connection with the development of the hæmoglobinuric paroxysm. The fact that hæmoglobinuria is rare early in the course of a malarial infection is well recognized; it is particularly common in individuals who have suffered from frequent and long-continued attacks. But when we consider the extensive degenerative changes which occur in the kidneys and in the liver in chronic and frequently repeated infections, it is not inconceivable that an increased permeability of the renal epithelium due to the grave alterations produced by the infection, together with a relative incapacity of the liver to carry out the extra work demanded of it, may represent important factors among the elements constituting the predisposition to hæmoglobinuria in such conditions.*

Let us now consider the conditions under which the hæmoglobinuric paroxysm occurs.

All observers agree that climate plays an important predisposing rôle. The greater prevalence of the process in certain special regions has been already mentioned.

Beyond this there is apparently an individual predisposition the nature of which is by no means clear. There are, however, certain general conditions which appear to be necessary for the development of the hæmoglobinuric paroxysm.

Hæmoglobinuria does not occur early in a malarial infection. It is seen usually in relapses or after oft-repeated attacks where the patient is in a more or less anæmic or reduced condition.

But, as Bastianelli † has insisted, it is not in the most

---

* Murri (Il Policlinico, 1895, ii, 340), who discusses this subject at length, insists especially upon the importance of grave renal lesions as necessary for the development of hæmoglobinuria.

† Ann. di med. nav. ann. II, 1896, xvi.

chronic cases of malaria that hæmoglobinuria occurs—that is, those cases where already a certain equilibrium has been established between the needs of the organism and the function of the hæmopoietic organs; it is in those cases where the melanosis and the anæmia are yet present— that is, at a period where the organism is actively engaged in freeing itself from the residua of the infection and in compensating for the loss of the elements of the blood.

If these be important factors in the predisposition above referred to, it is not surprising that it should be variable and transitory.

The factors which are necessary for the production of an hæmoglobinuric paroxysm are summed up as follows by Bastianelli : *

"1. Pre-existing alterations in the hæmopoietic organs due to preceding infections.

"2. Anæmic conditions of the blood.

"3. That one or more febrile attacks have preceded.

"4. An individual predisposition (idiosyncrasy).

"The above-mentioned factors create the transitory conditions which permit the attack which takes place through the action of

"5. A provocative agent."

The latter varies possibly in different cases.

Bastianelli has distinguished several different forms of hæmoglobinuria according to their relation to the stage of the infection in connection with which they occur.

1. Hæmoglobinuria occurring in association with the malarial paroxysm. The onset of the attack here coincides with

---

* *Op. cit.*

the sporulation of a group of organisms and with the fresh parasitic invasion.

Such attacks may be of relatively short duration. They may be intermittent, being repeated with successive paroxysms, or, in other cases, continuous or subcontinuous, just as may be the fever in infections with multiple groups of the parasites.

2. In other instances the attack may likewise come on during an ordinary malarial paroxysm in association with the sporulation of a group of parasites; the parasites, however, which were present at the onset disappear spontaneously during the paroxysm. Such attacks are often severe and of long duration, lasting several days after the disappearance of organisms from the blood. They may be followed by fever of some days' duration.

In these forms of hæmoglobinuria the exciting cause is evidently closely connected with the life history of the parasite; it is present only at the time of sporulation of a group of organisms and may very possibly be represented by some toxic substance set free at the time.

3. But there are other forms of malarial hæmoglobinuria which much resemble these clinically, but occur in patients whose blood and organs are free from parasites. There has, however, always been a recent infection. In other words, we have to do with a *post-malarial hæmoglobinuria*.

These post-malarial attacks may occur:

(*a*) Rarely as separate intermittent paroxysms.

(*b*) More commonly as a single, very severe, often fatal attack.

The direct exciting cause of such paroxysms is quite unknown. Interesting cases of this nature have been reported by Grawitz* and Bastianelli and Bignami.†

4. Lastly, as pointed out originally by Tomaselli, of Sicily,‡ and later by Grecian physicians, by Murri,# and especially by Plehn,∥ hæmoglobinuria may occur in individuals who are suffering or have recently suffered from malaria, as a direct result of the administration of quinine.

From a careful consideration of the reported cases Bastianelli shows that:

(*a*) It occurs only in individuals who have suffered from a previous malarial infection.

(*b*) In such cases the hæmoglobinuric attack follows every time that quinine is administered, whether it be during the occurrence of the malarial paroxysm (Tomaselli) or after the infection has run its course (Murri).

(*c*) Extremely small doses of quinine are capable of bringing on the attack.

(*d*) The hæmoglobinuria of quinine has been seen in patients who have already suffered from spontaneous hæmoglobinuria.

An important difference between the hæmoglobinuria of quinine and the spontaneous hæmoglobinuria of malaria is that in the former the predisposing conditions, whatever they may be, last usually for a considerable length of time, and while this predisposing condition exists the determining cause, quinine, produces the attack without fail every time that it is administered, be the dose ever so small. Tomaselli believes the predisposing condition to be a personal

---

* Deutsch. med. Woch., 1892.
† Bull. soc. Lanc. d. Roma, 1892, xii, 81.
‡ (*a*) I Cong. di med. int. Roma, 1888; (*b*) Clin. med. Firenze, 1895, 151.
# Policlinico, July 15, 1895. ∥ *Op. cit.*

idiosyncrasy; it has been observed to prevail in certain families.

With the spontaneous hæmoglobinurias of malaria the conditions are different. The attack here appears to be merely an episode. In relapses or succeeding malarial paroxysms, where, so far as we can see, the conditions are exactly the same, there may be no return of the attack.

Thus we may see hæmoglobinuria due to quinine:

1. Occurring during an acute infection.
2. After the organisms have disappeared (post-malarial).

Here, in the words of Bastianelli, "the preceding malaria creates the fundamental disposition; the existing malaria, the accidental disposition; the quinine, the provocative agent."

It may be that in addition to these two forms we must yet recognize a third type where quinine exercises its action only occasionally—"hemoglobinuria accessuale do chinino episodiche" (Bastianelli).

The clinical picture of an hæmoglobinuric paroxysm is fairly characteristic. It is never the first symptom of a malarial infection. Usually it appears in the course of a relapse, or, at least, the patient has had several paroxysms before the pernicious one appears. As has been above stated, the paroxysm may appear after the acute symptoms of the infection have subsided. It is commonest in individuals who have had repeated attacks and are more or less cachectic. Further predisposing causes may be anything tending to reduce the vitality of the individual. As has been mentioned above, certain individuals and certain families appear to be especially subject to hæmoglobinuric attacks. An individual who has once undergone an hæmoglobinuric paroxysm is not infrequently the subject of further attacks with subsequent infections or relapses.

CLINICAL DESCRIPTION OF MALARIAL FEVER. 163

The process usually begins with a severe chill, which is in marked contrast to the general rule in æstivo-autumnal infections, where the chill is so often abortive or absent. This chill is followed by intense headache and aching pains in the back and extremities, and usually by profuse and obstinate vomiting. The vomitus consists of a deeply bile-stained fluid. The face is flushed, the conjunctivæ injected; the pulse is usually rapid and small. There is a distinct icteric hue to the skin and conjunctivæ. The attack is generally associated with great mental anxiety and apprehension. There is commonly profuse diarrhœa.

The *urine*, at first of a reddish hue, becomes deeper in color, and finally an intense brownish-black, with something of a greenish hue. On shaking, there is a greenish-yellow foam. The *vomitus*, at first yellow, then green, becomes finally almost black. The *stools* are of a green or brown color, and are usually fluid, though in some instances there may be constipation.

The patient often falls into an algid condition. He is quite conscious, but in a state of profound collapse; often there is great anxiety and mental agitation. There may be severe epigastric pain, which is possibly associated in part with the repeated vomiting. The pains in the back and loins are usually excessive.

Kelsch and Kiéner* believe that these pains in the loins may be associated with the intense renal congestion. There is usually high fever, the temperature touching in some instances 41° C. (106° F.). The jaundice generally increases during the attack.

The *urine*, at the height of the process, is of a deep

---

* Maladies des pays chauds.

brownish-black color, and deposits, on standing, an abundance of reddish-brown sediment. The amount varies considerably in different instances. It may be extremely scanty, though at times it may amount to one thousand or fifteen hundred cubic centimetres. The specific gravity varies inversely to the amount of urine passed. It is usually above normal. The reaction varies, being generally feebly acid. Albumen is usually abundant. In some instances there may be a reaction for the bile-coloring matters. Kelsch and Kiéner believe this to be the rule at the height of the process, while Plehn, in eight instances, failed to obtain the test.

The *sediment* consists of mucus, bladder epithelium, numerous granules and masses of pigment, renal epithelial cells, and, almost invariably, hyaline and granular casts with epithelial cells adherent. In many instances blood-corpuscles may also be found, actual hæmorrhage taking place into the kidney.

The severity of the hæmoglobinuric attack varies greatly. In some instances the temperature may remain elevated for nine or ten hours, and then with profuse sweating fall rapidly to normal. The urine clears up, only a slight trace of albumen with occasional casts persisting for a few days. Complete recovery may follow a single such attack. There may be repeated intermittent hæmoglobinuric paroxysms, which may, as Plehn has shown, end in recovery under wholly expectant treatment.

Usually, however, the condition is more severe and the fever is prolonged. The vomiting and purging continue and increase in severity, and the jaundice becomes deeper. There may be slight intermissions, but the manifestations are often continuous. During intermissions the urine may show temporary changes for the better, but with the exacerbation of the symptoms it returns to its old condition. The amount of urine diminishes, the albumen increases, the patient becomes pale, the eyes sunken, the tongue dry, the pulse rapid and feeble, and finally a fatal result ensues. It is surprising, however, from what apparently desperate conditions patients may recover.

In other instances the course of malarial hæmoglobinuria is extremely rapid and fatal. A very grave symptom in these cases, which begin always with a chill, fever, vomiting, and diarrhœa, is suppression of urine. But a few intensely bloody drops may be passed; there may be complete anuria. There is great agitation, prostration, and profound collapse; death follows usually within a few days.

The hæmoglobinuric attack is always followed by nephritis. In the milder cases this may be transient and slight. Sometimes, however, the paroxysm has a definitely nephritic type. The initial suppression of urine never entirely clears up, the quantity remaining steadily below normal. The albumen and casts persist, and symptoms of uræmia, delirium, coma, and convulsions follow, leading to a fatal result.

The hæmoglobinuric attack is in itself one of the most fatal manifestations of pernicious malaria, yet it is very interesting to note how frequent are spontaneous recoveries with disappearance of the parasites. These facts suggest strongly the possibility that either the existence of the hæmoglobinæmia itself, or the presence of some other toxic substance in the blood, may act unfavorably upon the parasite during the time of the paroxysm. In many instances, however, where spontaneous recovery has been noted the process was probably a true *post-malarial* hæmoglobinuria, like the cases of Bastianelli and Bignami.

The hæmoglobinuric paroxysm due to quinine differs little

in its clinical manifestations from the spontaneous malarial hæmoglobinuria.

The Blood in Æstivo-autumnal Fever.—The blood in æstivo-autumnal fever shows the presence of the third variety of malarial parasites above described—the so-called æstivo-autumnal organism (*Hæmatozoon falciparum*, Welch). During the early part of an æstivo-autumnal infection the only forms which are seen in the circulating blood are the small ring-shaped or amœboid hyaline bodies. These, as will be remembered, are often smaller and somewhat more refractive than the younger forms of the tertian and quartan parasites. They frequently show a very marked ring-like appearance, though they may be disk-shaped and actively amœboid. Shortly before the onset of a paroxysm certain of these bodies are seen to have very minute dark-brown pigment granules, often only one or two. These are very commonly situated near the periphery or about the central lumen-like spot.

Just before and during the paroxysm organisms may be seen which are a little larger than the others, containing, in the middle, collections of fine, dark-brown pigment granules, or a single pigment block. Actual segmenting organisms are very rarely seen in the peripheral circulation. After the process has existed for from five days to two weeks, the larger ovoid and crescentic forms, with collections of coarse, centrally arranged pigment granules are usually to be found.

Where the crescents and ovoid forms are to be found we may often see also the round bodies which develop from them, and wherever these round bodies are present changes similar to those observed in full-grown tertian and quartan organisms may often be followed out:

1. Vacuolization. Either the crescentic or ovoid or round forms may show an accumulation of small circular bodies, the

development of which is usually associated with an increasing pallor and apparent disintegration of the parasites as a whole.

2. Pseudo-gemmation. The round body usually, though sometimes an ovoid or even crescentic form, gives rise to several small bud-like fragments.

3. Flagellation. The flagellate bodies, when they occur, always develop from the round forms.

Under quinine the organisms rapidly disappear from the circulation, with the exception of the crescentic, ovoid, and round forms, which may persist for weeks, or even months. Thus the writer has observed flagellate bodies over a week after the administration of quinine and the disappearance of all active symptoms of malarial fever.

The blood in *malarial hæmoglobinuria*, if the process occur in an acute infection, shows the æstivo-autumnal parasite.

In æstivo-autumnal fever *phagocytosis* occurs with less cyclical regularity than in tertian or quartan fever. This is due, probably, to the facts (1) that multiple groups of parasites are often present, segmenting at frequent intervals; and (2) to the fact that in many instances early degenerative changes are brought about within the red cells which render them practically foreign bodies in the circulation. Pigmented leucocytes are much more frequent during and just after the paroxysm, but may be found at any time during the course of the fever. They may contain granules or blocks of pigment, or in some instances complete parasites with central pigment clumps; shrunken and brassy red corpuscles, with or without included parasites, may be taken up. These latter bodies are often found within large mononuclear macrophages, elements such as are ordinarily only to be seen in the spleen and internal organs. A more accurate description of these forms will be given in the section upon phagocytosis.

Beyond the presence of the parasites the blood in æstivo-autumnal fever may show little that is remarkable. In severe cases, however, the anæmia may be considerable, while the pallor of the individual blood-corpuscles, the differences in size and shape, and the presence of nucleated red corpuscles may be notable.

The same reduction in the number of the leucocytes, with a relative increase in large mononuclear forms and diminution of the polymorphonuclears, is to be made out as in the regularly intermittent fevers.

I shall enter into a more extended discussion of this subject in the following lecture.

The blood in *malarial hæmoglobinuria* shows usually the evidences of a grave anæmia. There are marked differences in size between the individual corpuscles; there may be a moderate poikilocytosis. Occasional shadows of red corpuscles may be seen in the circulating blood, but they are rare. Nucleated red corpuscles may be fairly numerous.

In dried and stained specimens Bastianelli found numerous red corpuscles containing areas which stained with methylene blue.

Bignami and Bastianelli noted a marked increase in the number of the blood platelets which may be of unusually large size.

In some cases these observers believed that, in the presence of a large number of free parasites, they had found evidence of an early destruction by decolorization of a large number of parasitiferous corpuscles.

An important fact in connection with the blood in malarial hæmoglobinuria is that there is a marked leucocytosis, with an increase in the number of polymorphonuclear cells. This leucocytosis is otherwise never seen in uncomplicated malaria, except, perhaps, during the death agony. The leucocytosis begins with the attack and lasts a certain length of time afterward; it continues during the fever which sometimes follows the hæmoglobinuric paroxysm.

FEVERS WITH LONG INTERVALS.

From early times intermittent fevers have been described with intervals lasting materially longer than two or three days; thus, quintans, sextans, octans, nonans, etc., have been noted.

Now after Golgi had described the life history of the quartan and the tertian parasites, demonstrating clearly how the paroxysms every other day, or every fourth day, were definitely related to certain phases in the cycle of existence of the parasites, it is but natural that he should have looked forward to the discovery of other parasites, which in turn might give rise to fevers characterized by paroxysms with longer intervals. And, indeed, in 1889 * he stated his belief that the parasite which we now know as the æstivo-autumnal organism might, under certain circumstances, be associated with fevers with long intervals. He believed that the parasite underwent a slow development, passing through the crescentic form and finally segmenting, giving rise to paroxysms at intervals of ten days or more. He advanced this view only as an hypothesis, stating that he had not as yet been able to discover segmenting bodies.

In 1890, as will be remembered, Canalis,† from the study of the same organism, came to the conclusion that the parasite possessed two distinct cycles, a shorter and a longer. The shorter, associated with the forms which we now recognize to

---

* *Op. cit.* † *Op. cit.*

be connected with the ordinary cycle of development of the æstivo-autumnal parasite, lasted about twenty-four hours; while the longer cycle, associated with the development of the crescentic and ovoid bodies, lasted a considerably greater length of time, three or four days or more. Canalis, as well as Antolisei and Angelini, believed that they had found definite proof of the segmentation of crescentic parasites and their derivatives.

Further study and observation, however, has tended to bring these views into discredit, and there are probably, to-day, no observers who believe in the existence of a parasite whose regular cycle of existence lasts more than seventy-two hours. As we have seen in the description of the parasite, there is no proof whatever that the crescents and ovoid bodies are capable of segmentation. And indeed it is true, that while cases of fever with long intervals are not infrequent, the *regular* recurrence of the paroxysms—that is, a *regular* quintan, sextan, or octan, etc.—is extremely rare. That, however, paroxysms with intervals of *approximately* seven, eight, nine, ten, fourteen, twenty-one days do occur is unquestionable.

To what results have intelligent studies of the blood in these cases led us? Golgi, as has been noted, described such paroxysms occurring in patients with the æstivo-autumnal parasite. Bignami* and Pes,† however, showed that they might occur in connection with the tertian parasite, while Vincenzi ‡ has more recently shown that they may be observed in infections with any one of these three organisms.

---

* Riforma medica, 1891, iii, 169.
† (a) Riforma medica, 1893, ii, 113. (b) Riforma medica, 1893, ii, 759.
‡ (a) Bull. d. R. acc. med. d. Roma, 1891–'92, 631. (b) Arch. per le sc. med., xix, f. 3, 1895, 263.

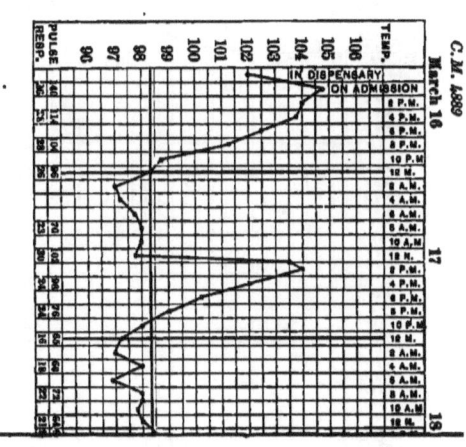

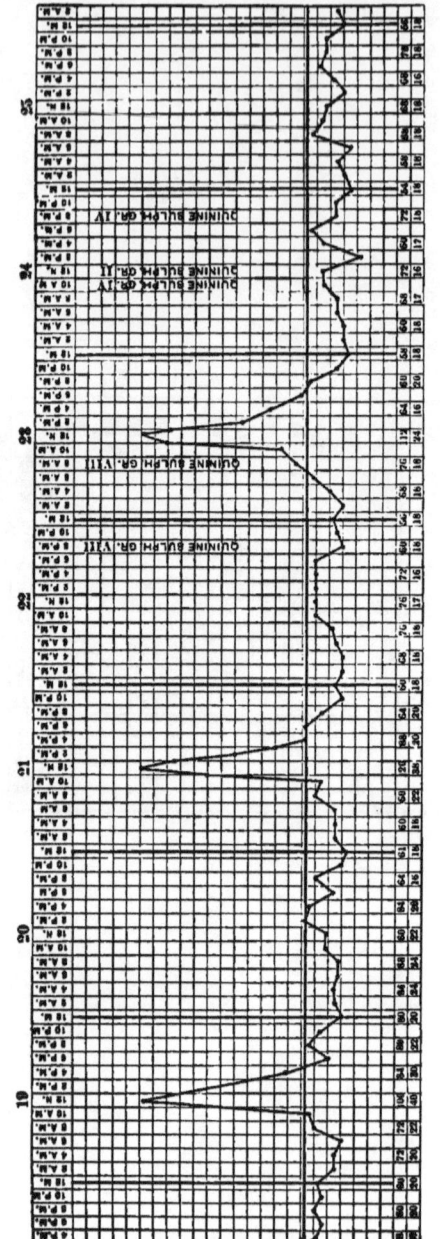

CHART XVII.

QUOTIDIAN AND TERTIAN FEVER—DOUBLE TERTIAN INFECTION.

Appearance of one group of parasites following a severe paroxysm, resulting in a change from quotidian to tertian fever.

These facts have been abundantly confirmed in our experience.

Bignami was the first to advance what is doubtless the true explanation of this phenomenon. It is self-evident that in infections, for instance, with the tertian parasite, if with each paroxysm every full-grown organism underwent segmentation and every segment attacked a new red corpuscle, the infection must of necessity soon reach such a degree of intensity that it would become pernicious and fatal. This, however, is not the case. A very considerable number of full-grown parasites do not even reach the segmenting stage, but undergo one or another of the various forms of degeneration above described. Furthermore, we have seen how frequently the segmenting bodies themselves may be engulfed by phagocytes.

It is doubtless true that with every paroxysm a large number of full-grown and segmenting forms as well as fresh spores are destroyed in the circulating blood, whether this be due to the normal activity of the blood serum, to the presence of some abnormal toxic substance, or to an active phagocytosis on the part of the colorless corpuscles. This destruction may be so great that, for instance, in a double tertian infection, one group of parasites may entirely disappear from the circulating blood, the fever type changing from quotidian to tertian (*vide* Chart XVII, facing page 171). Such a spontaneous cure is, however, usually but temporary. After a varying length of time, from a few days to several weeks, a recrudescence occurs. A few organisms have been left which, undergoing their ordinary cycle of development, eventually reach a number sufficient to produce again the characteristic clinical symptoms.

Sometimes, by a similar mechanism, a single tertian or

quartan infection may be associated with paroxysms at long intervals. The writer has observed one instance in which three or four paroxysms occurred thus at intervals of exactly eight days. After each paroxysm the destruction of the parasites was so great that a period of eight days passed before the group acquired sufficient strength to give rise to fresh manifestations. It is probable that in many of these cases, if very careful observations of the daily temperature were made, slight unobserved febrile elevations would be seen forty-eight hours, or seventy-two hours, or a day, according to the type of the infection, before the distinct paroxysm.

The same condition of things may be observed in quartan and æstivo-autumnal infections.

In some instances paroxysms with long intervals may owe their occurrence to the intermittent administration of quinine. In one of our cases a lady asserted that she had had several paroxysms at intervals of ten days, the last of which occurred under our observation. Immediately after each paroxysm she had taken a single dose of quinine, which had so far destroyed the group of tertian organisms present as to postpone the recrudescence for ten days.

It may then be asserted that fevers with long intervals are probably invariably due to recrudescences of partially cured tertian or quartan or æstivo-autumnal infections. We know, as yet, no organism which is associated regularly with fevers occurring at longer intervals than seventy-two hours.

COMBINED INFECTIONS WITH DIFFERENT VARIETIES OF THE PARASITE.

Combined infections with different varieties of the malarial parasite may occur, though they are uncommon. Out of sixteen hundred and eighteen cases occurring at the Johns

Hopkins Hospital, there were only thirty-one combined infections. The commonest combination observed in this climate by far is that of the tertian and the æstivo-autumnal parasites.

It is interesting that the clinical manifestations of these cases are usually dependent upon one or the other variety of the parasite, a complicated fever chart resulting from the combined action of both organisms being extremely rare. Usually one organism is markedly in excess, giving rise to the symptoms characteristic of that type of infection.

Vincenzi has observed that in combined infections which are untreated, an interesting alternation in the symptoms may occur, a period of tertian fever, for instance, being followed by a spontaneous recovery, which is in turn followed by a period of quartan fever; this again gives way of itself, and is followed by a recrudescence of the tertian manifestations.

It has also been observed by Di Mattei* that if a patient suffering with one variety of malarial fever be inoculated with the organisms of another type, the pre-existing infection appears to give way to the fresh, which rapidly replaces it. Such experiences are not dissimilar to what, as is well known, may be observed in the artificial culture of various other micro-organisms.

Rare cases are reported, however, where complicated fever charts, causing sometimes grave and pernicious manifestations, may be associated with the presence of two active groups of parasites of different types. Such a case we have never observed.

MASKED MALARIAL INFECTIONS.

There is an extensive and rather confusing literature upon the masked or so-called "larvate" forms of malaria. These

---

* *Op. cit.*

are supposed to be cases where, without fever, the intoxication manifests itself by a variety of symptoms; headache, neuralgias, urticaria, hæmorrhages, dyspepsia, asthma, etc. These may occur intermittently, and in some instances appear to yield to quinine.

The insight which we have recently gained into the true nature of paludism has shown us that many of these cases have no connection whatever with malaria. And yet in a certain number of instances malarial infections may cause distinct symptoms with little or no fever. These instances are not infrequent in improperly treated tertian and quartan infections, where the patient keeps about on his feet, taking, perhaps, an occasional single dose of quinine, enough to weaken but not to eradicate the infection. Here the process may, as it were, be kept in a permanent stage of incubation.

There are, however, other instances where for a considerable length of time there may be more or less marked subjective symptoms with little or no fever. The paroxysm is represented by a slight feeling of *malaise*, often associated with headache or neuralgia in various regions. Supraorbital neuralgia is generally described as particularly typical of these cases, though in my experience it is not a common manifestation of malaria.

During the abortive paroxysm there may be slight flushing, with a rise of temperature to a degree or so above normal, which may be followed by a little sweating; but usually fever is practically absent, the temperature really being subnormal during the greater part of the time.

We have observed the same condition in a number of instances of æstivo autumnal infection. These cases may show for some time a normal or even subnormal temperature, with more or less subjective symptoms. These symptoms are especially likely to be nervous—severe headache, neuralgias, and sometimes, indeed, other interesting nervous phenomena. In several instances the patients showed beside headaches a sensation of dizziness together with a markedly unsteady ataxic gait. The blood showed typical æstivo-autumnal organisms, both small amœboid, intra-corpuscular bodies and crescentic and ovoid forms. Torti has reported a case of æstivo-autumnal infection without fever where the symptoms suggested strongly multiple sclerosis.

Sometimes in true pernicious cases the temperature may fall and remain normal or subnormal for some days before the fatal issue. A case of this nature has been reported by Osler.*

There are, moreover, particularly in old individuals, cases where the gravest and most fatal infections may occur almost entirely without fever. An example of this nature is reported by Marchiafava and Bignami—a case of pernicious æstivo-autumnal malaria with hemiplegia and yet a practically normal temperature. The blood in these instances may contain a very large number of parasites. These masked pernicious cases may be most insidious in their origin, and, apart from the great number of parasites in the circulation, there may be at first little evidence either in the temperature or in the other symptoms of the gravity of the case. Marchiafava and Bignami have called attention to the analogy between the insidious development of the symptoms in these cases and that observed in other infections, especially in pneumonia in the aged and debilitated.

---

* Johns Hopkins Hospital Bulletin, vol. ii, 1891, p. 161.

THE URINE IN MALARIAL FEVER.

We have in this clinic made no elaborate analyses of the urine in malarial fever. Much of what follows is taken from the careful observations of Rem-Picci.*

Amount.—There are no very characteristic changes in the daily quantity of the urine during malarial fever. In the regularly intermittent fevers the amount, while within the limits of normal, is yet rather large; in the more continuous æstivo-autumnal fevers, where the conditions both with regard to the temperature, the nourishment, and the surroundings are more like those existing in the other continued fevers, the amount is diminished.

Interesting variations occur in the quantity passed at different periods during the infection. The greatest quantity of urine is, as a rule, passed during the early part of the febrile paroxysm, though the increased flow begins just before and continues a little after the fever. During the intermission a small amount of urine is passed.

There are occasional exceptions to this rule where the greater quantity of urine is eliminated after instead of during the paroxysm.

During convalescence from the regularly intermittent fevers there is often a well-marked polyuria. This may begin immediately after the end of the febrile period, or not until five or ten days later. It may last a few days or for some time, in one instance over thirty days; the amount is usually moderate, not exceeding two or three litres. This postmalarial polyuria is much less marked in æstivo-autumnal

---

* (a) Rem-Picci and Bernasconi, Policlinico, Roma, 1893-'94, i, 131. (b) Rem-Picci and Caccini, Policlinico, Roma, 1893-'94, i, fasc. 12°. (c) Rem-Picci, Bull. d. R. acc. med. d. Roma, 1896, xxii, 771.

fever than in tertian and quartan infections, though *a priori* on account of the previous diminution in urine one might expect the contrary.

Color.—The color of malarial urine is generally increased, resembling often that of an ordinary fever urine. In some cases the color may be excessively high. The deep reddish hue which is usually evident depends upon the increased quantity of urobilin which is derived from the transformed hæmoglobin of the destroyed red corpuscles. Not infrequently, as is stated elsewhere, the blood serum may contain actual bilirubin and the patient show a slight but distinct jaundice, while the urine is free from bile coloring matters, showing only an excess of urobilin. The transformation of bilirubin into urobilin in these cases occurs in all probability in the kidneys themselves.

In severe cases, however, the quantity of biliary coloring matters in the circulation may be so great that they are eliminated as such in the urine and become demonstrable by Gmelin's test. This is especially common in the hæmoglobinuric paroxysms, where both blood and biliary coloring matters are often demonstrable.

The color of the urine during the paroxysm is, according to Botazzi and Pensuti,* lower than that afterward. Rem-Picci, however, as a result of careful studies with more material, maintains that the opposite is the case, the febrile urine showing a distinctly higher color.

Acidity.—There is apparently no characteristic change in the reaction of malarial urine beyond the fact that owing to the moderate concentration the urine is often rather highly acid, as is the case in any acute febrile process. In a few

---

* Sperimentale, Firenze, 1894, xlviii, 232.

observations by Rem-Picci the acidity of the urine during the paroxysms was certainly not reduced.

Specific Gravity.—The specific gravity of the total daily quantity of urine in malarial fever varies in general in inverse proportion to the amount of urine, and passes little outside the limits of normal. The urine during the chill, which is increased in amount, is yet of a normal or even increased specific gravity, while that passed between the paroxysms has a lower density.

It is an interesting fact that the urine in post-malarial polyuria is of a relatively high specific gravity: 1015, for instance, with 3,000 cubic centimetres of urine. Botazzi and Pensuti, who assert that the greater quantity of urine is passed after the paroxysm, differ from Rem-Picci also with regard to the specific gravity, maintaining that that following the paroxysm has a greater density.

The Total Solids.—The total solids are somewhat increased, as in any fever urine. They are more abundant during the paroxysm, less in the intermission. They are markedly increased during the post-malarial polyuria.

The Urea and Total Nitrogen.—The total amount of nitrogen eliminated in twenty-four hours is almost always increased, though not excessively.

The urea and total nitrogen increase markedly during the fever, and more particularly during the early part of the paroxysm. The increased elimination may begin even before the actual onset of the fever. After the paroxysm there is a diminution in the urea, the quantity eliminated remaining relatively low until just before the onset of the next chill.

Ringer,[*] studying the urine in cases treated with quinine,

---

[*] Med.-Chir. Trans., 1859, xlii.

noted a rise in the nitrogen elimination at a time corresponding to that on which the succeeding paroxysm would have occurred without treatment, and Rem-Picci was able to observe this in one case.

In post-malarial polyuria there is also an increased nitrogen elimination.

Uric Acid.—The twenty-four hours' quantity of uric acid is not increased beyond normal limits. The variations in the excretion of uric acid at different periods of the malarial infection are strikingly slight when compared with those of urea and total nitrogen. In general, the amount excreted during fever is slight relatively to that eliminated during the intermission.

The fact that the urine of malarial patients not infrequently deposits a sediment of urates depends rather upon their greater or less solubility than it does upon their actual increase.

Chlorides.—The chlorides, which in so many other febrile diseases are diminished, remain stationary in malaria. They are increased during the febrile period, falling to a lower level afterward. They are increased in post-malarial polyuria.

Sulphates.—The twenty-four hours' quantity of the sulphates as well as the variations in the amount excreted at different periods of the disease correspond entirely to the variations in the excretion of urea and total nitrogen.

Phosphates.—The phosphates, earthy and alkaline, are often increased in the twenty-four hours' urine. Alone among the solids they show a marked fall during the febrile period, the maximum quantity being eliminated during the intermission, at which time the increased excretion more than compensates for the reduction during the fever. There is a marked increase in the elimination of phosphates in post-malarial polyuria.

The Bases. Sodium and Potassium.—Rem-Picci devoted himself especially to the study of the quantity and variations in the excretion of sodium and potassium as representing the chief bases of the urine. In normal individuals 1·5 to 2 parts of sodium are excreted to 1 part of potassium, while during continued fever or in fasting the potassium has been shown to be in excess. In convalescence there is a great excess of sodium over potassium.

In Rem-Picci's cases of malaria the total quantity of these two bases varied, sometimes being higher, sometimes lower than normal. It was very striking, however, that while sodium and potassium might be excreted in larger quantities than normal, the sodium was, as a rule, in excess of the potassium.

During the febrile period the sodium, while yet in excess of potassium, tends to fall slightly below its normal relation, while in apyrexia a small quantity of both solids is excreted with the potassium in excess. During convalescence there is a marked increase in the potassium salts in sharp contrast to what occurs to convalescence from other febrile diseases.

In patients with the *regularly intermittent fevers* the maximum elimination of sodium and potassium occurs always during the fever, when the quantity per hour is often above normal. In the apyretic periods the quantity is subnormal, not only as compared with that eliminated during the fever, but also as compared to normal urine.

In *æstivo-autumnal fever* the rule is not as sharply to be made out. In one half of Rem-Picci's cases the bases were diminished during the fever; in the other half during apyrexia. In an half, more sodium was eliminated during the fever than during the apyrexia; in the other half the opposite.

Botazzi and Pensuti believe that they have demonstrated peptone in both febrile and afebrile urine.

Iron.—Interesting researches have been made by Colosanti and Iacoangeli * concerning the excretion of iron in malaria. They have shown that the urine in malaria contains more iron than in the ordinary febrile diseases. The relative amount is greater after than during the febrile paroxysm; it is derived evidently from the products of the destroyed red corpuscles. They have further demonstrated the fact that the elimination of iron is proportionate to the destruction of red elements.

Albumen.—Albumen is usually present after severe paroxysms. In the regularly intermittent fevers it may amount only to a slight trace, while in severe infections it may be more abundant. The *sediment* here shows usually a few hyaline or granular casts. In the milder cases these are only to be found after the most prolonged and careful search. Where the albumen is more abundant they may be frequent.

Actual acute nephritis occasionally occurs in connection with or following the malarial infection. Here the sediment shows numerous hyaline, granular, and epithelial casts, and in some instances blood.

Malarial fever may be followed by severe chronic nephritis; here the quantity of albumen may be abundant (one half per cent or more), while the sediment may show numerous casts and renal epithelial cells.

---

* Atti di XI Cong. med. internaz. Roma, 1894, iii, farmacol., 42.

Ehrlich's diazo reaction is occasionally to be observed; it was found in 5·5 per cent of the cases analyzed by Hewetson and myself.

The urine in malarial hæmoglobinuria has already been considered.

LECTURE VI.

SEQUELÆ AND COMPLICATIONS.

SEQUELÆ.

Relapses.—The recrudescences which so frequently follow spontaneous recovery or imperfect and insufficient treatment have already been spoken of. There exist, however, cases where, after thorough treatment and apparently complete recovery, a reappearance of the symptoms of the disease occurs after months—nay, sometimes, probably, even after years. These cases, though not extremely common, are by no means very rare, and have given rise to the idea so general in malarious districts, that a patient once the subject of malarial fever never thoroughly recovers. Many instances, doubtless, of so-called relapses of malarial fever after very long periods of time are examples of mistaken diagnosis; chills occurring from any cause whatever in a patient who has once had malaria are very commonly and unjustly ascribed to the old process.

True relapses after really long intervals do, however, occur. A case of this nature I have already referred to in a previous publication; that of a physician who, some eighteen months after the last appearance of a malarial fever, over a year after he had been in a malarious district, had three characteristic tertian chills while in the mountains of the Tyrol. The patient was well acquainted clinically and pathologically with the manifestations of the disease, and studied his own case with interest, taking quinine only after the third tertian paroxysm. The treatment had an immediate effect, and now some ten years have passed without further recurrence of the symptoms. This case was probably a true relapse after a long interval.

How, with our present knowledge of the pathogenesis of malaria, are we to account for such cases? The specific organism must exist in some form within the economy during this long period of time. It is hardly conceivable that it should remain in the general circulation, passing through its ordinary cycle of existence without causing any symptoms whatever. Further, the failure of repeated examinations of the blood of patients who have previously suffered from malaria to reveal the presence of the parasite renders this most unlikely. We are forced to fall back upon some such supposition as that of Bignami, who believes that there must exist some, possibly encapsulated, form of the parasite which we have not discovered—a form, he suggests, which may not be brought out by our ordinary staining methods. In this state, possibly as a spore, the organism may remain perhaps within the cell body of certain phagocytes for long periods of time, only to be set free again as a result of some insult, the nature of which is not as yet appreciable to us.

It has been suggested that the recrudescences of malaria reported after injuries to the spleen may be explained in some such manner as this, the body containing the resting stage of the parasite being in some way or other injured by the shock, so as to set free its contents.

Changes in the Blood.—Post-Malarial Anæmia.—One of the earliest symptoms to be observed in most of the malarial fevers is the development of a more or less marked anæmia. The reason for this may be readily appreciated when we consider the nature of the malarial infection. With every period

SEQUELÆ AND COMPLICATIONS. 185

of sporulation an enormous number of red corpuscles is of necessity destroyed by the group of parasites, while also, as we have seen in considering the development of malarial hæmoglobinuria, there may well be other substances present in the circulation which result in the destruction of a considerable number of non-parasitiferous elements. The early development of an anæmia is a point upon which we shall insist later as of considerable value in the differential diagnosis between malarial fever and certain acute infections.

There are points about the anæmia occurring after malaria which are somewhat characteristic, and the study of the blood by a number of observers, particularly by Bignami and Dionisi,* has revealed to us several more or less distinct forms in which the anæmia may appear.

Let us consider the changes occurring in the formed elements and in the coloring matter separately.

(a) *The Red Corpuscles.*—From what has been said above, it may readily be conceived that examination shows a fall in the number of red corpuscles following each malarial paroxysm. This has been noted by a number of observers, Kelsch,† Kalindero,‡ Dionisi,# and others, while in our own clinic a number of counts made by Kirkbride under my observation tended to support these views. The fall in the number of corpuscles following a paroxysm varies greatly with its severity. It is relatively slight in the regularly intermittent fevers, while in æstivo-autumnal fever the loss may be very marked, over one million to the paroxysm. In malarial hæmoglobinuria it may be enormous. So far as I know, this has never been

---

* Arch. f. allg. Path. u. path. Anat., 1894, v, 422.
† Arch. de Phys., 1875, 690.
‡ Jour. de méd. et de pharm. de l'Algérie, 1889, xiv, 123.
# Lo sperimentale, 1891, 284.

carefully estimated, though how great it must be the degree of anæmia noted after these attacks testifies.

In the regularly intermittent fevers the regeneration of the red corpuscles occurs rapidly, the number approaching the normal point before the following paroxysm. It is only after a succession of paroxysms, as a general thing, that the anæmia attains any marked degree of severity.

In æstivo-autumnal fever, where the loss in corpuscles is so much greater, the regeneration is usually less active and prompt, and a grave anæmia may develop early in the course of the disease. It has been noted that where the fall in corpuscles has been great in the early paroxysms and a pronounced anæmia develops early, the subsequent paroxysms appear to be followed by relatively slight changes in the total number of corpuscles.

The anæmia following malaria may reach a very severe grade, Kelsch having observed as small a number as five hundred thousand red corpuscles to the cubic millimetre. From the more severe grades of malarial anæmia convalescence is often extremely slow, the patient remaining in a feeble condition for months after the disappearance of the fever.

(*b*) *The Hæmoglobin.*—The hæmoglobin follows in a general way the same course as the red corpuscles. As is common, however, in all secondary anæmias, it usually falls to a somewhat lower point, and in convalescence rises to normal more slowly than do the red corpuscles. The behavior of the hæmoglobin has been studied with particular care by Rossoni.[*]

(*c*) *Colorless Corpuscles.*—The behavior of the colorless corpuscles in malarial fever presents several rather important characteristics. In most of the acute infectious diseases with

---

[*] Lav. d. cong. d. soc. Ital. di med. int., II cong., Roma, 1889, 121.

which we are familiar there is a leucocytosis. To this there are two well-marked exceptions—typhoid and malarial fevers. Excepting in certain very grave pernicious paroxysms the number of colorless corpuscles in malaria is almost invariably subnormal.

Attention was first called to this point by Kelsch,* while it has since been studied with particular care by Bastianelli † and Billings. ‡ These observers agree entirely in tracing a fairly characteristic course for the total number of colorless corpuscles in the circulating blood in relation to the malarial paroxysm. While the number of corpuscles is almost always normal or slightly subnormal, there occurs a more or less rapid reduction in the number during and immediately after the paroxysm. Following this there is a slow, gradual rise until just before the beginning of the succeeding febrile elevation, when there occurs a rather rapid increase in number, to be followed again toward the end of the paroxysm by a fresh fall.

It is also interesting and important to note that on more careful study the relative proportions of the different varieties of leucocytes one to another have been found to show a distinct and constant deviation from the normal. There is a diminution in the relative percentage of polymorphonuclear elements, with a corresponding increase in the large mononuclear forms. The following tables show the percentages obtained by Billings in sixteen cases, as compared with the normal mean:

	Normal.	Malarial fever.
	Per cent.	Per cent.
Small mononuclear............................	18	16·90
Large mononuclear and transitional...........	6	16·90
Polymorphonuclear...........................	74	65·04
Eosinophilic.................................	2	0·96

* Arch. de Phys., 1876, 490.
† Bull. d. R. accad. med. d. Roma, 1892, xviii, 487.
‡ Johns Hopkins Hospital Bulletin, 1894, 105.

This change, it will be seen, is exactly similar to that first pointed out by Uskov * and confirmed by Khetagurov † and the author, ‡ in typhoid fever. Such a condition is in marked contrast to that which we usually see in those forms of disease most commonly confounded with malaria, such as pneumonia, influenza, tuberculosis. In all these conditions a well-marked leucocytosis, with an increase in the relative percentage of the polymorphonuclear leucocytes at the expense of the small mononuclear varieties, is the rule.

In rare instances, as mentioned by Bastianelli,# a pernicious paroxysm may be associated with an increase in the number of leucocytes. Excepting, however, in malarial hæmoglobinuria and during the death agony, this is usually an evidence of a complicating infection.

A remarkable instance of leucocytosis in pernicious fever occurred under our observation. This was the case of algid malaria referred to above. Here the blood count an hour before death showed fifty thousand leucocytes to the cubic millimetre. It is extremely interesting to note that, despite this leucocytosis, the differential count showed the characteristic changes mentioned above. The differential count showed:

Small mononuclear .... 23·0 per cent.
Large mononuclear and transitional forms..... 18·4 "
Polymorphonuclear.... .... 58·6 "

Bignami and Dionisi ‖ have recently studied the post-malarial anæmias, dividing them into four fairly distinct types.

(1) The first of these types is that observed after ordinary acute malarial fever, and differs from the usual secondary

---

* The Blood as a Tissue, 8vo, St. Petersburg, 1890.
† Virchow's Archiv, Bd. cxx, F. xii, B. vii, 187.
‡ Johns Hopkins Hospital Reports, iv, 83.   # *Op. cit.*
‖ Centr. f. allg. Path. u. path. Anat., 1894, v, 422.

anæmias only in the behavior of the leucocytes. There is a more or less well-marked diminution in the red corpuscles, a moderate degree of leucocytosis, and the presence of nucleated red corpuscles, according to the degree of anæmia. The hæmoglobin is usually diminished to a somewhat greater extent than the corpuscles. The leucocytes, however, instead of being slightly increased, as is the case in most secondary anæmias, are usually somewhat diminished in number, and often show characteristic changes in the relative proportion of the different varieties—namely, a diminution in the polymorphonuclear elements, with a corresponding increase in the large mononuclear forms. The prognosis in these instances is favorable.

(2) In another class of cases the anæmia may be progressive and fatal, while the blood shows those changes characteristic of pernicious anæmia—a great diminution in the red corpuscles, marked poikilocytosis, the frequent presence of very large red elements, and a diminution in hæmoglobin relatively less than that of the corpuscles. Nucleated red cells, when present, are in great part gigantoblasts. The leucocytes, diminished in number, may show an increase in the small mononuclear forms.

(3) There is another type of case in which the course is also rapidly fatal. These cases show in the beginning the same general characteristics as in Class 1, excepting for the complete absence of any regenerative forms (nucleated red corpuscles). This form of pernicious anæmia, due to the complete absence of regenerative activity in the blood-forming organs, is exactly similar to the cases described first by Ehrlich,* occurring sometimes after severe hæmorrhage. I

---

* Charité Annalen, xiii. Jahrg.

have observed the same condition of the blood in two fatal instances of purpura hæmorrhagica.

(4) There may be grave chronic secondary anæmias, the main characteristics of which are those of Class 1, excepting for the practical absence of nucleated red corpuscles and the marked reduction in the number of the leucocytes. These cases are particularly common in chronic malarial cachexia, and are doubtless due, in part at least, to the grave secondary degenerative changes which occur in the blood-forming organs after repeated or long-continued malarial infections.

There are, it should be said, some post-malarial anæmias, usually after short-lived infections, where recovery is very rapid and a leucocytosis similar to that seen in most other acute secondary anæmias occurs.

Chronic Malarial Cachexia.—When one considers the grave anæmias which of necessity follow frequently repeated attacks of malaria, and when one further remembers the marked changes which take place in the various internal organs, it is easy to imagine that repeated or long-continued attacks might lead to grave general consequences, and such, indeed, is the case. In severely malarious districts cases of profound cachexia may occur due to frequently repeated or chronic infections. These usually follow imperfectly treated malaria. The patient very often takes with each paroxysm a single large dose of quinine, or only a few, and then, feeling quite well, abandons treatment until again, after a certain length of time, the symptoms are renewed.

In the course of time grave general results follow. There is marked anæmia; the skin assumes a sallow, grayish-yellow color; there are frequent severe headaches or facial neuralgia; there is marked dyspnœa on exertion, with œdema of the dependent parts. The tendency toward œdema and transudations is rather characteristic of these instances of chronic malaria. Gastro-intestinal symptoms are frequent—nausea, vomiting, and persistent and annoying diarrhœa.

There are often frequently recurring slight febrile attacks, and commonly a regular evening exacerbation of temperature, rising as high as from 100° to 102°.

On physical examination, the pallor, and more particularly the splenic enlargement, which may here reach an excessive degree, are the chief symptoms of note. The liver is often somewhat enlarged. The patient may be reduced to a most distressing condition, where he is a prey to any secondary infection.

Chronic malarial cachexia is more frequently due to the presence of the æstivo-autumnal parasites. Here the symptoms are more irregular and not quite so amenable to treatment, while not infrequently mild continued æstivo-autumnal infections may for some weeks present no marked febrile reaction, or only abortive and irregular paroxysms.

In young children and infants chronic malarial cachexia is particularly common. This is probably due to the fact that the ordinary symptoms of the paroxysm are so frequently missed that the true nature of the case is often misunderstood and proper treatment is not carried out. The picture presented by such a child is very striking. There is often extreme emaciation and great pallor; the patient may present the most marked degree of infantile atrophy. The eyes are sunken; the face drawn; the yellow, parchment-like skin hangs in folds about the extremities; the voice is weak and husky, and the child altogether presents a most pitiful appearance.

There may be mild febrile attacks with nausea and vomiting, and possibly an occasional slight convulsion. Gastro-intestinal symptoms are particularly common; vomiting and diarrhœa. The spleen is almost invariably enlarged, while a well-marked increase in the size of the liver is to be made out.

The adult patient rarely dies of chronic malarial cachexia itself, though at times, after a long-continued infection, pernicious symptoms may develop. Ordinarily, the fatal results of chronic malarial cachexia are indirect, depending upon secondary intercurrent affections.

The condition of the *blood* varies according to the nature of the case. If the cachexia be due to a continued uncured tertian or quartan infection, we may by careful search find an occasional characteristic parasite. Often, though, between febrile attacks it may be impossible, on ordinary examinations, to discover any organisms. Not infrequently occasional pigment-bearing leucocytes may be found; these are fairly characteristic when one is once familiar with the appearance of malarial pigment. If the infection be with the æstivo-autumnal parasite, crescentic and ovoid forms are frequently met with.

If the treatment with quinine has been well instituted, we may scarcely expect to find more than an occasional pigmented leucocyte, or if the case be of æstivo-autumnal infection, a few ovoid and crescentic bodies.

Malarial Nephritis.—As is the case with most other acute infectious diseases, malarial fever is not infrequently accompanied by albuminuria. In the cases classified by Hewetson and the author, albuminuria was present in 133 instances out of 335 cases. Our subsequent observations, however, would lead us to believe that it is really much more frequent than was indicated here; it was noted in over fifty per cent of the last 300 cases treated in the Johns Hopkins Hospital.

In a like manner, just as with other infectious processes associated with the presence of circulating toxic substances, malaria may be accompanied or followed by a more or less severe nephritis. The most severe nephritides occurring with malaria are those associated with hæmoglobinuria. Here, as has been stated, the nephritis may be rapidly fatal. In a considerable number of instances, however, milder malarial attacks may be followed by more or less serious renal disturbances. The course of these cases of post-malarial nephritis is usually favorable, provided that treatment by quinine is early instituted.

In other instances, however, one of which we have recently observed, malarial fever may apparently be the starting point of a grave chronic nephritis.

The symptoms are usually those of an ordinary acute or subacute nephritis, coming on with headaches, gastro-intestinal disturbances, and general œdema. In one instance of grave renal disturbance, for which no origin other than the malaria could be discovered, the symptoms were those of a chronic diffuse nephritis.

The *urine* is at first usually diminished in quantity; the specific gravity is not especially altered. It is often reddish or smoky in color, containing a considerable quantity of blood. Sometimes, however, blood may be absent.

The sediment shows, generally, numerous tube casts, hyaline, granular, and often blood casts, together with degenerated epithelial cells.

Amyloid Degeneration.—Frerichs and Marchiafava and Bignami have described cases of amyloid degeneration following malarial infection. These cases were for the most part associated with the symptoms of chronic malarial cachexia, presenting in the end the evidences of a grave chronic nephritis. Such instances are very uncommon, excepting in the graver malarious districts. The cases studied by Marchiafava and Bignami followed a long series of febrile paroxysms in æstivo-autumnal or obstinate quartan infections.

The *blood* in some of these cases shows the condition first noted by Ehrlich to be of grave portent—i. e., a severe anæmia with a complete absence of nucleated red corpuscles; a reduction in the number of leucocytes with an excess of lymphocytes; an absence of eosinophilic cells. The marrow of the long bones is found to show no evidences of an attempt at blood regeneration.

Atrophy of the Gastro-intestinal Mucous Membrane.—Pensuti * reports a case of atrophy of the gastro-intestinal mucosa which Baccelli agrees with him in ascribing to malaria. The possibility of such a result following the gastro-intestinal localization of the parasites would certainly seem not very unnatural. This is, however, so far as I know, the only instance reported. In this case the acute malarial attack was followed by obstinate diarrhœa. The patient became much debilitated, and died after three months of a broncho-pneumonia.

Malarial Hepatitis—Malaria and Cirrhotic Processes.—Many observers believe that malarial fever plays an important part in the ætiology of cirrhosis of the liver. There is, however, little evidence in favor of this view, at least in so far as it relates to the ordinary atrophic cirrhosis. Most of the cases of so-called malarial cirrhosis occur in individuals who have been subjected to one or more of the other conditions which are recognized as common causes of this change.

Distinct changes in the liver associated with enlargement

---

* Gaz. med. di Roma, 1893, xix, 121.

of the organ and an increase in the amount of connective tissue—a chronic hepatitis—do unquestionably follow repeated malarial infections; this condition has been well described by Bignami. There are, however, no distinctive clinical symptoms. This subject will be further discussed in the lecture on pathological anatomy.

Malarial Paralyses.—That various transitory paralyses may occur during pernicious paroxysms has been stated in a previous lecture. The paralyses occurring during acute malarial infections are usually cortical in nature and clear up rapidly under treatment with quinine. They are due probably, for the most part, to circulatory disturbances induced mechanically by the parasites. The nervous symptoms in acute malaria are more commonly irritative than paralytic.

It is readily conceivable that under certain circumstances a malarial paroxysm might be the exciting cause of the rupture of a cerebral vessel or the dislodgment of a fragment of a thrombus in an individual with cardiac or arterial disease.

Such an instance has come under my observation. The patient, a colored man fifty-three years of age, with somewhat thickened arteries, became suddenly unconscious during a paroxysm of tertian fever, developing a right-sided hemiplegia with aphasia. He was brought into the hospital unconscious, and the malarial infection was not suspected until the following paroxysm. The infection yielded immediately to quinine, but the hemiplegia, though showing a marked improvement, had not wholly cleared up at the time of the discharge of the patient. In this instance the malarial fever was probably only the remote cause of the hemiplegia.

A certain number of cases has been reported where, in association with a malarial infection, symptoms have occurred which were suggestive of disseminated sclerosis; with the disappearance of the parasite under quinine recovery has followed.

Torti* reported a case of this nature which pursued an entirely afebrile course; the nervous manifestations were the only symptoms of the infection.

Da Costa † has described an interesting case of paraplegia with intention tremor, severe headaches, bi-temporal hemianopsia, and mental symptoms where the blood showed æstivo-autumnal parasites. Recovery followed the administration of quinine. Kahler and Pick's ‡ cases of "acute ataxia" were probably of malarial origin.

Bastianelli and Bignami # report a case showing the symptoms of the so-called "electric chorea" or "Dubini's disease," associated with an æstivo-autumnal infection. They ascribe the symptoms to "lesions secondary to the cerebral localization of the parasites."

Most of these processes are essentially favorable in their course if the treatment be begun early. According to Boinet and Salebert,∥ however, permanent paralysis may follow malarial infections.

A few instances of *peripheral neuritis* have been reported after what was thought to be malarial fever. In none of these cases has the parasite been found, so that definite proof of the malarial origin is wanting. From what we know, however, of the general pathology of malaria, it is but natural to suppose that such cases may occur. Jourdan △ has recently reported an interesting case of multiple neuritis following

---

* Bull. d. Soc. Lanc. d. osp. d. Roma, 1891, xi, 217.
† Internat. Clinics, Philadelphia, 1891, iii, 246.
‡ Beiträge z. Path. u. path. Anat. des Centralnervensystems, Leipzig, 1879.
\# *Op. cit.* ∥ Rev. de méd., Par., 1889, ix, 933.
△ Gaz. des hôpitaux, 1896, 603.

what was in all probability malarial fever; no mention is, however, made of the presence of the parasite.

Raynaud's disease has been thought by some to be relatively common in malarial fever. No such instance has ever come under our observation.

Poncet described a retinitis and retino-choroiditis due to emboli of melaniferous leucocytes.

Mental Diseases.—Just as in the case of any other severe acute infection, malarial fever may be followed by psychoses, mania, melancholia, delusional insanity.

One of our cases of tertian fever was followed by an attack of delusional insanity of several months' duration.

Other Post-malarial Phenomena—Post-malarial Auto-intoxications (?).—Marchiafava and Celli,* in 1887, reported a fatal case of malarial fever where the coma lasted four days, the number of parasites in the circulation progressively diminishing. This fatal outcome despite the disappearance of the parasites is not, they say, remarkable when one reflects "that the same occurs with the agents of other infectious diseases (for example, the typhoid bacillus). In these cases we must take into consideration the consecutive toxic products and the chemical and anatomical changes in the organs—for instance, in the case above cited, the numerous punctiform hæmorrhages."

Kelsch,† in 1876, noted that an increase in the severity of an anæmia might take place after all other signs of the infection had disappeared; while Dionisi,‡ in 1890, showed that this progressive aggravation of the anæmia might continue for eight or ten days after the parasites had disappeared from the circulation.

---

* *Op. cit.* † *Op. cit.* ‡ *Op. cit.*

In 1890 Bastianelli and Bignami* reported a case of rapidly developing fatal anæmia pursuing a lethal course despite the diminution of the parasites under quinine.

The same observers, in 1892,† report cases showing that, on the one hand, malarial hæmoglobinuria beginning during a paroxysm may continue after the organisms have disappeared from the circulation, while on the other hand the process may *develop* after all evidences of the infection have disappeared—a true post-malarial hæmoglobinuria. These conditions they believe to be due to "alterations of the blood, secondary to the recently preceding acute infection, and continuing after the disappearance of the parasites." Concerning the nature of these alterations, whether they depend upon the persistence of the intoxication or upon some other cause, they abstain from speculating. A similar case of post-malarial hæmoglobinuria is reported by Grawitz,‡ while Bastianelli # has recently again called attention to the importance of those cases.

A remarkable post-malarial phenomenon came under our observation during the spring of this year. Several cases of æstivo-autumnal fever were admitted to the Johns Hopkins Hospital during the month of April—an unusual occurrence in this climate. All the patients were seamen from one steamer; they had contracted the disease in Central America. After nine days' treatment in the hospital they were discharged, apparently well.

One of these patients, who had had paroxysms off and on for nearly two months before entry, returned to the hospital a second time eleven days later. He had been living at a sailors'

---

* Bull. Soc. Lanc., Roma, 1890, ann. ix, x, 179.
† *Ibid.*, 1892, xii, 81.
‡ Berlin. klin. Woch., 1892, 138.
# Annali di medicina nav. ii, 1806, fasc. xi.

SEQUELÆ AND COMPLICATIONS. 199

boarding house during the interim, and had appeared to be quite well. The day before entry he had complained of a headache on going to bed. During the night he conversed with his roommate on several occasions. In the morning, however, he was found unconscious, with stertorous breathing and high fever; he was brought to the hospital in the afternoon. On entrance he was comatose, breathing stertorously. The pupils were equal, of medium size; there was no apparent paralysis; physical examination otherwise negative.

The peripheral *blood* showed no malarial parasites; there was a leucocytosis of 24,000. On puncture of the spleen an occasional ovoid and crescentic æstivo-autumnal organism was found on careful search. Considerable pigment was noted in the white elements—large blocks and clumps. No forms whatever of the active cycle of the parasite were found.

The *urine* was very high-colored; specific gravity, 1030; acid; no sugar; trace of albumen; sediment considerable; hyaline and finely granular casts; mucous cylindroids; diazo reaction not present.

The temperature ranged between 104° and 106° F. Despite cold baths, stimulation, and quinine hypodermically, the patient remained comatose, and died twenty hours after admission.

The autopsy showed the evidences of a recent malarial infection. There were most extensive areas of necrosis in the liver, some visible to the naked eye, one or two nearly half as large as the head of a pin. These areas dated probably from the preceding malarial infection. The brain, beyond a rather marked injection of the vessels, showed nothing abnormal. Beyond an occasional crescentic parasite in the spleen, no malarial organisms were found. Cultures from all the organs were negative. Microscopical examination of the organs by Prof. Flexner showed extensive necroses in the liver and spleen, and every evidence of the existence of an intense toxæmia. The case will be reported in full later.

The weather at this time was very hot, and the suggestion was made that the case might be one of thermic fever. There are, indeed, facts which might lead us to believe that individuals suffering from malarial fever or having recently recovered from an infection are unusually sensitive to high temperatures. The manner of the onset which occurred during the relatively cool night would speak against this idea in the present case.

It is not impossible that these post-malarial phenomena may be due to different causes. In some instances, such as Marchiafava and Celli's case of long-continued coma, the symptoms may depend upon the persistence of the toxæmia or on the actual anatomical changes—capillary thromboses—punctiform hæmorrhages.

In other cases—for example, post-malarial hæmoglobinuria or instances such as the above-described case—one is tempted to suspect that the anatomical and chemical changes in the economy produced by severe or repeated infections may be so extensive as to leave the organism in, as it were, a state of extremely unstable equilibrium where slight insults (exposure to heat?) may produce the gravest effects, resulting possibly, in some instances, in fatal perversions of the normal body metabolism.

May it be, perhaps, that some of these inexplicable phenomena occurring in the subjects of recent malarial infections are to be classed as true *post-malarial auto-intoxications?*

COMPLICATIONS.

Mixed Infections.—There are but few branches of the literature of malaria where more confusion exists than that which has to do with the complications. Like any other acute infectious disease, malaria may be associated with a variety of other pathological processes, and, within certain limits, each of the coexisting affections may be more or less modified by the presence of the other. The term malaria has been, however, very loosely used, and the medical public even to-day speaks of "malarial pneumonia," "malarial dysentery," "malarial orchitis," and "typho-malarial fever" as processes almost specific in nature, showing a characteristic complex of symptoms due in many instances to a malarial infection alone.

In an earlier lecture I have spoken of the frequency with which acute intestinal symptoms may be associated with certain malignant malarial infections. The fact, likewise, that pernicious fever may at times assume a form suggesting, by its symptoms, acute pneumonia has also been mentioned. It has furthermore been noted how similar many cases of irregular æstivo-autumnal fever may be in their general symptoms to typhoid.

The choleraic form of malaria, however, has nothing to do with Asiatic cholera; the pneumonic form of pernicious fever is in no way associated with pneumonia; and the continued fever in æstivo-autumnal infections has no connection with typhoid. Infection with the malarial parasite can not of itself produce pneumonia, or typhoid fever, or Asiatic cholera. There is nothing more specific or characteristic about a pneumonia complicating a case of malarial fever than there is in a pneumonia associated with typhoid fever, nor in the cases of typhoid fever in an individual suffering from a malarial infection than in a case of typhoid occurring, perhaps, in a patient suffering from pulmonary tuberculosis. The terms "malarial pneumonia," "typho-malarial fever," "malarial dysentery," etc., are misleading and incorrect, and the sooner they are abandoned the better.

Pulmonary Complications—Pneumonia.—Malarial fever is not infrequently complicated by acute pneumonia, as is the case with any severe acute infectious disease. There is nothing unusual in the course of such a process. The pneumonia is always produced by the specific micro-organism—the pneumococcus *—whether it be associated with malarial fever or not. The high temperature of the pneumonia may or may not mask the malarial paroxysm. The course of the complicating pneumonia is the same as under other conditions, excepting that it is frequently severer on account of the reduced condition of the patient. The malarial fever pursues its usual course, yielding as it always does to quinine, which naturally has no effect whatever upon the pneumonia. A case of this nature Hewetson and the author have already published.

These instances of pneumonia complicating malarial fever must not be confused with the occasional cases of pneumonia with intermittent febrile manifestations. Such cases have been described by a number of observers. They are quite distinct from malarial fever, with which they have no connection.

Pleurisy.—Pleurisy may occur in individuals affected with malarial fever. A good instance of this nature has been recently reported by Geppener.† There is nothing particularly characteristic in the course of such a process. The administration of quinine is followed by the disappearance of the malarial infection, while the pleurisy is unaffected.

Typhoid Fever.—Malarial fever is occasionally complicated with typhoid fever. A patient with a chronic or rela-

---

* Perhaps rarely the Friedlaender diplo-bacillus. † *Op. cit.*

tively latent malarial infection may develop typhoid fever, or at some time during the course of the convalescence from typhoid fever a relapse from a preceding malarial attack may occur; in some instances perhaps the two infections may be coincident in time. A fresh malarial infection during typhoid is probably rare.

It is unusual for well-marked symptoms of the two diseases to be present at the same time. More commonly the malarial paroxysms appear during convalescence from typhoid fever. Even these instances, however, are not common. Gilman Thompson* has recently published some interesting charts showing the actual complication of the two diseases during the height of the process. Here the malarial paroxysms were well made out against a background of the continued fever of typhoid. These cases, however, are very unusual. Under quinine the malarial parasites and the symptoms due to them quickly disappear.

It is very important to recognize the fact that intermittent fever with chills is not an infrequent symptom in typhoid fever, particularly during defervescence and convalescence. These intermittent chills, however, in the great majority of cases have no connection whatever with malarial fever. They are due to secondary infections or to auto-intoxications of a nature as yet unknown.

It may be well here to say a few words about the term so commonly employed in medical literature—*typho-malarial fever*. It has been supposed in past years that there existed a process due in some way or other to a combination of the typhoid and malarial poisons, which manifested itself by a continued fever with marked remissions; this fever was sup-

---

* Trans. Ass'n. Amer. Phys., 1894, 110.

posed to be extremely resistant to quinine. With our modern methods of diagnosis, and the recent advances in our knowledge of the intimate nature of both typhoid and malarial fevers, we now know that no such condition exists. Moreover, it is, I think, safe to say that the great majority of these instances are nothing more nor less than simple typhoid fever.

It is important that the profession should recognize this fact—important from a very practical point of view. The mere use of the term "typho-malarial fever" has indicated to many the advisability of the administration of quinine, and not infrequently this drug is used for days and for weeks in cases of uncomplicated typhoid fever in doses which can not but be injurious to the patient. This is a matter of really grave importance. It is one of the positions in which the physician actually has done and does do to-day really serious harm to his patient. There is no excuse for cinchonizing an individual with continued fever who after three or four days shows no change in the symptoms, while the blood is free from malarial parasites. There is no such disease as typho-malarial fever in the ordinary sense in which the term is used. The term, as has been said before, is incorrect and misleading and should be abandoned.

Intestinal Complications.—Malarial fever may be complicated or followed by grave intestinal disturbances. Acute dysenteric symptoms may, as has been previously mentioned, be one of the important manifestations of severe malarial infection, and it is easy to understand how, in connection with the changes which must of necessity accompany such a process, grave secondary infections might occur; and such infections do occur. Their course is not different from that of any other ordinary acute dysentery.

Sometimes the pathogenic agent of the complicating process may be readily demonstrable, in the presence in the fæces of the amœba coli. These cases, of which we have observed six at the Johns Hopkins Hospital, are particularly interesting not only as affording examples of coincident infection with two different forms of protozoa, but in that they suggest the possibility that the amœbic ulcers may in some cases form a port of entry for the malarial parasite.

In none of these cases where there is a true mixed infection does the ingestion of quinine by the mouth affect the complicating process, excepting in so far as by removing the malarial infection the general condition of the patient is improved.

Tuberculosis.—There has been widespread belief that tuberculosis and malarial fever are antagonistic one to the other, and that a complication of the two processes is impossible or most unusual. Boudin,* who upheld this view with vigor, asserted that tuberculosis is rare in countries where malarial fever is common, and the converse. This is by no means the fact. It is true that, as a general rule, tuberculosis is more common in northern countries where malarial fever is unusual. There are, however, many regions where tuberculosis and malarial fever are both, alas, only too common—such, for example, is the eastern coast of the United States. Cases where tuberculosis and malarial fever exist together in the same patient, while not common, do occur, and occasionally give rise to confusion in diagnosis. Geppener † has recently reported a good observation of this nature.

Marchiafava,‡ who has looked into this question carefully,

---

* Traité des fièvres intermittentes, 8vo, 1842, 69.
† Meditsinsk. Pribav. k. Morsk. Sbornik., 1895, i, 67.
‡ Bull. d. soc. Lanc. d. osp. d. Rom., xi, 1891, 186.

speaks emphatically against the idea of the incompatibility of the two diseases. He asserts, indeed, that chronic or frequently repeated malarial attacks with cachexia are important predisposing causes of tuberculosis.

Orchitis.—There is a fairly widespread belief in certain regions in the occurrence of orchitis and epididymitis of malarial origin. There is, however, absolutely no pathological proof of this supposition. Some instances of so-called "malarial orchitis" are suppurative (!). On looking through a number of cases in the literature one is struck by the fact that the notes with regard to a previously or concurrently existing gonorrhœa are generally insufficient, while often the existence of the malaria itself is not proven. We know that the malarial parasite is not of itself a pus producer, and in those instances where suppuration occurs there must at least be a mixed infection.

There is, of course, no reason theoretically why, in some instances, a special localization of the parasite should not occur in this region. In nearly two thousand cases, however, observed in the last six years the author has not seen a single instance of malarial orchitis, and in the entire absence of any proof that those cases already reported are really malarial in nature, it seems quite reasonable to believe that this condition, like malarial pneumonia and other supposed malarial complications, is usually a mixed infection.

Post-partum and Post-operative Malarial Fever.—Under the heading of the complications of malarial fever we may perhaps speak of those cases which occur during the puerperium or shortly after surgical operations. It is generally believed that the occurrence of malarial fever under these circumstances is not rare—hence the special terms post-operative and post-partum malaria, so frequently employed. It is a matter of common observation that individuals who have recently suffered from malarial fever are not infrequently subject to fresh outbreaks of the infection whenever their surroundings are such as to depress the vital forces. Such conditions are present during the puerperium and after severe operations. It is thus not unnatural that occasional outbreaks of malaria should occur under these circumstances. These manifestations may be quite alarming.

I have observed recently an interesting example. A man had been subjected to a severe surgical operation, the greater part of the tongue having been removed for carcinoma; tracheotomy had been performed. For several days the patient did fairly well, having a moderate irregular fever, but a good pulse. Suddenly, on the evening of the fifth day after operation, he had a violent chill. When seen, the patient was cyanotic; the face was pinched; the hands and extremities cold and blue; the respiration rapid and convulsive; the pulse small and uncountable at the wrist, above 175; the temperature 105·8°. Examination of the blood showed the presence of æstivo-autumnal parasites; small amœboid hyaline bodies and glistening rings. One gramme (gr. xv) of muriate of quinine and urea was given hypodermically, and immediately followed by an intravenous injection of 0·5 (gr. vijss) of bimuriate of quinine (Baccelli's method). Six hours later muriate of quinine and urea, 1· (gr. xv), was repeated hypodermically, and thereafter administered in doses of 0·325 (gr. v) by mouth every four hours. The recovery was uninterrupted. On questioning the patient, it was found that he had had malarial fever within a month. My colleague, Russell,* has recently reported several interesting cases of this nature.

---

* Bull. of the Johns Hopkins Hosp., 1896, vii, 204.

One example of *post-partum malarial fever* which was proved to be such by the discovery of the parasite, and a number of others which were probably malarial, may be found in the thesis of Nuñez y Palomino.*

It should be said, however, that the terms "post-operative" and "post-partum malaria" are seriously misused. But a small proportion of the cases referred to by these titles are, in all probability, truly malarial in nature. The majority are instances of septic infection. Very few cases of post-operative malarial fever have been observed in the surgical department of the Johns Hopkins Hospital.† The abuse of the term is even more frequent in puerperal cases than after the ordinary surgical operations, and it would be well if the medical public recognized more clearly that intermittent pyrexia with rigors may depend upon many other causes than malarial infection.

Parotitis.—Parotitis may occur in association with malarial fever, as indeed it may with any severe and long-continued febrile process. It is in no way specific in its course. The immediate cause of its origin is probably the same as in the parotitis occurring in typhoid fever—namely, the entrance of pathogenic organisms from a foul mouth through Steno's duct. The only instance which the author has observed occurred in a case of severe continuous æstivo-autumnal fever.

Other Mixed Infections.—Numerous other mixed infections may occur. Various observers report the complication of malaria with the *exanthemata*. This complication certainly

---

* Tesis, Habana, 1895.

† It may be said that the careful observation of cases before operation has revealed the existence of a malarial infection in a number of instances where, if the operation had been immediately performed, the case would have been classed as one of post-operative malaria.

may occasionally exist, though most of the cases reported are unproven.

General *furunculosis*, *tonsillitis*, and *acute rheumatism* have been observed. In one of our cases studied by Barker there was a general infection with the *Streptococcus pyogenes*.

Insolation.—In a recent publication Bastianelli and Bignami * call attention to the fact that in Italy a considerable number of cases of what doubtless is simple insolation are generally regarded as pernicious comatose forms of malaria. Several of their cases occurred in individuals who were either the subjects of a mild malarial infection or else showed signs of a recent attack.

Kelsch † has shown that insolation may occur in individuals suffering from malarial fever, and has drawn attention to the fact that owing to the great similarity between the symptoms of comatose pernicious fever and ordinary insolation the diagnosis may at times be extremely difficult. He further suggests that an existing or recently passed malarial infection may, by depressing the vital forces of the individual, render him more susceptible to the influence of heat, just as is the case in subjects of alcoholism, pneumonia, or any other exhausting process.

Our own observations would lead us to believe that this hypothesis of Kelsch is just. During a recent hot spell I have had occasion to observe four or five instances of prostration in patients suffering from relatively mild malarial infections—infections which, judging from the ordinary criteria (the number of parasites in the peripheral circulation and in the spleen), would scarcely have been expected to show such grave symptoms.

---

* *Op. cit.* † Traité des maladies des pays chauds, 1889, 8vo, p. 488.

It is a well-recognized fact that in severe malarial infections comatose paroxysms are especially likely to follow exposure to the sun. It may be that in some manner this exposure may tend to determine the cerebral accumulation of the parasites, so that grave symptoms may result even in infections with a moderate number of the organisms. On the whole, however, it appears more likely that a pre-existing or present malarial infection renders the organism unusually susceptible to those grave changes—auto-intoxication (?)—which may follow exposure to the rays of the sun or to unusually high temperatures.

LECTURE VII.

MORBID ANATOMY.

Anatomical changes occurring in acute malarial infections—Anatomical changes following repeated or chronic infections—Cirrhotic processes and malaria—Malarial pigment.

The favorable course pursued by the regularly intermittent fevers renders the study of the pathological anatomy of such cases extremely difficult, and our knowledge of the anatomical changes produced by malarial infections is based almost entirely upon the study of specimens derived from two sources: First, from the organs of cases of acute pernicious malaria; and, secondly, from individuals who, having suffered from repeated or chronic infections, have finally died from some other cause.

A number of valuable studies of the pathological anatomy of malarial fever have been made during recent years, especially by Laveran,[*] Councilman and Abbott,[†] Guarnieri,[‡] Bignami,[#] Dock,[||] Barker,[▲] Monti,[◊] and Bastianelli.[‡] Much of what I shall say will be taken almost directly from the comprehensive publications of Bignami.

We shall take up the description of the anatomical changes produced by the malarial infections under two main headings:

---

[*] *Op. cit.*
[‡] Atti. d. R. acc. med. d. Roma. s. ii, vol. iii, 247.
[||] Am. Journ. Med. Sci., April, 1894.
[◊] Bull. d. Soc. med. chir. d. Pavia, 1895.
[†] *Op. cit.*
[#] *Op. cit.*
[▲] *Op. cit.*
[‡] *Op. cit.*

1. Anatomical changes occurring in acute malarial infections.

2. Anatomical changes following repeated or chronic infections.

1. THE ANATOMICAL CHANGES FOLLOWING ACUTE MALARIAL INFECTIONS.

The lesions in acute pernicious malarial fever differ very markedly according to the distribution of the malarial parasites and the anatomical changes produced by them. This variation in the distribution of the organisms is an extremely characteristic point, and, as has been shown in the description of the parasite and of the clinical symptoms, it exerts a marked influence upon the outward manifestations of the disease.

In a general way the point in the gross pathology of malarial fever which is most likely to impress the observer is the deep, slaty-gray coloration which is shown by many of the internal organs. This pigmentation or melanosis, as it is called, results from the accumulation of the pigment produced by the parasites from the hæmoglobin of the red blood-corpuscles. Excepting in very acute infections the pigment is always present, though it may vary markedly in quantity. It is more evident in older infections. Its localization may vary considerably, as in the case of the parasites.

The Brain.—The most marked changes in the brain are usually to be found in those cases which during life have shown cerebral symptoms. This is particularly the case in well-defined comatose pernicious fever. In some instances, however, of pernicious malaria the changes in the brain may be but slight. There may be no melanosis, though often

MORBID ANATOMY. 213

there is a slight sub-pial œdema with hyperæmia of the cerebral substance, and not infrequently punctate hæmorrhages. Generally the gray cortex shows a considerably deepened, somewhat chocolate color. This coloration may be excessive. The vessels are injected, and in numerous areas punctate hæmorrhages may be found.

Here, under the microscope, the cerebral capillaries are crowded with parasites; they may form a complete injection of the vessels. The organisms may be in all stages of development, though usually one of the phases is more conspicuous. Sometimes when death occurs during the paroxysm actual thrombi of segmenting parasites may be seen. In other cases the organisms are not so numerous, though evidence of their previous existence is usually to be found in free clumps of pigment and swollen pigmented endothelial cells, as well as in leucocytes containing pigment and red blood-corpuscles. The endothelium of the vessels is often granular and fatty, and frequently contains pigment; some endothelial cells may be greatly swollen, almost occluding the lumen of the vessel. These cells, as Golgi and Monti have pointed out, may contain apparently well-preserved parasites in various stages of development. The organisms may be young forms lying within shrunken and brassy colored-corpuscles, or, in other instances, full-grown and free bodies.

Not infrequently, large macrophages almost occluding the lumen of the capillary are to be seen. These cells, as Monti asserts, may represent endothelial elements which have broken loose and are free in the blood current. It is not impossible that the punctate hæmorrhages so commonly observed are largely dependent upon changes such as the above described.

Different parts of the central nervous system may be differently affected. In a case studied by Marchiafava,* there was noted a special localization of the changes in the medulla oblongata. During life the patient showed well-marked symptoms of bulbar paralysis.

In other instances there may be but few changes in the brain. The capillaries are almost free from parasites, while the endothelium is relatively intact.

The changes occurring in the nervous elements of the gray cortex have been studied recently by Monti.† While in some cases no marked changes were to be made out, in others Golgi's stain showed interesting pictures. These changes were chiefly found in cases which showed during life grave nervous symptoms. They were generally of a focal nature, and never affected all the elements in a given area. Usually, cells more or less profoundly altered were found among other cells and fibres which were quite normal.

The changes were chiefly in the protoplasmic prolongations of the cortical nerve cells, which at times appeared thin and studded with fine nodes. Often the alterations were limited to the more delicate and distant branches, though it was not difficult to find cells where all the dendrites presented a beaded appearance exactly similar to that observed in the nerve cells of animals dead of inanition. In other areas the alterations consisted of simple irregularities of contour in dendrites which were much thinned and arose from cells the bodies of which, while sometimes normal, were generally swollen, or, more rarely, were thin, shrunken, or atrophied.

Coarser alterations were, however, to be found. Certain cells showed dendrites with coarse varicosities and very

---

* *Op. cit.* † Bull. d. soc. med. chir. d. Pavia, July 12, 1895.

marked constrictions, appearing as if formed of protoplasmic masses connected only by the finest filaments. Similar changes have been described by Monti in the brains of animals in which artificial embolism was produced by injection of lycopodium.

In most of Monti's cases the axis cylinders were well preserved, the principal lesion appearing to be the alterations of the protoplasmic prolongations. Sometimes, however, especially in a case of severe comatose pernicious fever, changes were made out as well in the axis cylinders which showed in many areas, both in the gray cortex as in the cerebellum, small nodes or, more rarely, larger swellings instead of the ordinary regular smooth appearance. In this instance the general alterations were more extensive than in the other cases, the dendrites being more generally affected. Monti believes that these changes are due to the grave circulatory disturbances, the occlusion of the capillaries, lesions of their walls, the stasis, and the hæmorrhages produced by the malarial parasites.

The Spleen.—The spleen is always enlarged. In the early cases it may present the characteristics of an acute splenic tumor, being soft and almost diffluent. It is commonly cyanotic and dark in color, and in older cases it is almost black. The enlargement may be so great that rupture with fatal hæmorrhage may result.

Under the microscope the pulp is seen to be crowded with red corpuscles, many of which contain parasites which may be in various stages of development. Sometimes in the same organ different areas show different groups of parasites in different stages of development. This is particularly true in æstivo-autumnal infections, in which most of the studies of the pathological anatomy of malaria have been made. Usually large numbers of intra-corpuscular parasites with central pigment clumps and blocks and segmenting bodies are to be found, while free forms are relatively rare.

The splenic pulp is crowded with phagocytes, some of which are small and similar to mononuclear leucocytes, while others are extremely large, containing a single large nucleus and occasionally a very coarse eosinophiloid granulation. These cells, which may reach an enormous size, are laden with pigment, either in the shape of large blocks and clumps, or in small spheres or rodlets, or very fine granules. The granules may show the same arrangement which they previously had in the body of the engulfed parasite.

In other instances the pigment may be distributed in delicate lines throughout the protoplasm of the macrophage; it often seems to vary in color in different parts of the cell, but, on focusing, this appearance is found to be due to differences in the plane. These large cells also contain red corpuscles which are often partially or completely decolorized and contain parasites. Further, they may include entire small phagocytes with their contained pigment or corpuscles, as well as clumps of hæmoglobin of the color of old brass, and fragments of degenerated red blood elements.

Golgi and Monti have called attention particularly to the frequency with which these macrophages contain apparently well-preserved parasites in different stages of development. They believe that the shrunken and brassy parasitiferous red corpuscles are seized by the macrophages, as would be any foreign body, while the included parasites continue their development within the cells. Not infrequently these large macrophages show evidences of necrosis. In some places there may be actual focal necroses of the pulp very similar to those which may be seen in typhoid fever. Excellent descriptions and drawings of these changes may be found in the article of Barker.*

Free malarial pigment may be found in the intercellular spaces in the pulp. Pigment-bearing polymorphonuclear cells are relatively rare. The small mononuclear elements and the lymphocytes of the follicles never contain pigment. The capillaries are usually filled with corpuscles containing parasites, while on the other hand the splenic veins show relatively few, though pigment-bearing phagocytes and fragments of red corpuscles are always to be found.

The Liver.—The liver is usually somewhat enlarged, and, if the infection has lasted for any length of time, is always of a dark, slaty-gray color; this color, depending upon the amount of pigment present, may be very striking. The distribution of the pigment in acute malarial infection is different, as will be pointed out later, from that characteristic of repeated attacks. There is always a striking cloudy swelling.

On microscopical examination the capillaries are usually found to be crowded with white elements, many of which are phagocytic. Some of the largest macrophages are to be observed here. Undoubted evidence of phagocytosis on the part of the endothelial cells is usually to be noted. Numerous pigment-bearing cells may be found in the perivascular tissue in the portal spaces, while frequently the liver cells may contain clumps of pigment derived from the blood, and altered red blood-corpuscles. As a rule, the vessels contain few intracorpuscular parasites. These are more numerous in the interlobular branches of the portal vein, while in the intra-lobular veins the macrophages are more commonly found.

Not infrequently disseminated areas of focal necrosis of

---

* Johns Hopkins Hospital Reports, vol. v, 1895.

the liver elements, with fragmentation of the nuclei, wandering in of leucocytes, and sometimes with evidences of proliferation of the cells in the surrounding tissue, may be found. These focal necroses may be so large as to be readily visible by the naked eye. One can not but be impressed by the similarity between these changes and those which have been already described in typhoid fever and other acute infectious diseases, and shown by Flexner * to be pathognomonic of certain general intoxications.

The occurrence of these foci in the liver was first described by Guarnieri,† who believed them to be due to the cutting off of the nutrition by the extensive blocking of the intra-lobular capillaries with pigment-bearing phagocytes. Barker ‡ has described and pictured capillary thromboses in association with these areas.

The Lungs.—On gross examination there is nothing in the lungs characteristic of acute malarial fever. The alveolar capillaries often show large numbers of phagocytes, which are, however, smaller than the largest macrophages of the liver and spleen. They not infrequently show evidences of necrosis. The endothelial cells of the capillaries and smaller veins may also contain pigment, but in much less quantity than the capillaries of the brain or of the liver. Pigment-bearing leucocytes are very rarely found within the alveoli. The phagocytes are for the most part mononuclear. Polymorphonuclear pigment-bearing leucocytes, when present, contain usually finer, smaller particles of melanin. The macrophages collect usually about the periphery of the smaller veins. The endoglobular parasites show often all stages of development.

---

* The Johns Hopkins Hosp. Reports, vol. vi.   ‡ *Op. cit.*
† Atti d. R. acc. med. d. Roma, 1887, s. ii, vol. iii, 247.

The endothelium of the capillaries and small veins is almost free from pigment, in sharp contrast to what one sees in the brain and in the liver. In the areas of broncho-pneumonia which are not infrequently found, ordinary polymorphonuclear leucocytes and alveolar cells only are present; pigmented elements are extremely rare. The capillaries of the septa may, however, be filled with pigment and macrophages. Bignami suggests that this fact is due to the diminished vitality of the pigment-bearing cells, which have to a certain extent lost their motile power, and are thus less able to pass through the vessels.

The Kidneys.—The changes in the kidneys in acute malaria are relatively slight, as compared to those in the liver and spleen. The macroscopical appearance is often almost normal. On gross examination there may be no evidence of pigmentation. The parasites and phagocytes are generally present in small numbers, the quantity being out of all proportion to the alterations which may be found in the parenchyma. Ordinarily, however, there is considerable pigment in the glomeruli. This pigment is found in large colorless cells within the vessels; sometimes, however, in the glomerular epithelium. Intra-corpuscular parasites are rarely seen in the capillaries of the glomeruli. They are more common in the intertubular vessels, but are rare even there.

The most important lesions are the exfoliation and degeneration of the capsular epithelium. Albuminous exudates within the glomeruli were found by Bignami only in algid pernicious fever. Sometimes, however, there may be extensive focal necroses of the epithelium, especially that of the convoluted tubules.

The Gastro-intestinal Tract.—Under ordinary circumstances few changes are to be found in the stomach and intestines beyond a moderate degree of melanosis. In this connection it should be remembered that the intestinal mucous membrane may be of a very dark, slaty-gray tinge in conditions other than malarial fever. In other instances, however, marked changes may be made out; great injection, superficial necroses, and ulcerations.

Under the microscope a considerable number of parasites may be found. These are generally full-grown and segmenting organisms, and lie in the capillaries of the mucous membrane together with numerous pigmented cells and a few pigment clumps. As a rule, however, the gastro-intestinal mucous membrane contains relatively few parasites.

There are cases, however, as pointed out particularly by Marchiafava and Bignami, where the main seat of the localization of the infection may be in the gastro-intestinal tract. Macroscopically, there may be intense hyperæmia with punctate hæmorrhages in the gastro-intestinal mucosa, while a very distinct, dark, slaty tinge may also be observed. The capillaries throughout the gastro-intestinal tract are crowded with parasites, both free and contained in red blood-corpuscles or in phagocytes. Actual thromboses may exist, as in the cerebral capillaries, with resulting necrosis of the endothelial covering and ulceration. In such cases there are often severe gastro-intestinal symptoms which may closely simulate Asiatic cholera.

The Bone Marrow.—The marrow is generally of a dark, slaty color; it may be almost black. Microscopically, the small vessels may show large numbers of endoglobular parasites with central pigment blocks or clumps, while in the periphery of the vessels are collected numerous macrophages, including pigment and red blood-corpuscles. Bignami describes also ovoid or round bodies lying about between the corpuscles, which from their size and staining characteristics he believes to be free segments. The parasites are found in greater or less number both within and outside of the vessels. Macrophages are particularly numerous even in the pulp, while free pigment clumps may be observed.

Suprarenal Capsules.—Barker * has shown that the adrenal glands may be the seat of pronounced alterations. There are irregular areas of vascular dilatation with numerous parasites in the distended vessels. Macrophages with varying contents may be present in considerable numbers. The endothelial cells of the vessels may be phagocytic, and malarial pigment and infected corpuscles may be inclosed by true adrenal cells.

There is little that is characteristic in other organs.

Anatomical Changes in Malarial Hæmoglobinuria.—Bastianelli † has recently published some careful observations upon the anatomical changes in the organs in cases of malarial hæmoglobinuria. Besides those changes which one might expect in or after acute infections, or in more chronic cases, according to the time at which the hæmoglobinuria has occurred, there are other changes, due especially to the hæmoglobanæmia, to the polycholia, and to the elimination of hæmoglobin and bile pigments.

Liver.—In some cases the distention of the gall bladder and the abundance of bile in the intestine are the only evidences of polycholia. In other instances the bile capillaries are filled in such a manner as to cause the most wonderful microscopical injection of the finest rootlets. The endothelial cells of the capillary blood vessels, even non-pigmented elements, often show degenerative changes and fragmenta-

---

* *Op. cit.*   † Annali d. med. navale, anno II, fasc. xi, 1896.

tion of their nuclei. The capillaries are dilated, the liver cells thinned, while in some places they have in great part disappeared, the few remaining being filled with large fat drops. These degenerated areas are generally rather extensive, occupying sometimes as much as one third or one fourth of an hepatic lobule.

Progressive changes are rarely seen. In one instance only Bastianelli noted an extraordinary number of karyokinetic figures in preparations from all parts of the liver. This can not, apparently, be regarded as an attempt to repair the damage done by the extensive necroses. Similar pictures were not found by Bignami in chronic cases with extensive tracts in the process of regeneration, nor were they present in Bastianelli's cases where the degenerative changes were most marked. Where they were present, however, the injection of the bile capillaries was conspicuous—an appearance interpreted by Bastianelli as evidence of hyper-function of the liver. Marchiafava and Bastianelli both agree in believing that this multiplication of the hepatic cells is an attempt on the part of the liver to meet the increased demands for work in eliminating the detritus of hæmoglobin.

The quantity of rusty-colored masses and remnants of red corpuscles contained in the hepatic cells is not greater in hæmoglobinuria than in ordinary malarial infections.

Spleen.—Nothing remarkable is found in the spleen excepting, perhaps, the considerable number of nucleated red corpuscles, which, however, are also found in the circulating blood. A greater or less number of globuliferous cells are to be found, while granules of hæmoglobin are present in the endothelium.

Bone Marrow.—The marrow of the long bones shows the characters of normal functionally active red marrow. Besides the presence of nucleated red corpuscles, there are found hæmoglobin containing cells and cells containing blocks and granules of an ochre-colored pigment.

Kidneys.—In some cases the alterations due to the hæmoglobinæmia, hæmoglobinuria, and to the bile pigments are very scarce; but in other cases there may be found grave degenerative changes.

In those cases where the alterations are conspicuous one may observe in the *glomeruli* a slight melanosis of the endothelium, while the epithelium of the loops and the capsules is normal; there may be a slight desquamation of the capsular epithelium.

The *convoluted tubules* show cloudy swelling or sometimes almost total degeneration of the epithelium; a few of the epithelial cells may be impregnated with hæmoglobin. The lumen of the tubules contains rarely hæmoglobin, but more commonly bile pigment, either in round masses of a greenish color about half the size of a red corpuscle, or in long filaments with rosary-like varicosities. Mitoses may be observed among the cells of the tubules.

Henle's loops are usually filled with detritus of hæmoglobin; this may consist of the finest granules, or of masses resulting from the fragmentation of epithelial cells coming probably from the tubule, whose protoplasm contains hæmoglobin. The epithelial cells of Henle's loops are generally well preserved—a fact which would lead one to suspect that the detritus of hæmoglobin which is here met with comes from above. Masses of biliary pigment may also be found in Henle's loops. The epithelium of the loop may be impregnated with bile, in which case the cells are usually altered and necrotic. This, however, is not the rule; more commonly the epithelium is preserved and the biliary pigment is present as a hollow cylinder within the lumen of the tube. Sometimes karyokinetic figures may be made out in the tubular epithelium.

In the *straight tubules* casts of hæmoglobin are more abundant than in any other part of the kidney; the cells of the tubules are well preserved.

The vascular endothelium contains black pigment or granules of hæmoglobin, while the interstitial tissue shows generally no alterations. Kelsch and Kiéner,* however, have noted severe interstitial hæmorrhages, while the escape of blood into the renal tubules, causing an actual hæmaturia, is not uncommon.

Neither in the circulating blood nor in the venous and capillary blood of the organs are to be found red corpuscles in the process of hæmoglobinæmic degeneration; shadows are usually very scanty. In some cases Bastianelli found a stasis of lymphocytes in the liver. The accumulation of the leucocytes in the renal vessels was notable.

2. Changes following Repeated or Chronic Infections—Chronic Malarial Cachexia.

Changes similar to the above described, of greater or less extent, occur thus with every acute malarial infection, and it is but natural that continued or repeated infections should result in important permanent changes in various of the organs. These changes have been studied with particular care by Bignami,† from whom the following description is largely taken:

The Spleen.—The spleen is always enlarged. It may reach below the umbilicus, even touching the pubes. It is

---

* Arch. de phys., 1882.
† Bull. d. R. acc. med. d. Roma, 1892-'93, xix, 186.

usually firm, with a sharp border. The capsule is thickened, showing often white fibrous cartilaginoid plaques upon the surface. On section, the surface is usually of a somewhat slaty color, while the trabeculæ are very prominent. The course of development of these changes has been ably sketched by Bignami. The acute splenic tumor results largely from:

(a) The aggregation in the pulp of the spleen of great numbers of red blood-corpuscles, which have become shrunken and brassy colored or decolorized. These are found included in colorless elements of the spleen as brassy colored fragments or hyaline masses.

(b) The continuous accumulation from all parts of the body of colorless elements which contain pigmented red corpuscles or parasites, and are often necrotic.

(c) The presence of large numbers of red corpuscles containing parasites, some of which apparently pass through the vessel walls by diapedesis and seek the columns of the pulp, where they are for the most part inclosed by the epithelioid cells.

As a result of these processes a considerable number of the proper elements of the spleen become necrotic, while others, as well in the pulp as in the follicles, undergo karyokinetic division; all this is followed by marked hyperæmia and acute tumor of the splenic pulp. Thus, the spleen is converted into a sort of tomb for the deposit of cadavers, while at the same time, during the same infection, processes of regeneration begin to appear.

When the actual infection is at an end and the acute hyperæmia of the spleen has passed away, the tissues bordering upon these collections of necrotic elements, or those surrounding the necrotic areas of the splenic pulp, begin to show changes, which on the one hand tend toward permanent alterations, and on the other toward a partial reparation of the part. In those parts where a considerable portion of the splenic tissue becomes necrotic or disappears, being carried away by the leucocytes, the vessels become dilated, forming a network of venous lacunæ which are separated by thin layers of pulp, giving rise to a tissue simulating that of an angioma.

In those instances where a more marked destruction of the splenic substance has occurred, and where every trace of the pulp is gone, there are left extensive areas of a tissue consisting of cavernous sinuses, whose septa are represented by a very delicate connective tissue rich in giant cells, similar to that of the bone marrow. Occasionally follicles become necrotic and fibrous.

At the same time a process of regeneration yet more extensive takes place, starting from the splenic pulp. The follicles through hyperplasia reach sometimes three or four times their normal size. This newly formed lymphatic tissue, starting from the follicles, may surround necrotic areas of splenic substance, which, becoming smaller and smaller, finally disappear. In the neighborhood of the hyperplastic follicles occurs an hyperplasia also of the pulp, while the reticulum becomes thickened so as to give rise in preparations to very clear and beautiful figures such as are not to be seen in the normal spleen. The pigment and probably the greater part of the necrotic elements are carried onward and collected about the periphery of the follicles, so that the diffuse melanosis of the pulp is followed by a perifollicular melanosis.

The pigment then passes on into the lymphatic vessels of the sheaths of the arteries and of the connective tissue of the septa. There results, on the one hand, a thickening of the vascular sheaths and of the septa, and, on the other hand, the appearance of single or multiple lymphatic cysts, causing a lymphangiomatoid picture, and resulting in chronic lymph stasis. When one considers that each new infection is accompanied by fresh processes similar to this, it is easy to appreciate the gradual development of the enormous splenic tumors, in which sometimes it is difficult, even histologically, to recognize the original structure of the organ.

The Liver.—The changes found in the liver of chronic malaria may in like manner be traced from those occurring in acute infections. In acute infections the capillary network of the organ is invaded by large numbers of phagocytes containing pigment or corpuscles, and coming in great part from the spleen, while the parasites are usually scanty. The circulation becomes slow, the capillary network dilates, while a certain amount of pigment is taken up by endothelial cells of the vessels, and later by Kupffer's cells. The pigmented endothelium becomes swollen and in part necrotic, while from these vascular changes new areas of stasis result.

Many of the liver cells at the same time undergo alterations, either an acute atrophy from pressure or a coagulative necrosis. Such areas are often quite extensive. Numerous cells are found filled with blocks of yellowish iron-containing pigment, resulting from the early death of many red blood-corpuscles. Together with this, a certain number of liver cells, Kupffer's cells, and endothelial cells undergo multiplication by karyokinesis. The result of all this is the acute hepatic tumor, and the increase in functional activity—polycholia.

Only a small part of the great number of pigmented elements which enter the liver escapes, passing through the branches of the supra-hepatic veins. The greater part, taken up by endothelial and perivascular cells, brings about a distinct melanosis of the vessels, consecutive to the previous melanæmia. Passing onward out of the capillary network into the perivascular lymph channels, the pigment becomes collected in the form of large blocks within white cells. Within these cells the pigment is carried through the lymph channels to the periphery of the lobules, so that the melanosis of the entire lobule is followed by a perilobular melanosis. The process extending, the masses of pigment are to be found three or four months after the end of the infection in large blocks, for the most part intra-cellular, in the perivascular lymphatic tissue of Glisson's capsule.

While this migration of pigment is going on there occur in the lobules, on the one hand, permanent alterations, and, on the other hand, regenerative processes. In those places where the dilatation of the lymph and blood vessels and the degeneration and pigmentation of the vascular elements are most marked, no regeneration may follow the atrophy and necrosis of the epithelial and liver cells. The dilatation of the vessels increases and becomes permanent, while the greater part of the remaining liver elements disappears, only a few remaining in an atrophic condition, leaving an angiomatoid tissue consisting of an ectatic vascular network about which may be recognized a stroma consisting of Kupffer's cells. Small lymphatic cysts may occur where there is a special dilatation of the lymph vessels.

In certain parts of the liver where, after the disappearance of the pigment and the necrotic masses in general from the endothelial cells of the vessel walls, the normal blood current becomes restored, there occurs an active regeneration of the tissue elements about the atrophic or necrotic liver cells. The young hepatic cells become arranged with great regularity in long rows on both sides of the old elements; thus, when the stroma remains intact complete regeneration of the lobule may occur. These regenerative processes are accompanied by the appearance of giant cells with budding nuclei similar to those found in the embryonic liver. Such regenerative processes never appear in parts of the liver which have not been entirely freed from the collections of pigment and parasites. The migration and collection of the pigment in the perilobular tissue is followed by an hyperplasia in this area so that the surroundings of the lobules are more distinct.

Such destructive and regenerative changes result, then, in a distinct increase in the size of some lobules and a diminution in size and atrophy of others. If we consider that every acute infection is associated with a process of this nature, it may be easily appreciated how the chronic perilobular, monolobular hepatitis of malaria arises, that process which is characterized by the presence of zones of hyperplasia or of atrophy of the parenchyma, by chronic blood and lymph stasis, by the formation of areas of angiomatoid tissue, by lymphectasis and lymphatic cysts. Thus, then, arise the familiar large livers with smooth surface and lobules of irregular size.

Bignami divides these processes in the liver into four stages:

1. The liver is congested, while the lobules are not sharply distinguishable, and show in severe cases a decreased melanosis. The macroscopical characters are about the same as those in the liver in acute malarial infections. Microscopically, at this period, a little after the termination of the acute infection, it may be noted that the parasites have disappeared from the capillaries, the pigmented endovascular macrophages have in great part disappeared, while the pigment is entirely

collected in the endothelium and in Kupffer's cells. Those parts of the lobules where necrosis or degeneration has occurred become markedly atrophied, the necrotic and degenerated elements being carried away by the phagocytes, while the vascular network becomes dilated.

2. At a more advanced stage the lobules are distinct on gross examination. The melanosis continues to be diffuse throughout the lobule, but prevails at the periphery. The liver is still congested. The particular features of this stage are, on the one hand, the fact that the hepatic lobule frees itself from the accumulation of pigment and the necrotic remains which become collected toward its periphery, while, on the other hand, an active regenerative process begins in the parenchyma.

3. Here the diffuse melanosis of the lobule, with the prevalence of pigment at the periphery, is followed by an exclusively perilobular melanosis. The liver is enlarged; the consistency somewhat increased; the surface smooth. On section, all the lobules are seen to be surrounded by a slate-colored line, in the neighborhood of which the lobular substance itself is somewhat brown. The slaty lines marking out each lobule form generally an exquisite network. The size of individual lobules varies greatly, some being two or three times as large as normally, others distinctly small. Microscopically, the degenerative alterations may be seen to have led in some areas to the formation of false angiomata and of lacunæ or cysts of lymphatic nature. Other lobules through degenerative processes have increased notably in volume. The pigment has become extra-vascular. Its transport through the capillaries and perilobular lymphatics is accomplished by colorless mononuclear and polymorphonuclear cells.

4. In cases where the acute infection has been past for several months—in one case only three months—the pigmentation may be so greatly diminished as to be scarcely visible by the naked eye. There is marked enlargement and congestion of the liver; the surface is smooth; the consistency is increased. On section, the lobules are well marked and surrounded by a most delicate reddish-brown border.

Microscopically, the melanosis is seen to have become exclusively perivascular.

5. Lastly, we arrive at the terminal form of the chronic malarial hepatic tumor. Macroscopically, the liver is enlarged and increased in weight, sometimes greatly. The surface is smooth; the capsule a little thickened. The appearance on section is finely granular, the lobules being well marked, somewhat prominent, and surrounded by a zone of slightly pinkish tissue.

Microscopically, all the malarial pigment has disappeared, while the alterations of the parenchyma are similar to those described in the last two stages. The lobules, of varying size, are surrounded by hyperplastic perilobular connective tissue. On the other hand, the connective tissue of the larger septa is of about normal volume. The capillaries are notably dilated, while there is still more or less stasis of the colorless corpuscles. There is an alteration in the form of the hepatic cells in those zones where there is most marked dilatation.

These lesions differ in extent considerably in different cases; thus, in some instances, despite the great increase in the weight of the organ there may be no very marked dilatations of the capillaries, no false angiomata nor lymphatic stasis, while, on the other hand, there may be a more extensive hyperplasia of the perilobular connective tissue with decided increase in the volume of many lobules. There may be an evident hyperplasia of the parenchyma, as testified to by multinuclear hepatic cells and nuclei rich in chromatic substance. In other cases, however, the stasis and false angiomata may be excessively developed. They may constitute one of the chief factors in the hepatic enlargement.

The Bone Marrow.—After numerous relapses or repeated attacks of malarial fever the marrow of the long bones—for example, that of the femur in the upper and lower fourths—is usually red, and of a consistency greater than is generally seen in acute infections. Microscopically, there are various alterations, generally the signs of an acute proliferation of the proper marrow elements. This is followed by an increase in the hæmatopoietic activity of the marrow. Marked degenerative and destructive alterations may, however, take place in the bone marrow during acute infections; these may result in considerable injury to the blood-forming functions of the marrow. In certain rare cases it may present the features of the marrow of acute pernicious anæmia, showing particularly the presence of numerous megaloblasts (gigantoblasts).

Finally, in some instances the new formation of hæmatoblastic marrow may be entirely lacking. In these latter cases the post-malarial anæmia is usually progressive.

The Blood.—Bignami and Dionisi,* as has been mentioned elsewhere, have described several distinct types of post-malarial anæmia which correspond more or less with the above-mentioned changes in the bone marrow.

1. Cases where the blood shows alterations similar to those observed in ordinary secondary anæmia. The chief difference is in the fact that the leucocytes here are diminished in number. The prognosis in these cases is favor-

---

* *Op. cit.*

MORBID ANATOMY. 233

able, though in a few instances fatal results have been reported.

2. Cases where the blood is like that of pernicious anæmia, showing the presence of gigantoblasts (megaloblasts). The prognosis here is bad.

3. Cases of progressive anæmia due to the lack of compensation by the marrow for losses brought about by the infection. In such instances the marrow of the long bones is poor in nucleated red corpuscles.

4. Chronic anæmia of the cachectic. These forms differ from the above-mentioned in that the special symptoms of malarial cachexia prevail, while post mortem there is a sclerosis of the bone marrow. In the long bones the marrow is red, of an increased consistency, while the giant cells, many of which are necrotic, are very numerous. Nucleated red corpuscles are rare, and polymorphonuclear leucocytes are scanty.

The Kidneys.—No great changes are, as a rule, to be found in the kidneys of chronic malaria. Two varieties of kidney have, however, been described by Kiéner as sometimes met with in chronic paludism :

1. The congested kidney.

2. The atrophic kidney.

1. The engorged kidneys are increased in size and weight, and of firm consistency. The surface is smooth, the color a deep red, the congestion being particularly marked in the pyramids. Owing to the excessive congestion of the vessels, interstitial hæmorrhages or the escape of blood into the tubules may occur. There is a marked granular degeneration of the tubular epithelium, while desquamation is common. Hyaline casts may be found.

2. The atrophic kidneys are small. The surface is irregu-

lar, the capsule adherent, the consistency increased. The color is usually of a maroon or mahogany tinge, and often there is a blotchy appearance. Small cysts are common. Microscopically, alterations are to be found in the interstitial tissue as well as in the tubular epithelium.

Amyloid Degeneration.—A few instances of amyloid degeneration of various organs have been described as following chronic or repeated malarial infections. Laveran found amyloid degeneration of the kidneys in two instances of chronic malarial cachexia, though each case was complicated with chronic broncho-pneumonia and bronchiectasis.

Frerichs * described three cases of amyloid liver.

More recently, several cases have been studied by Marchiafava and Bignami.† In these instances, which were of æstivo-autumnal or obstinate quartan fever, a long period of febrile attacks was followed by symptoms of a nephritis and a rapidly developing cachexia, the patient dying in a few months. Anatomically, there was found to be a grave anæmia and a marantic condition of the organs, a chronic nephritis, and a diffuse amyloid degeneration. The amyloid change was most marked in the kidneys, where, besides the affection of the vessels of small and medium size and of the glomeruli, there was a considerable involvement of the walls of the tubules. The degeneration of the interstitial tissue and the renal parenchyma may be very grave.

After the kidneys the most severe lesions were found in the *intestines* and *spleen*. In the bowel the vessels of the villi were chiefly affected, though those of the sub-mucosa were also the seat of changes, and to a less extent those of the other intestinal coats. In the spleen the process was par-

---

* Klinik der Leberkrankheiten. † *Op. cit.*

ticularly marked in the vascular network of the periphery of the follicles. Great blocks of amyloid substance may be found here, while in the trabeculæ of the pulp the process may be in its earliest stages or entirely absent.

In the *liver* the changes are less extensive than in the kidneys. Irregularly disseminated islands of hepatic tissue are involved; an island, for instance, the size of a lobule or larger, where the liver substance has entirely disappeared and the vascular network shows grave amyloid changes, may lie in the midst of apparently normal hepatic substance. In the first small zones the amyloid change is found usually, according to Bignami, at the periphery of the lobules, from whence it spreads.

Cirrhotic Processes and Malaria.

In many text-books of medicine malarial fever is placed among the more frequent causes of atrophic cirrhosis of the liver, while sometimes other chronic cirrhotic processes in the lung, endocardium, and central nervous system are ascribed to the same cause.

Cirrhosis of the Liver.—By far the most common cirrhotic process ascribed to malaria is the ordinary atrophic cirrhosis of the liver, and yet in going over the statistics of any considerable number of cases, or in looking through the literature, we can find little basis for such a statement. No one has ever definitely traced the development of an atrophic cirrhosis from the changes following acute or chronic malarial fever.

Frerichs, in his Diseases of the Liver, mentions particularly the infrequency of cirrhosis in individuals dying from chronic malaria, though in five instances this was the only probable cause to which he could ascribe the changes.

Laveran has observed only two cases of atrophic cirrhosis following malarial fever, and he is by no means positive as to the causal relation of the latter process.

Welch has seen but one instance of atrophic cirrhosis in which there seemed any reason to ascribe the process to previous malarial infection.

Kelsch and Kiéner* enter into a rather lengthy description of the hepatitis which may follow malarial fever, distinguishing three characteristic forms, and two groups of malarial cirrhoses:

1. Insular cirrhosis with nodular hepatitis, and insular cirrhosis with diffuse parenchymatous hepatitis.

2. Annular cirrhosis with nodular or diffuse parenchymatous hepatitis.

The general appearance of the liver under these circumstances differs little from those of the ordinary atrophic cirrhosis.

Bignami † discusses this subject at length, concluding that there is insufficient evidence to prove that atrophic cirrhosis is a frequent sequence to malarial fever. He describes the development of the chronic hepatic tumor of malarial cachexia, and says in conclusion: "It is easy to understand from this that it is not difficult to make a differential diagnosis between this form of chronic tumor, or of chronic hepatitis, as one might say, from the other forms of cirrhosis. There are no facts or reasons sufficient to cause us to believe that ordinary cirrhosis may follow a chronic tumor. The structure in the two cases is absolutely different. In the one we have an extensive new formation of connective tissue, multilobular in nature, contracting about the included lobules;

---

* *Op. cit.* † *Op. cit.*

in the other, a more scanty formation of perilobular connective tissue about a single lobule, not contracting, together with grave alterations of the lobules themselves, especially of their vascular and lymphatic systems, not depending, as we have seen, upon the new formation of perilobular connective tissue, but due to lesions primarily local.* Atrophic conditions of the liver exist in malaria, but are simple atrophies, and occur in patients who are exhausted—for example, by diarrhœa, etc.—or in cases which I have described as progressive post-malarial anæmia. They depend upon the complete want or almost complete absence of any process tending toward regeneration as a result of grave and diffuse regressive alterations."

More recently two observers in particular have come forward in support of the association of malaria with atrophic cirrhosis of the liver. Childe † reports a case occurring in a woman of forty, where the liver was connected by "dense adhesions to the diaphragm ; capsule thick, and nodular irregularities on surface ; liver very small and squeezed up ; its shape distorted, and much fibrous tissue throughout it." There is, however, no mention of a possibility of the previous existence of syphilis, and the absolute proof that the process is of malarial origin is wanting.

A more striking case is that reported by Lodigiani.‡ In this instance, occurring in a woman of twenty-eight, who

---

* It must be said that there is little evidence in support of the old idea that the ordinary atrophic cirrhosis is the result of a primary new formation of connective tissue. The primary changes here are doubtless in the parenchyma, the connective-tissue increase representing, probably, an attempt, imperfect though it may be, on the part of the organism to compensate for the damage done to the liver cells.

† Trans. Grant Coll. Med. Soc., Bombay, 1896, 49.

‡ Il Morgagni, January, 1896, Ann. XXXVIII, Pt. I, No. 1, 59.

showed no evidences of syphilis and gave no history of alcoholic habits, though a definite account of attacks of malaria off and on for eighteen years, there developed a typical atrophic cirrhosis. Splenectomy was performed on account of a large movable spleen at a time when the existence of cirrhosis was unsuspected. The patient died on the following day. The spleen, upon macroscopical and microscopical examination, showed the characteristic changes described by Bignami in chronic malarial infection, while the liver presented changes in every way similar to those of an ordinary atrophic cirrhosis. This case would appear to be the strongest support afforded by literature for the idea that typical atrophic cirrhosis may follow malaria.

In Barker's recent contribution, above referred to, the relation of malarial infections to cirrhotic processes is discussed. The author emphasizes the fact that many conditions exist in the organs in malarial fever which might well be the starting point for extensive cirrhotic changes.

It is interesting to note in connection with this the similarity between the necrotic areas found after malarial infections, and those artificially produced by Flexner* in animals after the injection of blood serum and other soluble toxic substances. In many of these instances Flexner has been able to follow the subsequent development of most characteristic atrophic cirrhosis of the liver and of the kidneys.

It may be said, then, that while we have as yet hardly sufficient evidence to justify us in assuming that ordinary atrophic cirrhosis is a frequent sequel of malarial infections, secondary cirrhotic processes in the liver, spleen, bone marrow, and other organs are, however, common.

---

* The Med. News, Philadelphia, August 4, 1894.

Malarial Pigment.

The Dark Pigment contained within the Parasites.—The dark pigment existing in the blood and in the organs in malarial fever has been known for many years. It was first described in the blood by Meckel* in 1847, and shortly afterward by Dlauhy, Virchow † and Hischl. ‡ These observers, as well as Frerichs in 1858, believed that the pigment was formed chiefly in the spleen and in the liver.

Planer, # in 1854, was the first to note that it arose in the circulating blood; an observation which was confirmed by Arnstein ‖ in 1874.

Arnstein went further, showing that this pigment originates in the red blood-corpuscle itself; an observation which was afterward confirmed by Marchiafava and Celli ▲ in 1879.

In the following year Laveran ◊ demonstrated the fact that the pigment arises within the malarial parasite as a result of destruction of and changes in the hæmoglobin of the red corpuscle. This melanin exists in small granules, at the most one micromillimetre in diameter, of a dark-brown or copper color. The pigment, as has been stated, seems to have a slightly different color in different forms of the parasite. This, however, is a point about which it is very hard to speak positively. Thus, while the granules in the young tertian organisms appear to have a lighter and more yellowish brown shade than the corresponding granules of the quartan parasite, it is impossible to say whether this may not in great

---

* Zeitschr. f. Psych., 1847, 198.
† Virch. Archiv, 1849, ii, 587.
‡ Zeitschr. d. k. k. Gesellschaft der Aertzte in Wien, 1850, 338.
# Zeitschr. d. k. k. Gesellschaft der Aertzte in Wien, 1854, 127, 280.
‖ Virch. Archiv, 1874, Bd. lxi, 494.
▲ Commentaria clin. di Pisa, 1879. ◊ *Op. cit.*

part depend upon the fact that they are much more minute. Certainly the difference in color between the granules of the full-grown tertian parasite and of the full-grown quartan organism, granules which are of nearly the same size, is very much more difficult to determine.

The minute granules of the young tertian parasite examined in the fresh unstained specimen appear to have a somewhat lighter color than those of the æstivo-autumnal parasite, which are no less minute.

In the tissues, especially in the spleen, the granules are often agglomerated in masses of irregular contour. These conglomerate masses may be really of a very considerable size; in some instances almost one half as large as a normal red corpuscle.

The pigment is resistant to the action of strong acids. Alkalies, however, especially potassium and ammonium salts, decolorize it; it is readily dissolved by sulphide of ammonium. The nature of the dark pigment of malaria is quite unknown. Arising, as it doubtless does, from the hæmoglobin of the red corpuscles, one might naturally expect that it would contain iron, but this reaction is not to be obtained by any method which we now know.

The Yellow Pigment.—Besides the dark granules of melanin, there is to be found in the tissues a considerable quantity of yellowish pigment which gives a good reaction for iron, both with sulphide of ammonium and ferrocyanide of potassium and hydrochloric acid; it corresponds with the pigment termed by Neumann[*] *hæmosiderin*. This yellowish pigment is found not so much about the periphery of the vessels as in the case of the true malarial pigment, but

---

[*] Virch. Archiv, Bd. cxvi, p. 318.

infiltrated throughout the proper tissue elements, more especially in the spleen, liver, and bone marrow.

This substance may exist as (a) extremely fine granules, the color of which is not to be made out excepting when they exist in large quantity, as in the renal tubules; (b) as large granules of an ochre or rusty color in the liver and pancreas; (c) as voluminous blocks of a pale yellow, or gold yellow, or brownish yellow in the spleen, bone marrow, and kidneys.

The direct origin of this pigment, at least of the larger blocks, from the shrunken, brassy-colored red corpuscles may readily be traced; marked changes have, however, taken place in the hæmoglobin.

This substance is insoluble in water and alcohol; it turns black with sulphide of ammonium, and gives the blue hæmosiderin reaction with ferrocyanide of potassium and hydrochloric acid, while it resists the action of strong acids and caustic potash.

Now while the black pigment *in the blood* clearly arises within the parasites, directly from the hæmoglobin of the corpuscles, it is, however, rather difficult to explain the large accumulations of black pigment which are to be found *in the tissues* in some cases where the parasites show but very little melanin. Marchiafava * noted the disproportion between the quantity of pigment in the spleen, liver, and bone marrow in such instances, and the slight melanæmia, and suggested that the pigment might also be elaborated within the tissues by the colorless cells.

While Dock † was unable to find evidence of such a process, Bignami ‡ has published some interesting observations relating to this point.

---

* Atti del II cong. di med. int., 1889.   ‡ *Op. cit.*
† Amer. Jour. Med. Sci., April, 1894.

He noted that the yellow iron-containing pigment is much more frequent in acute splenic tumors, while in the chronic melanotic tumors of the spleen and liver the reaction for iron is less marked, especially if there have been no recent attacks. The extensive siderosis of the acute tumors in great part disappears, leaving, however, a considerable accumulation of brown or black pigment.

Now it is not uncommon to find in the large phagocytes containing pigment blocks a blue reaction, either diffuse or surrounding the black masses; sometimes it forms a regular blue frame to the clumps of melanin. Similar pictures have been obtained in this clinic by Barker,* and by Macallum † in the organs of malarious birds.

These appearances suggest to Bignami the possibility that a part of the black pigment may come from changes taking place in the hæmosiderin which is formed during the acute infection, being derived in great part from the transformed hæmoglobin of the brassy corpuscles.

This supposition is certainly ingenious and plausible. It has an analogy in the experimental observations of Schmidt, who studied the modifications which the blood undergoes when injected into the trachea, finding that at first there arise masses of pigment, giving the characteristic hæmosiderin reaction, while after several weeks the pigment takes on a red-brown or black color and loses, little by little, its power of reacting to ferrocyanide of potassium and hydrochloric acid.

An interesting point in favor of this idea is the fact, as Bignami mentions, that in examining especially the fresh splenic juice we find a considerable number of bodies of a

---

* *Op. cit.* † As yet unpublished observations.

round form, in size up to about that of the red blood-corpuscles, which have a yellowish color and contain a number of black pigment granules; often they appear as simple masses of black pigment which seem to lie in a slightly yellowish body. The granules may be in active Brownian movement. These bodies Bignami believes to be masses of hæmosiderin which are in the process of change into melanin.

Bignami concludes: " That the melanæmia, index of an acute infection, is derived only from the direct transformation of hæmoglobin into melanin through the action of the parasites within the red corpuscles (as Marchiafava and Celli have demonstrated).

" That the melanosis of the viscera (spleen, liver, bone marrow), index of a previous infection, has a double origin. In chief part it is derived from the melanæmia—that is, from the deposition in the viscera of the black pigment formed during the acute infection in the circulating blood ; in part it has a local origin—that is, it is derived from the slow transformation of the blocks of ochre-colored pigment which are deposited or formed in the spleen and in the other viscera from the enormous quantity of altered red blood-corpuscles which, in grave infections, die before the direct action of the parasites has transformed their hæmoglobin into black pigment."

Welch justly observes that an objection to Bignami's conclusion is furnished by the fact that hæmosiderin is found in the liver, spleen, and· bone marrow very commonly in anæmias, but that the black pigment without micro-chemical iron reaction, which characterizes malarial infections, does not appear under these conditions. He suggests as an hypothesis that the malarial parasite may produce some chemical change in the substance of the red corpuscle which permits the transformation of the specifically altered hæmoglobin into black malarial pigment within certain cells of the body.

In conclusion, then, it may be said that there exist in the blood and tissues in malarial fever two main varieties of pigment:

1. The black granules and masses of granules which give no reaction for iron.

2. Yellowish ochre or rusty blocks or masses as well as fine granules which give the iron reaction (hæmosiderin).

The black pigment arises probably for the most part within the bodies of the parasites, though there is some evidence which might suggest its possible elaboration within the tissue elements from masses of hæmosiderin.

The second variety is derived doubtless from the fragments and remains of destroyed corpuscles, especially from the shrunken brassy-colored elements characteristic of certain malarial infections. This form of pigment is found only in the tissues.

LECTURE VIII.

GENERAL PATHOLOGY.

General pathology of the main symptoms of malarial fever—Infection with multiple groups of parasites—Mechanism of defense—Phagocytosis—Spontaneous recovery.

As has been shown in the preceding lectures, many of the clinical symptoms of malarial fever bear a direct relation to certain stages in the life history of the parasites in the blood.

Upon what does this relation depend, and how are we to account for the clinical manifestations?

The Intermittent Fever.—Let us first consider the malarial paroxysm. We know by observation that the paroxysm always follows the segmentation of a group of parasites. By what mechanism is this produced? Why should the parasites give rise to febrile manifestations at this stage only?

Numerous answers have been given to these questions.

Laveran, who does not wholly accept Golgi's views concerning the association of paroxysms with segmenting organisms, believes that the febrile elevation depends upon the irritability of the nervous system. "The degree of irritability of the nervous system, which varies with individuals and with the date of infection, seems to play an important rôle in the determination of the form and of the type of the fever. If it be a vigorous individual who is suffering from his first attack of malarial fever, the nervous system reacts actively, and one observes a continuous or at least a quotidian fever. If the patient be anæmic, enfeebled already by numerous previous attacks, the nervous system having become less susceptible, then it is a fever with long intermissions which is observed. The nervous system becomes accustomed to the presence of the hæmatozoa and reacts less and less. With individuals who have lived for a long time in malarious regions, or who have had numerous attacks of malarial fever, the febrile paroxysms are generally rare and mild, while with the new-comers the febrile reactions occur with great energy."

Richard,* in 1883, suggested that the fever represents the reaction of the organism against the parasites. The high temperature he believed to be directly injurious to the hæmatozoa; "they [the parasites] excite the fever, the fever destroys them, and falls in its turn." The few parasites still remaining after the paroxysm multiply, and when, as a result of this multiplication, the accumulation reaches a certain degree, there occurs another febrile reaction on the part of the organism. In typhoid fever, where temperatures of 40° and 41° do not destroy the pathogenic agent, the fever is continuous; in malarial fever a relatively short paroxysm destroys so many of the specific micro-organisms that for the time being the exciting cause of the fever is removed; hence the intermittent character of the manifestations.

To the majority of observers who have accepted Golgi's theories concerning the development of the malarial organisms, their arrangement in groups, and their definite cycles of development, these views are not wholly satisfactory. Golgi, in his first articles, assumed that the paroxysm was due to the entrance into fresh red corpuscles of the new group of parasites resulting from segmentation.

Antolisci † later on, however, called attention to the fact

---

* *Op. cit.* † Riforma medica, 1890, Nos. 12, 13, pp. 68, 74.

that if quinine be given shortly before the time at which the sporulation of a group of organisms is to be expected, the segmentation may still occur, followed by the paroxysm, and yet no new group of organisms is found within the red cells; all are killed by the quinine in circulation at the time of sporulation. The whole group of parasites is destroyed before entering upon a new cycle of intra-corpuscular existence, and further symptoms dependent upon the group fail to appear. From this fact Antolisei concluded that it is not upon the invasion of the red corpuscles by a new group of parasites that the paroxysm depends, but upon some other cause. This cause he believed to be intimately associated with the act of segmentation itself.

Baccelli * suggested that the paroxysm is due to a circulating toxic substance which is set free by the parasites at the moment of segmentation. He maintains that the symptoms of malarial fever depend upon two main causes: (*a*) a morphological hæmodyscrasia and (*b*) a chemical hæmodyscrasia. The former depends upon the progressive destruction of the red corpuscles by the parasites which live at their expense. The latter is manifested in a much more intense and rapid manner, and depends upon the entrance into the circulation of as yet undetermined chemical poisons which are set free at the time of sporulation—poisons due either to the act of sporulation or to substances set free from disintegrated red corpuscles. These toxic substances are injurious to the nervous system, and especially to the vaso-motor ganglia. It is to their liberation that the febrile paroxysms are due. The duration of the paroxysm depends probably upon the time required for the elimination of the

---

* Deutsch. med. Woch., Aug. 11, 1892, No. 32, 721.

toxic substances by the kidneys, skin, liver, and lungs. During the paroxysm many of the spores are destroyed, but a certain number survive to begin again their cycle of existence.

Golgi * in 1892 accepted this theory of the toxic origin of the febrile manifestations.

This explanation from analogy with what we know of the pathogenesis of other infectious diseases is certainly the most satisfactory, and, indeed, there are facts which speak strongly in its support.

Particularly suggestive of the presence of toxic substances in the circulation at the time of the paroxysm are the observations of Brousse and Roque and Lemoine, demonstrating the increased toxicity of the urine during malarial fever.

Brousse,† studying the effects following the injection of the urine of cases of malarial fever into animals, arrived at the following conclusions: "1. The urotoxic coefficient calculated by Bouchard's formula, the mean coefficient being 0·464, rises during the paroxysm, and the physiological effects observed are those which usually follow the injection of urine—dyspnœa, myosis, fall of temperature, exophthalmos, and, furthermore, convulsions. 2. This toxicity is diminished during the period of convalescence in intermittent fever very much below that of the urine during the paroxysm, and, moreover, below that of the normal urine." ‡

Roque and Lemoine # studied the urine in three cases of malarial fever—one a case of tertian fever and two cases of

---

* Deutsch. med. Woch., 1892, 661, 695, 707, 729.
† Quoted from Laveran, Du paludisme, etc., Paris, 1891.
‡ Société de méd. et de chir. pratiques de Montpellier, 14 Mai, 1890, cited from Laveran.
# Revue de méd., 1890, p. 926.

pernicious comatose malaria. Their conclusions were as follows:

"1. The pathogenic agents of paludism form in the blood a large quantity of toxic products, a great part of which is eliminated by the urine. This elimination is at its maximum immediately after the paroxysm, and lasts, generally, twenty-four hours, at least in the paroxysms of tertian fever.

"2. Sulphate of quinine acts by favoring the increase of this elimination.

"3. In certain pernicious fevers, a complete absence of toxicity of the urine depends probably upon alterations in the kidneys and liver, and the return of the urinary toxicity should be considered a good prognostic sign.

"4. Finally, it may be noted that in two cases recovery has followed a more increased elimination of toxines than that observed after the preceding paroxysms."

In discussing this paper, Lépine justly remarked that injections should be made not only with pure urine, but also with a solution of the salts of the urine made after calcination. This alone can give a reliable idea of the toxicity of the urine dependent upon organic compounds.

More recently Botazzi and Pensuti* have made a control research, and, while finding the same general results as Roque and Lemoine, dispute their conclusions, believing that there is not sufficient evidence of the formation of a specific toxic substance. Their conclusions are as follows:

"We think that we have demonstrated:

"1. That in the malarial fevers the febrile urine is less toxic than that passed during the apyretic stage.

---

* Lo sperimentale, Firenze, 1894, xlviii, 232, 254.

"2. That the urine emitted during the period of apyrexia is more toxic than normal urine.

"3. That the toxicity of the urine of malarial patients augments constantly with the succession of febrile attacks, though in some cases this augmentation appears in the form of unexpected and irregular exacerbations.

"4. That, as there is nothing specific in the course of the intoxications produced in rabbits with malarial urine, there is no need to suppose the presence of specific toxines or substances of the nature of leucomaines, for the salts of potassium, phosphoric acid, the urinary pigments, the peptones—all of which substances are eliminated in increased quantities—are a sufficient explanation.

"5. That the injection of febrile urine is followed by a slower intoxication, characterized by sopor, by increased diuresis, by diarrhœa, and mydriasis, while the apyretic urine produces a more acute effect, sometimes fulminating, characterized by clonic and tonic spasms, myosis, 'exhorbitisme,' spastic expiration.

"6. That to explain this different picture one may suppose that with febrile urine the polyuria and diarrhœa are due chiefly to the increased richness in urea, while the peptones may contribute to the production of sopor. In the afebrile urines the salts of potassium, the phosphoric acid, the urinary pigments, and especially the urobilin, manifesting themselves as substances essentially convulsive, determine an hypertoxicity.

"7. Finally, besides the hæmocytolysis, the destruction of the cellular elements of the tissues, and the formation and elimination of toxic substances, there must exist intermediate factors which account for the absence of increased toxicity after the first febrile paroxysms, and the irregular elevation and diminution in the urotoxic coefficient in some other cases."

Laveran also speaks conservatively concerning these experiments as a proof of the existence of a specific toxine.

A suggestive research relative to the excretion of toxic substances during the malarial paroxysm was carried out by Queirolo,* who injected into guinea-pigs sweat collected from individuals suffering from various infectious diseases, including malarial fever. The sweat in the latter cases was obtained during the paroxysm. Malarial sweat produced extremely toxic results in doses which were quite without effect when the sweat of normal individuals was used. Almost all the animals died as a result of the inoculations.

In four instances sterilization of the sweat before inoculation did not diminish its toxic power.

The theory of the toxic origin of the paroxysms has been expanded in an interesting manner by Plehn.† This observer reports several cases where individuals who were exposed at night in most malarious districts developed severe paroxysms immediately following the exposure, without the presence of parasites in the peripheral circulation. Later, however, in the course of ten days or two weeks, several of the cases developed typical malarial fever, the blood showing characteristic micro-organisms.

Plehn suggests that the initial paroxysm may have been caused by the absorption of some toxic substance which had been produced by the parasite outside of the body at the same time that the primary infection took place. At the end of the ordinary incubation period the typical fever developed.

---

* Lav. d. II Cong. d. soc. Ital. d. med. int., 1889, 134.
† Virchow's Archiv, 1892, cxxix, 285.

The observations are interesting and the explanation ingenious, but purely hypothetical.

The strongest evidence, however, in favor of the toxic origin of many of the symptoms of malarial fever is furnished in the existence of areas of focal necrosis in the spleen, liver, and other internal organs, closely similar to those seen in diphtheria, typhoid fever, and other acute infectious diseases. These areas, at least in diphtheria, have been shown by Welch and Flexner* to owe their origin to a circulating toxic substance rather than to the presence of micro-organisms in the affected areas; while the results of Reed's † studies of the liver in typhoid fever speak in favor of a similar origin for the typhoid necroses. Recent observations by Flexner ‡ tend to show that these disseminated focal necroses may be regarded as conclusive evidence of the existence of a general toxæmia.

What conclusions, if any, are we then justified in forming concerning the pathogenesis of the intermittent fever?

We know that the paroxysms occur always in direct association with a certain definite stage in the cycle of existence of a group of malarial parasites—the period of sporulation.

Golgi's original idea that the exciting cause of the paroxysm is the invasion of red corpuscles by a fresh group of parasites, has been clearly disproved.

There is, however, in the increased toxicity of the urine and sweat, as well as in the anatomical changes—focal necroses—occurring in the internal organs, strong evidence of the presence of a toxic substance or substances in the circulation.

---

* Johns Hopkins Hospital Bulletin, 1892, iii, 17.
† Johns Hopkins Hospital Reports, vol. v.
‡ Journal of Experimental Medicine, 1897.

GENERAL PATHOLOGY. 253

There are many reasons, then, from the facts which we have before us, and from analogy with other similar conditions, to believe that the febrile paroxysms are due to the presence of toxic substances in the circulation—substances which appear only at a certain stage in the life history of a group of parasites—that of sporulation.

Now, since the organisms are arranged in large groups, all the members of which are practically at the same stage of development, and since the cycles of existence of these groups vary from twenty-four to seventy-two hours according to the type of parasite, sporulation, the liberation of toxic substances, and the resulting paroxysms occur, consequently, at intervals of from twenty-four to seventy-two hours.

Acknowledging, then, the strong probability that the febrile manifestations are excited by the presence of circulating toxic substances, the questions at once arise: What are these toxic substances, and what is their origin?

Let us consider just what takes place in the circulation at the time of sporulation of a group of malarial parasites. There occurs at this period:

1. The segmentation of a large number of full-grown parasites into fresh young organisms, while the pigment, and possibly some small quantity of the cytoplasm of the parasites, are left behind.

2. The liberation of a multitude of full-grown and segmenting organisms, with the destruction and disintegration of the including red corpuscles and the escape of a certain amount of hæmoglobin into the general circulation.

3. The fragmentation and degeneration of a certain number of full-grown extra-cellular 'parasites, which, with the remnants of the segmenting forms, are usually engulfed by phagocytes.

4. The rupture and disintegration, possibly, of uninfected corpuscles, with the escape of their hæmoglobin.

We have, then, before us three main possibilities:

(*a*) The toxic substances arising at the time of the paroxysm result from the destruction and disintegration of a large number of red blood-corpuscles.

(*b*) They are liberated by the parasites themselves at the time of sporulation, and possibly also by the fragmenting fullgrown forms which are usually observed at this period.

(*c*) Both of the above factors may play a part in the process.

It is very possible that the destruction and disintegration of a large number of red corpuscles may exert a toxic influence on the organism, though in most instances where this takes place it is difficult to separate the effect of the blood destruction from that of the exciting cause. Extensive disintegration of red blood-corpuscles is, however, by no means always associated with a febrile paroxysm. In poisoning by chlorate of potassium or carbon monoxide, where great numbers of red blood-corpuscles are destroyed, with consequent hæmoglobinuria, fever may be practically absent.

Hence, despite the lack of absolute proof, we are inevitably led to the conclusion that the most important exciting cause of the malarial paroxysm is the liberation of some toxic substance by the specific parasites at the time of their sporulation. While, very possibly, toxic substances may arise as a result of the disintegration and destruction of red blood-corpuscles which occur at this period, it is improbable that these play the primary part in exciting the paroxysm.

The intermittent character of the fever is due to the intervals present between the sporulation of groups of parasites.

In some infections where multiple groups of parasites are

present, as is not infrequent in the case of the æstivo-autumnal organism, the intervals between the sporulation of different generations may be slight or even absent, while the fever, as one might expect, is remittent or subcontinuous.

As to the intimate nature of the toxic substance or substances we are wholly ignorant.

The Anæmia.—One of the most striking symptoms of all varieties of malarial fever is the well-marked secondary anæmia which always follows, sooner or later, if the attack be of any duration. The onset is in some instances rapid and acute; in others, more gradual. These anæmias depend probably upon three main causes:

1. The direct mechanical destructive action of the parasites on the blood-corpuscles.

2. The destruction and disintegration of uninfected red blood-corpuscles occurring at the time of the paroxysm.

3. The structural changes in the blood-forming organs resulting from the infection.

When we consider the manner in which the parasites develop within the red corpuscles, destroying them with their growth, as well as the probability that in some instances a considerable number of uninfected corpuscles are also destroyed at the time of the paroxysm, it is easy to appreciate how acutely these anæmias may arise; and careful studies by a number of observers have shown that following each paroxysm there is a marked fall in the proportion of red corpuscles to the cubic millimetre. In the milder, regularly intermittent fevers this fall is followed by a rapid regeneration. In the more severe fevers, however, the regeneration is often much slower. The main characteristics of these anæmias have been fully entered into in a previous lecture.

While the cause of the acute anæmia following the paroxysm is thus readily appreciable, the obstinacy of many postmalarial anæmias is equally explicable when we consider the changes brought about in the blood-forming organs by the infection itself. It is probable that the slow regeneration in the graver post-malarial anæmias is definitely due to the extensive necroses and resulting fibroid changes in the bone marrow, for, as has been shown, the bone marrow and the spleen are often in these very cases the main seats of localization of the infection. The accumulation of great quantities of malarial pigment in these organs, as well as the aggregation in them of large numbers of macrophages, may also be mentioned as possible causes of interference with function.

The Pain in the Bones.—The severe pains in the course of the long bones, associated so commonly with malarial fever, have been ascribed to the changes produced in the bone marrow—an interesting suggestion, but purely speculative. These symptoms are not essentially more marked in malaria than they are in any other severe acute infection.

The Jaundice.—The jaundice which is so frequently present is doubtless due to the extensive destruction of the red blood-corpuscles. The products of the disintegration of large numbers of erythrocytes are taken up by the liver; this is shown by the enormous quantity of iron-containing pigment which is accumulated here in acute malarial infections.

Most of the pigment is probably disposed of through the bile. A marked polycholia results; more bile is produced than can readily be carried away by the ducts, and finally from its accumulation and backing up an actual reabsorption with jaundice follows.

The jaundice here, as in other conditions associated with extensive blood destruction (pernicious anæmia), is hæmatogenous probably only in its remote origin.

The blood serum may contain bilirubin even in mild cases where the bile coloring matters are not demonstrable in the urine.*

Cerebral Symptoms.—Among the most important symptoms associated with grave malarial infection are the cerebral manifestations—headache, delirium, coma, and convulsions. These symptoms may be due to (a) general causes, (b) local causes.

(a) General causes. Some of these manifestations are in all probability due to the presence of circulating toxic substances; indeed, it can not be denied that the most serious symptoms, perhaps even coma, may depend wholly upon this cause.

(b) Local causes. Other symptoms, however, are doubtless to be traced to definite mechanical local causes. While the spleen and the bone marrow appear in most instances of æstivo-autumnal fever to be the main points at which the parasites are accumulated, a marked tendency toward variations in the localization of the foci of infection has been noted by many observers.

As long ago as 1854 Planer † called attention to the fact that in comatose pernicious fever he had found the capillaries of the gray cortex filled with masses of black pigment, which in some instances actually occluded the vessels. To this mechanical obstruction Planer ascribed the symptoms of coma. This pigment has been since recognized to lie almost invariably within malarial parasites or within phagocytes, and, as has been shown by numerous observers, there may exist

---

* The coloring matter is excreted here as urobilin, the change occurring, in all probability, in the kidneys. For an excellent discussion of this question, *vide* Rho, La malaria, secondo i più recenti studi, 8vo, Torino, 1896, Rosenberg & Sellier.   † *Op. cit.*

actual thrombi of malarial organisms, often in the stage of segmentation, throughout extensive areas of the cerebral cortex. These accumulations of the malarial parasites exert probably a mechanical influence by shutting off the circulation, while further changes follow in the surrounding tissues—perivascular exudation and punctate hæmorrhages.

It is, then, natural that in some instances the patient should show clinically manifestations pointing to local irritation. In one interesting fatal case reported by Marchiafava,* where the patient showed, among other symptoms, evidences of an acute bulbar paralysis, the vessels of the medulla were found to be crowded with malarial parasites, while the surrounding substance showed numerous small hæmorrhages and extensive perivascular infiltration.

A third explanation of the coma was suggested by Guarnieri,† who first described the extensive accumulation of the parasites in the capillaries of the liver and the numerous areas of focal necrosis. This observer called attention to the similarity existing between the symptoms in comatose malaria and those which result in animals from artificial interference with the portal circulation. He suggested that the coma of malarial fever might be due to the extensive blocking of the hepatic vessels by phagocytes. It seems, however, scarcely probable that the hepatic changes have so important a bearing upon the symptoms.

Gastric and Intestinal Symptoms.—Vomiting is a common symptom in the ordinary intermittent fevers, as it is in many acute infections; it depends probably for the most part upon the toxic substances circulating in the blood. A slight diarrhœa is also not uncommon, particularly in children. In

---

* *Op. cit.* † *Op. cit.*

some severe pernicious fevers, however, the gastric and intestinal symptoms may be the main features of the case, which may closely simulate Asiatic cholera.

In cases of this nature Marchiafava * has found the capillaries of the gastric and intestinal mucous membrane crowded with malarial parasites. In some instances this has gone so far as to produce actual thrombosis with superficial necrosis and ulceration—a condition which readily explains the clinical symptoms. Barker † has reported a similar case, while a second instance has more recently come under our observation.

The Origin of Infections with Multiple Groups of Parasites.—In some forms of malarial fever, especially, as has been repeatedly noted, in æstivo-autumnal infections, the presence of multiple groups of parasites is common.

In many instances it is probable that the original infection was with several generations of organisms. In others, however, one is led to suspect that the condition may be due to the anticipation or retardation in the development of a certain number of organisms in an originally single group; these parasites which have been unduly hasty or delayed in their segmentation give rise eventually to new groups, until finally the sporulation of such groups occurs at so frequent intervals that the temperature curve becomes complicated, eventually showing a remittent or subcontinuous course.

Theoretically, it appears easy to account in this manner for the development of multiple groups of parasites in æstivo-autumnal fever. With tertian and quartan infections, however, the question is by no means so simple.

It has been mentioned repeatedly in earlier lectures that, in the regularly intermittent fevers, infection with more than

---

* *Op. cit.* † *Op. cit.*

one group of parasites is not infrequently observed. It has been also noted that in tertian fever infections with more than two groups of parasites are rare, while in quartan fever more than three groups are very uncommon. Furthermore, it will be remembered that when, for instance, in tertian fever two groups of parasites are present, the hour of onset of the paroxysm on successive days is usually very similar. Often slight constant differences in the hour of onset—an hour or so, several hours at the most—are to be made out, but the occurrence of one paroxysm in the morning, and that on the following day, for instance, in the afternoon, though occasionally to be noted, is rather unusual. Not infrequently in cases of single tertian infection, a second group of parasites may make its appearance a considerable length of time after the onset of the clinical symptoms, perhaps, indeed, only with a relapse or recrudescence of the process.

One can not but ask: What is the origin of this second group of parasites? Do they enter the organism at the beginning of the infection and remain latent until late in the course of the disease, or does the second group arise, for some reason or other, from members of the original single generation which have anticipated or lagged behind in their development?

These are questions which can not at present be definitely answered.

A very considerable number of cases are assuredly double infections from the beginning, but there are others where the late appearance of the second group certainly suggests the possibility of its origin from one original generation. We are immediately, however, brought face to face with the question: If multiple groups develop from an original single group through anticipation or retardation in the sporulation of a certain number of parasites, why should this anticipation or retardation usually be of almost exactly twenty-four hours?

If in tertian fever we were accustomed to see the development of fresh groups whose hour of sporulation came about three, or four, or five, or six hours before or after that of the larger original group, it would be very simple to explain such a process through the anticipation or lagging behind of a few parasites from the larger mass; but this is not the case, or at least such a course of events is but rarely observed.

From a purely morphological point of view it is interesting to see what a difference there may be in the size of the parasites and the number of segments present in different members of a single group of tertian organisms. While the majority of parasites have, before segmentation, reached a size nearly equal to that of the red blood-corpuscle and have wholly decolorized the red cell, yet there are often others which are materially smaller, so much so that had we seen them just before sporulation we should scarcely have considered them more than half or two thirds developed. This suggests the possibility that when the majority of the organisms in a group begin to sporulate, the remaining parasites, even though they may not have reached as advanced a stage of development, may by some unknown influence be dragged into line and brought to segment with the rest.

If one should suppose the existence of some such exciting influence as this, it would be possible to imagine that a few organisms which had lagged far behind the other members of their generation might remain without segmentation until the maturation of another large group of parasites should by its influence, whatever that may be, induce sporulation. In other words, we might imagine one or two organisms dropping from one group into another in an originally double infection.

Suppose, however, only one group of organisms exist in the beginning. In such a case we can only suspect some such course of events as the following: With the segmentation of every group of parasites a certain number of organisms which have not as yet reached full development are by some influence drawn into precocious segmentation. Sometimes, however, parasites may be so far behind as to escape this influence; but such forms are practically half-grown organisms, and would not naturally reach maturity for nearly twenty-four hours. Any bodies further advanced than these would be drawn into segmentation with the original group.

But why should the hour of segmentation of the second group be so nearly the same as that of the original?

This is a question not easy to answer. It is, however, by no means the rule for the hour of onset of paroxysms due to two different groups to be exactly the same. Differences of a few hours are common, while occasionally we see double infections where the paroxysms occur on one day in the morning and on the next in the afternoon (*vide* Chart No. IV, page 117). The majority of tertian and quartan infections are associated with paroxysms beginning between eight in the morning and one in the afternoon, and taking any number of cases at random the hours of onset of the paroxysms agree fairly well; indeed, it is not wholly clear that in the long run this agreement may not be nearly as close as that between the hours of onset of the paroxysms due to different groups in an equal number of double infections.*

---

* In seventeen consecutive cases of double tertian fever there was an average difference of 2·89 hours between the time of onset of the two different groups of parasites. In thirty-four consecutive cases of single tertian

And this brings us to the question, What is the reason that the paroxysms in the regularly intermittent fevers tend to occur so commonly in the morning hours?

But the consideration of such questions, tempting though they be, would lead us too far into the domain of pure speculation.

The explanation offered by Pes * of the development of double from single tertian infections is interesting, but it seems to us a little far-fetched. This observer suggested that certain organisms which have entered unusually small red corpuscles become mature sooner, and thus anticipating the others in their segmentation, form eventually a second group.

The possibility that the second group may be due to anticipation rather than to retardation, as we have been tempted to suspect, must be borne in mind.

Here, however, again we are brought face to face with the same problem as to why the anticipation should be of almost exactly twenty-four hours.

May it be that there is some inherent tendency in the parasite, or some influence from without, which is constantly tempting the organism to segmentation in the morning hours?

And may it be that if a few tertian parasites, for instance, have been unusually precocious in their development, they may actually be drawn into segmentation in twenty-four instead of forty-eight hours, and thus eventually by multiplication give rise to a new group?

And if such an influence exist, what may it be? These are interesting but unsolved questions.

---

fever, each successive two cases being compared one with another, there was an average difference of only 3·92 hours between the time of onset of the paroxysms.

* Riforma medica, 1893, vol. ii, 759.

MECHANISM OF DEFENSE—PHAGOCYTOSIS—SPONTANEOUS RECOVERY.

In the previous remarks about the morphology of the parasites, the presence of pigment-bearing leucocytes has been frequently referred to. They are, in fact, a constant feature in malarial infections.

Tertian and Quartan Fever.—In tertian and quartan fever pigment-bearing white elements are to be seen at distinct periods in the cycle of existence of the parasites—namely, at the time of sporulation during and just following the paroxysm. The cells observed in the circulating blood are not only the ordinary polymorphonuclear leucocytes (neutrophiles), but also a considerable number of large mononuclear elements resembling the mononuclear leucocytes of the blood, or at times somewhat larger. Indeed, the mononuclear phagocytes seem to be more numerous than those with polymorphous nuclei. This is an interesting point, for in the fresh specimen the amœboid movement of these mononuclear elements is extremely feeble, and while active phagocytosis by the neutrophiles may often be observed, we have never seen a similar performance by the large mononuclear white corpuscles.

The contents of these cells are usually scattered granules or blocks of pigment; sometimes, generally in very large mononuclear elements, there may be larger masses and accumulations. More rarely entire parasites or fragments of parasites may be contained within the phagocyte.

' In the fresh specimen the leucocytes may be seen to engulf:

(*a*) The extra-cellular fragmented forms which are seen with particular frequency in tertian fever.

(*b*) Free pigment clumps and the remains of segmenting organisms.

(*c*) Flagellate bodies.*

(*d*) Segmenting forms.

Inclusion of the parasites while yet contained within the red cell I have never observed in tertian and quartan infections.

When we consider the forms which are most readily attacked by the leucocytes, the periodicity of the phagocytosis is easily comprehensible, for it is just at the time of the paroxysm that these stages of the parasite are most commonly present in the circulation.

Æstivo-autumnal Fever.—In the irregular æstivo-autumnal fevers the periodicity of phagocytosis is not nearly so marked. Pigment-bearing white elements are to be seen with greatest frequency during and shortly after the paroxysm, but they are often present throughout the course of the fever, as Bastianelli † in particular has shown. The reasons for this are:

1. The frequent presence of multiple groups of parasites resulting in more or less continued segmentation.

2. The fact that in many instances an early necrosis of the red corpuscles—shrunken and brassy-colored elements (*globuli rossi ottonati*)—takes place, owing to which they may be engulfed by phagocytes at a time when the parasites are as yet immature.

3. In the regularly intermittent fevers flagellate bodies developing from mature parasites are met with only at a cer-

---

* This may, indeed, be observed in the majority of instances. I have seen as many as three leucocytes enter the field of the microscope and simultaneously attack a flagellate body.

† Bull. d. R. acc. med. d. Rom., xviii, 1892, 487.

tain period in the cycle of the organism—i. e., at or about the time of sporulation. In the æstivo-autumnal fevers, on the other hand, after crescentic and ovoid bodies have begun to appear, flagellate forms may be met with at any time. The frequency with which flagellate bodies are engulfed by phagocytes has been mentioned.

This brings up the question: Do flagellate bodies develop in the circulation? The question is by no means settled. We have never seen flagellate forms until some time after the preparation of the specimen, though Laveran asserts that they may be found immediately upon the first inspection of the slide. If we accept the view held by many, that the flagellate forms develop only outside of the body, then the third explanation of the frequency of pigment-bearing leucocytes in æstivo-autumnal fever would apply only to the fresh specimen of blood.

Here we may see not only ordinary neutrophiles and mononuclear leucocytes containing pigment, but occasionally much larger mononuclear phagocytes, sometimes true macrophages, ten times as large, perhaps, as the white blood corpuscles. The phagocytes may include not only the forms above described, but also entire red corpuscles containing parasites; these elements are always shrunken and brassy-colored or decolorized. At times, within the large macrophages, there may be entire leucocytes with included pigment or parasites, free or in red corpuscles. Some of these macrophages may show distinct evidences of necrosis.

As may be suspected from this description, these elements are in every way similar to those which have been described in the spleen, liver, and bone marrow, from whence it is not impossible that they have escaped into the circulation. Some of them may be of endothelial origin.

The existence of phagocytosis in malaria was first demonstrated by Golgi* and Metschnikoff.† Golgi,‡ accepting Metschnikoff's ideas, ascribed to the process an active curative influence upon the malarial infection, believing that a constant combat is waged between the leucocytes and the parasites. It is through the engulfing and destruction of the latter that spontaneous cure occurs. A more careful examination into the conditions of phagocytosis will show us, however, that this conclusion is not to be too hastily made.

Let us consider, again, the elements which are to be found within phagocytes. These are:

1. Free pigment and the remains of segmenting bodies.
2. Fragmented extra-cellular parasites.
3. Shrunken, crenated, brassy-colored red blood-corpuscles, and fragments of blood-corpuscles with and without included parasites.
4. Flagellate organisms.
5. Whole segmenting forms.
6. In very rare instances crescentic bodies.#

It can not but strike one who considers this list that the elements which are engulfed are all extra-cellular, with the exception of the parasites included within the brassy and shrunken corpuscles of æstivo-autumnal fever, where doubtless the corpuscle itself, having become necrotic, acts as a foreign body in the circulation. In other words, the parasites are never attacked by the leucocytes while contained within the relatively normal erythrocyte.

Now the question may be asked whether these forms which

---

* *Op. cit.*
† Russk. Med., 1887, No. 12, 207; ref. in Centr. f. Bakt., i, 1887, 624.
‡ Arch. Ital. de biol., xi, 1889.
# So far as I know, the only mention of the phagocytosis of crescentic bodies is in Osler's article, in 1887 (Brit. Med. Jour., I, 556), where the process is pictured.

are engulfed are really living parasites possessed of their full functional activity. The free pigment and the fragmented extra-cellular bodies are assuredly lifeless or at least degenerate elements. The shrunken, brassy red blood-corpuscles represent, doubtless, necrotic structures, and are attacked by the phagocytes on their own account rather than because of the contained parasite. It should be added that many observers, notably Marchiafava and Bignami, believe that the parasites themselves die with the necrosis of the surrounding cell. The flagellate bodies, as is well known, are considered by many to be degenerate and dying forms. The segmenting bodies might be regarded as living and active, and yet we must remember that it is at this stage that the organism is most readily destroyed by anti-malarial treatment; in other words, is most vulnerable.

Have we any proof, then, that the elements which are engulfed are really living, and, if so, are they possessed of their normal vitality? May they not have been previously affected by some hostile influence in the circulation? The rôle of phagocytes in general as active combatants against infection we can not enter into at length. There are, however, certain other points in connection with the course of ordinary malarial infection which would certainly suggest that this rôle has been overestimated. If the spontaneous cure of malarial fevers depends upon active phagocytosis alone, the phagocytes attacking the vigorous organisms, how are we to explain the ordinary course of an untreated malarial infection, say of the tertian or quartan type?

Bastianelli * has ably discussed this question.

It has been shown by careful observation that many of the

---

* Bull. d. R. acc. med. d. Rom., xviii, 1892, 487.

milder malarial infections pursue a definite cyclical course, beginning gradually, increasing in intensity, reaching a climax, and then again diminishing, going on to spontaneous recovery, which is, to be sure, usually followed by a relapse. This sequence of events may repeat itself through months.

Why, if we are dealing with phagocytes alone as combatants against the infection, should we observe this cyclical course?

Why should not the phagocytes put an end to the infection in its earliest stages when the parasites are relatively scanty?

Does it not rather suggest that against the vigorous parasites the phagocytes are relatively powerless, but that, after some other influence has come into play, the organisms, the vitality of which is diminished, are more readily overcome?

Is there, indeed, any actual proof that any organisms, other than degenerate, dead, or dying forms, fall prey to these cells?

In the present state of our knowledge these questions can not be positively answered. It must, however, be acknowledged that the distinctly cyclical course so often pursued by the fevers, as well as analogy with other acute infections, would lead us rather to assume that the more important rôle in spontaneous cure is played by some parasiticidal substance or substances circulating in the blood serum. These substances, to be sure, may be of cellular origin.

May it not be possible that in some instances the parasite is injured by the products of its own growth?

Rather suggestive of this idea is the sudden termination of some tertian infections. We may see, for instance, the entire disappearance of a group of parasites immediately following a severe paroxysm, notwithstanding the presence of numerous segmenting bodies in the peripheral circulation. I have seen such an instance in a case of double tertian fever, where, after an intensely severe paroxysm, with a large number of segmenting organisms, no fresh intra-corpuscular bodies were to be found, the case pursuing its course afterward as a single tertian infection (*vide* Chart No. XVII, page 171).

Such cases certainly suggest that the destruction of the new group of organisms may depend upon the presence of some toxic substance produced at the time of the paroxysm itself.

While in the great majority of instances the organisms within phagocytes, if living at the time of inclusion, are rapidly destroyed and disintegrated, it must yet be remembered that there are appearances which have suggested to certain observers that this may not by any means be the universal rule. Golgi* and his school maintain that organisms thus included may often continue their development within the phagocytes, pass on even to the segmenting stage, and finally accomplish the destruction of their host. This assumption is based upon the fact that in the spleen and marrow and endothelial cells, more particularly in the brain and liver, one notices so frequently all stages of the development of the parasite within phagocytes, while a considerable number of these phagocytes show well-marked evidences of necrosis.

These organisms are not supposed to grow free within the body of the engulfing leucocyte, but to continue development within the corpuscle in which they lie at the time of the phagocytosis.

Previously to Golgi's introduction of this idea, Bignami †

---

* Arch. Ital. de biol., 1893, xx, 288; also Monti, Boll. de Soc. med.-chir. di Pavia, 1895.

† Atti del R. acc. med. di Rom., xvi, 1890.

had suggested that it might be in the form of some resistant spore within the bodies of phagocytes that the malarial parasite is preserved in those cases where relapses occur after long intervals. These are both interesting hypotheses, but as yet are without definite proof.

In conclusion, it may be stated that while phagocytosis is a regular accompaniment of malarial infection, occurring at definite periods in the cycle of existence of the specific organisms, it is as yet by no means an entirely settled fact that it plays an active curative rôle. Indeed, there is much which suggests that the rôle of the phagocyte in spontaneous cure is secondary to that played by some other influence which primarily injures the vitality of the parasites.

LECTURE IX.

DIAGNOSIS, PROGNOSIS, TREATMENT, PROPHYLAXIS.

DIAGNOSIS.

The Regularly Intermittent Fevers.—Tertian and Quartan Fevers.—The diagnosis of tertian or quartan intermittent fever is usually a relatively simple matter. The regularity of the manifestations, and the occurrence usually of the paroxysm with its three characteristic stages—the chill, the fever, and the sweating—render the diagnosis clear. The presence of herpes upon the lips or nose may be of important assistance. Herpes may, of course, occur under a number of other circumstances, particularly in pneumonia, but the frequency with which it is noted in malaria is great, probably far above that shown by most statistics.

The presence of a well-marked anæmia may also be of distinct help, chiefly in distinguishing malarial infections from tuberculosis, where the mucous membranes are usually of fairly good color, though the face may be pale.

The spleen is almost invariably demonstrably enlarged. At times a slight enlargement of the liver may also be made out. An important point is the peculiar grayish-yellow color of the skin, which is more or less characteristic.

In a number of other conditions, more especially *septic* in nature, paroxysms simulating those of malaria may occur.

CHART XVIII.

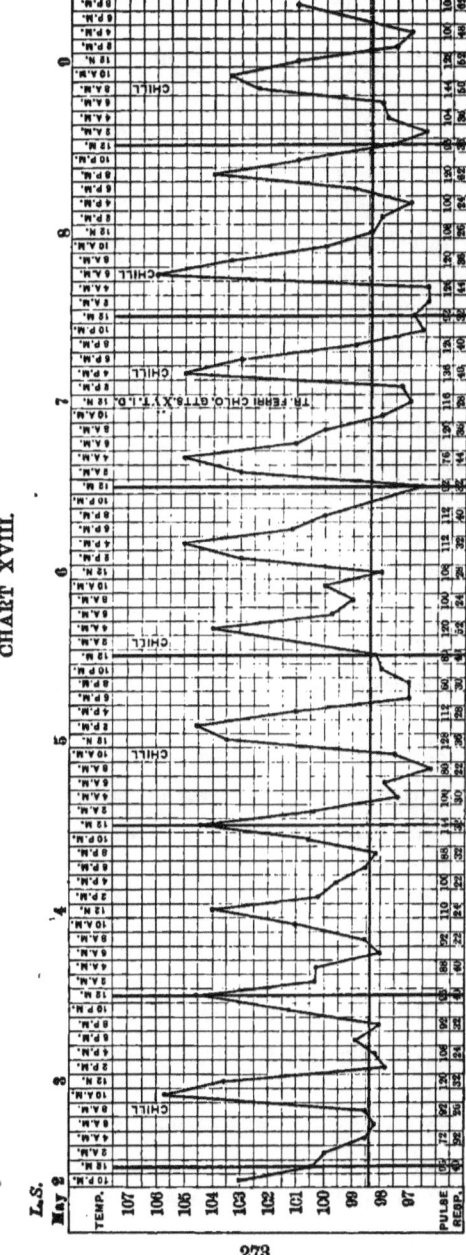

INTERMITTENT FEVER—GONORRHŒAL ENDOCARDITIS.

There are, however, often slight differences. Estimating the period elapsing between the time when the temperature passes 99° and reaches this point again, the average duration of the malarial paroxysm is a little under eleven hours.

In other infections, however, while exactly similar paroxysms may occur, they are often distinctly shorter. A paroxysm in which the temperature reaches a point above 104°, the entire duration of which is under six hours, is uncommon in malarial fever, and not infrequent in septic infections (*vide* Chart No. XVIII, page 273).

In a great majority of instances the processes which are likely to be confused with malaria do not show the same regular periodicity; chills occur at irregular intervals. Sometimes, however, the temperature curves may be curiously similar to those of paludism (*vide* Chart No. XIX, page 275).

The one process above all others which is confounded with malarial intermittent fever is *pulmonary tuberculosis*. As I have recently stated in a communication elsewhere, it is safe to say that the majority of cases of pulmonary tuberculosis occurring in malarious districts in this country are, at some time in their course, mistaken for malarial fever. This confusion occurs at the stage usually present at some time in the course of phthisis, where intermittent fever, often associated with chills, is present. The patient very frequently ascribes these symptoms to malarial fever, and with this diagnosis the physician all too frequently acquiesces.

The differential diagnosis may be readily made. In tuberculosis, apart from the pulmonary lesions which careful investigation will generally reveal, there is an absence of the

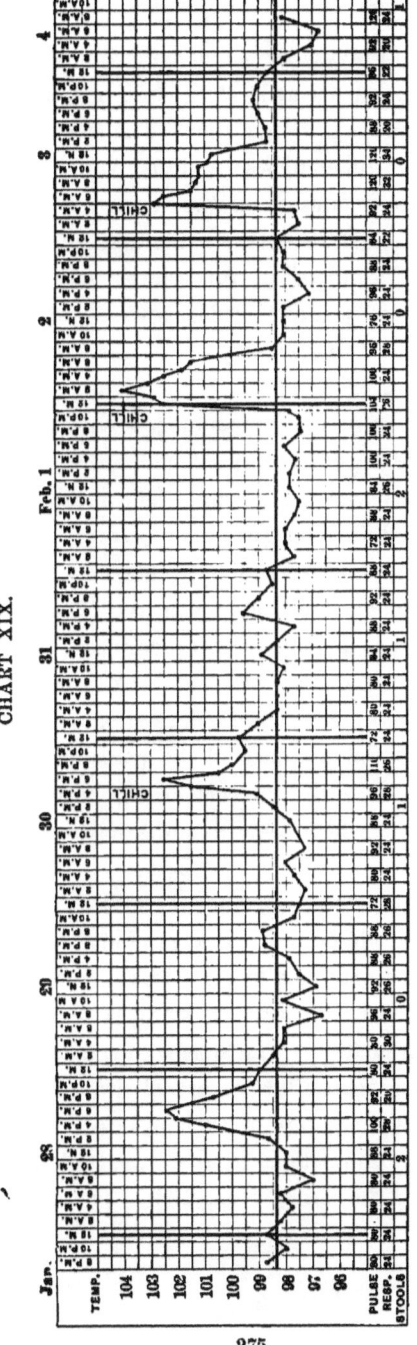

CHART XIX.

INFLUENZA.

Tertian and quotidian intermittent fever simulating malaria.

sallow, yellowish-gray color so common in malaria. The mucous membranes are usually of good color, while in malaria there is almost always a slight pallor. The spleen is generally undemonstrable in tuberculosis; almost invariably palpable in malaria. Herpes is unusual in the former, common in the latter. The examination of the sputa and blood will settle the question. The blood in tuberculosis with intermittent fever shows, generally, a distinct leucocytosis, which is absent in malarial fever. The discovery of the parasites is, however, the deciding point.

Chills occurring in the course of *gonorrhœa*, or following *catheterization* or the passing of a sound, are not infrequently confused with malarial paroxysms. The urethra should always be examined in doubtful cases. Grave and fatal cases of septicæmia may, however, follow gonorrhœa, while there is little or no evidence of an acute urethritis. The examination of the blood here, as in pulmonary tuberculosis, will settle the question. In both gonorrhœa and tuberculosis there is a distinct leucocytosis; in malaria a normal or reduced number of leucocytes and the presence of the parasites. The examination of the blood is the one certain method of diagnosis— the only manner in which a positive diagnosis of malaria is to be made.

In rare instances tertian infections may show, for a time, continuous fever which may be confounded with *typhoid*. The diagnosis here may be difficult. In three cases which the author has observed the parasites were extremely scanty in the peripheral circulation. The anæmia, the color of the skin, the frequent presence of herpes, are all important points in favor of the malarial nature of such an infection, while careful and repeated examinations of the blood will always reveal the true nature of the case.

DIAGNOSIS.

The discovery of malarial parasites renders the diagnosis positive. In the great majority of cases the organisms are readily made out. In very mild infections or in certain rare instances of tertian fever, where the parasites appear to behave as do the æstivo-autumnal organisms, being aggregated in the internal organs, they may be extremely scanty in the peripheral circulation. Here the presence or absence of a leucocytosis is an important diagnostic sign. In almost all conditions which simulate intermittent fever there is well-marked leucocytosis, while in malaria the absence of a leucocytosis, indeed even a reduction in the number of leucocytes, is the rule. *The presence of an appreciable leucocytosis is strong evidence against the existence of uncomplicated malarial fever.* At times, where very few parasites are present, pigment-bearing leucocytes may be an important aid to diagnosis; the skilled observer can usually distinguish malarial pigment from extraneous particles.

The differential diagnosis between tertian and quartan infections is readily made in the fresh specimen, though it is somewhat more difficult in the stained. The tertian organisms are larger, paler, more active; the pigment, especially in the younger forms, finer, brownish, more vigorously dancing; the segments in the sporulating organism are more numerous and less regularly arranged; the surrounding corpuscle becomes decolorized and expanded with the growth of the parasite. The quartan organism is smaller, more sharply outlined, lazier in its movements; the pigment coarser, darker, less motile, and often peripherally placed; the segments less numerous and more regularly arranged; the surrounding corpuscle retracts about the parasite, and becomes, if anything, of a deeper color.

The following table may serve to emphasize these distinctions:

TERTIAN PARASITE.	QUARTAN PARASITE.
Substance excessively pale, hyaline and transparent; outline often difficult to distinguish.	Substance more refractive; outline sharp and distinct.
Pigment granules smaller and of a lighter brownish color, especially in the younger forms; in active dancing motion.	Pigment coarser, darker, and only slightly motile, excepting in the very youngest forms; marked peripheral arrangement of the granules.
Amœboid movements very active during the first twenty-four or thirty-six hours.	Amœboid movements slow and lazy, excepting in the very youngest forms.
Red blood-corpuscle becomes expanded and decolorized with the growth of the parasite.	Red blood-corpuscle tends to retract about the parasite and has a somewhat deeper color.
Full-grown bodies as large or nearly as large as the red blood-corpuscles.	Full-grown bodies distinctly smaller than the red corpuscles.
Segmentation sometimes occurs before the entire collection of the pigment into one clump or block; no radial arrangement of the pigment as it gathers together.	In the early stages of segmentation the pigment flows in toward the middle of the parasite in radial lines. Segmenting forms with scattered pigment rarely or never seen.
The regular geometrical figures shown by the quartan segmenting bodies may be wanting; the parasite may divide into spores irregularly throughout its substance; 15 to 30 segments.	Segments are usually arranged in a regular rosette form about the central pigment clump; 6 to 12 in number.

The presence of two groups of parasites is readily recognizable.

In stained specimens the motility of the pigment and of the parasite is of course absent, while the differences in the shade and size of the pigment granules are not as clearly to be made out, but in other respects the distinction between the two types of organism is easy.

Combined infections with quartan and tertian organisms occur, but are unusual in this climate. I have never seen such an instance.

If, for any reason, it be impossible to make a microscopical examination of the blood, we may in most instances rely upon the therapeutic test—the rapid disappearance of the paroxysms under quinine. In the regularly intermittent fevers, if the patient be put to bed, there is rarely any recurrence of the fever after forty-eight hours from the beginning of the administration of quinine. In the majority of instances of tertian infection all traces of the fever disappear under these circumstances in twenty-four hours.

The Æstivo-autumnal Fevers.—While the diagnosis in the regularly intermittent fevers is usually a simple matter, the same can not be said in the case of the more irregular æstivo-autumnal infections. During the early manifestations of æstivo-autumnal fever, while the paroxysms are yet distinctly intermittent, the diagnosis may be clear; but later on, when more marked irregularities become evident, and a remittent or continued temperature ensues, confusion with various other pathological processes is common. Sometimes, indeed, in an æstivo-autumnal fever which is pursuing a regularly intermittent course the length of the paroxysm, amounting sometimes to nearly forty hours, may give rise to serious doubt as to the nature of the condition.

The process with which æstivo-autumnal fever is most commonly confused is *typhoid* fever. In certain instances the continued fever, the dull, apathetic condition of the patient, the pains in the head, the loins, and extremities, the coated tongue and the enlarged spleen, all closely simulate enteric fever. To such instances, the "remittent fever" of this country, Baccelli has given the name *subcontinua typhoidea.* Often, however, certain distinctive points may be made out. Usually, though the fever may be continuous, if one follow the case through several days, evidences of abortive paroxysms are to be recognized.

Though no actual chill may occur, there are periods of slight coldness or blueness followed by exacerbations of the fever. The occurrence of these at similar hours on successive days, or at intervals of about forty-eight hours, may serve to turn one's suspicions toward the true nature of the process. Again, the history of distinct intermittent fever at the beginning of the illness would be suggestive. Moreover, prodromal symptoms are usually less frequent and severe, as a rule, in malaria than in typhoid fever. Of the physical signs, the presence of a slight anæmia, of a sallow, yellowish hue to the skin, or herpes upon the lips, are all important evidences of the malarial nature of the process.

Bronchitis is more common in typhoid than in malarial fever, as are also abdominal symptoms, though they may occur in both conditions. The appearance of the characteristic typhoid roseola may be the deciding point. Urticaria is not very infrequently observed in malaria; it is unusual in typhoid. The diazo reaction is almost always present in the urine of typhoid fever after from seven to ten days, while it is unusual in malarial fever, occurring in but 5·5 per cent of our cases.

The examination of the blood usually settles the question. The small ring-shaped and amœboid hyaline æstivo-autumnal parasites, with or without occasional pigment granules, are to be found, while, if the process has lasted a week or more, pigmented ovoid and crescentic bodies are usually present. Not infrequently the parasites are very scanty, particularly if we examine just before or during a paroxysm, and every now and then we may hunt for a long period of time without finding any organisms. Here the presence of pigment-bearing leucocytes is an important diagnostic help. It is rare, however, in severe infections not to find the parasites after a short search. The presence of a diminished number of leucocytes is not here of the same assistance that it is in the differential diagnosis between malaria and the septic infections, since the leucocytes in typhoid fever show essentially the same changes in number and in differential relations one to another as they do in malaria.

If we are unable to obtain a microscope, the therapeutic test will give us the diagnosis in almost all instances. No malarial fever which we now know resists large doses of quinine for more than three or four days. It is quite safe to say that if the process be malaria the temperature will be quite normal, or at least will have shown a marked break by the fourth day, usually earlier. If quinine fail to influence the fever, we may rest assured that the process is either nonmalarial or else that a complication exists.

The following table, taken in part from Rho,[*] may be of assistance in bringing out the contrast between the two processes:

CONTINUED MALARIAL FEVER—REMITTENT FEVER.	TYPHOID FEVER.
Onset generally intermittent. Irregular remissions.	Onset gradual and progressive. Regular, though very slight morning remissions, with evening exacerbations of temperature.
The temperature may arrive at 40° C. (104° F.) at the end of the first day.	The temperature does not reach 40° C. (104° F.) before the third or fourth day.
Headache rare in the beginning; of a neuralgic character, pulsating, variable in its position and intensity. Sclera subicteric from the onset.	Headache from the beginning; permanent, severe, frontal. Sclera white.
The apathetic expression of the face, the dryness of the tongue, sordes upon the teeth, are not very marked.	These symptoms well marked and progressive.

---

[*] La malaria secondo i più recenti studi, Torino, 1896, 8vo.

Breath foul.	Breath has a peculiar mouse-like odor.
The delirium may come on in the early days; it is recurrent, but changes with the exacerbations of temperature and the other symptoms, and may give way to grave symptoms related to other organs.	Delirium appears only when the disease is well pronounced; it is often persistent, and variable only in degree.
If there be pulmonary congestion the cough and other symptoms come on suddenly; the areas affected change from one to the other lobe or lung, and may disappear and reappear again with varying intensity; dyspnœa is very pronounced; circulatory disturbances are marked, even syncope.	Pulmonary congestion is gradual and persistent; always hypostatic (the bases and dorsal surfaces of the lungs); the dyspnœa is less pronounced and later in appearing, depending more upon the abdominal conditions (tympanites, etc.).
There is usually restlessness and anxiety (*jactatatio corporis*).	There is usually relaxation, prostration, stupor ($\tau\bar{v}\phi o s$).
Peculiar grayish-yellow color of skin; sometimes a slight jaundice.	No jaundice.
Herpes common.	Herpes rare.
Anæmia often more or less marked early in the course.	Anæmia absent excepting in later stages.
No characteristic exanthem; urticaria not uncommon.	Characteristic roseola.
At times there may be transient tympanites or ileo-cæcal gurgling; they are but slightly pronounced and paroxysmal; diarrhœa is slight or absent, and has not the characters of that in typhoid fever.	Tympanites, gurgling, diarrhœa appear slowly and may become well marked.
No distinct course.	Has a fairly characteristic course.
Urine high colored; may show a trace of bile; Ehrlich's diazo reaction rarely present.	Urine high colored; bile absent; diazo reaction present during the height of the process.
Blood shows no leucocytosis; eosinophiles not notably diminished; serum does not cause agglomeration of typhoid bacilli (Pfeiffer, Durham, and Widal); malarial parasites and pigmented leucocytes present.	Blood shows no leucocytosis; eosinophiles diminished or absent; serum causes agglomeration of typhoid bacilli; malarial parasites and pigment absent.
Fever disappears under quinine.	Fever uninfluenced by quinine.
Is an endemic disease, occurring particularly in rural districts, rarely epidemic.	Usually epidemic; prevailing commonly in cities.

Confusion with *typhus fever* might arise; examination of the blood will here settle the question.

The differentiation of the fever from *tuberculosis* or various *septic processes* rests upon the same general rules as in the case of the regularly intermittent fevers. The examination of the blood shows in malaria an absence of leucocytosis and the presence of parasites, while in tuberculosis and most other acute febrile processes a well-marked increase in leucocytes is to be observed.

It should be remembered that occasionally the parasites in the peripheral circulation may be very scanty notwithstanding the existence of well-marked symptoms.

Baccelli * thus asserts : "(*a*) That sometimes severe fevers of a malarial nature occur during which it is impossible to make out the presence of the pathogenic organisms in the blood. . . .

"(*d*) That when they have been at last found, they may appear in so small a number that there is no question of any relation between the number of endoglobular parasites † and the severity of the fever.

"(*e*) That in the beginning of the attack . . . neither sporulating forms nor new forms are to be made out in the red blood-corpuscles; the latter begin to appear only when the paroxysm is advanced. . . .

"(*f*) That in cases of experimental paroxysms which we have produced, some of which, indeed, developed with severe symptoms, there were at the onset of the fever no pathogenic micro-organisms to be found in the red blood-corpuscles.

---

* Verhandl. d. XI. Cong. f. inn. Med., Leipzig, 1892.
† In the peripheral circulation (W. S. T.).

"(g) That these forms were found remarkably late and were very scanty."

We have repeatedly observed that in intermittent æstivo-autumnal fever parasites were very scanty during the early hours of the paroxysm and just before. And, indeed, in some cases of more or less continuous fever they have been at times surprisingly hard to find. If, however, we miss parasites on the first examination, it is very rare that a second examination several hours later fails to reveal their presence.

Pernicious Malarial Fevers—The Comatose Type.—Comatose paroxysms may be mistaken for sunstroke, uræmia, or cerebral hæmorrhage. The differential diagnosis from sunstroke may be extremely difficult. Bastianelli and Bignami, as has been mentioned, have recently noted the fact that in Italy many instances of uncomplicated insolation have doubtless been regarded as cases of pernicious malaria. It has been demonstrated by their autopsies that insolation may occur in individuals who have recently passed through a malarial attack, or who, indeed, may be subjects of a mild or unsuspected infection. In such instances it may be extremely difficult, without examination of the blood, to determine the true nature of the paroxysm. Jaundice, anæmia, and an enlarged spleen would particularly suggest the malarial nature of the process, while hyperpyrexia—temperature as high as 108° or 110° F.—would rather testify in favor of sunstroke.

In case of comatose symptoms in an individual where examination of the blood from the peripheral circulation and from the spleen reveal but few organisms, it may be extremely difficult to determine the cause of the manifestations. In such an instance quinine should be administered as if the case were one of pernicious fever; while hyperpyrexia, if present, should be combated by ice baths, just as in a case of uncomplicated sunstroke. In some such instances the question whether or not insolation has played a part in the symptoms is impossible to settle.

The *tetanic, meningeal, eclamptic,* and *hemiplegic* types of malaria are to be recognized by the condition of the blood.

The Algid Paroxysm.—In some instances, where the temperature is subnormal or but slightly elevated, while (from the actual condensation of the blood?) the anæmia may not be apparent, the diagnosis may not at first be suspected. A sallow color of the skin and an enlarged spleen would, however, be suggestive of malarial fever, while examination of the blood will settle the question. It is in these doubtful cases of pernicious malaria that the life of the patient may at times be saved by the physician who systematically examines the blood of his patients. This was the case in the instances of postoperative malaria above referred to. There was little in the appearance of the patient to suggest malaria, and had Dr. Livingood neglected to examine the blood, the patient's life would very possibly have been lost.

The Hæmorrhagic Type.—The diagnosis in some instances of this type of fever must be made between malaria and yellow fever. The spleen is often but little enlarged in the latter affection, while albumen and casts appear unusually early in the urine. In some instances we must depend entirely upon the examination of the blood.

Malarial Hæmoglobinuria.—The diagnosis here must be made between yellow fever, ordinary paroxysmal hæmoglobinuria, acute nephritis from some other toxic origin, and probably also from the hæmoglobinuria which at times follows quinine. The chief reliance must be placed here upon the examination of the blood.

The appreciation in each case of the relation of the hæmoglobinuric attack to the malarial infection is of the greatest importance for treatment.

In that class of cases where the attack is one of the manifestations of the malarial paroxysm, and the parasites remain in the circulation, the diagnosis is clear.

Where, however, the organisms disappear spontaneously with the paroxysm the diagnosis may be by no means as easy. Usually, a few parasites, possibly only crescentic and ovoid forms, are to be found.

In the cases of true post-malarial hæmoglobinuria the diagnosis may be extremely difficult. We must rely here much upon the history of the case and the evidences (enlarged spleen, anæmia) of an antecurrent infection.

Lastly, under the heading of malarial hæmoglobinuria, come those instances—rare apparently in temperate climates—where the paroxysm is due to quinine.

In those cases which follow quinine given during an acute malarial infection with parasites in the blood, we should be very cautious in our diagnosis; we should remember that many such instances are doubtless *post hoc* simply—not *propter hoc*. The history of previous attacks, or of family or personal susceptibility to the drug, is important.

Where the association of the paroxysm with quinine has occurred in more than one instance the diagnosis is easier.

Post-partum and Post-operative Malaria.—Various puerperal and post-operative septic infections must here be excluded. The diagnosis is generally evident from a study of the chart; the sequence of the paroxysms is usually irregular in septic infections. Besides the irregularity in succession of the septic paroxysms, they are often of relatively brief duration as compared with the malarial attack. Enlargement of the spleen is usually present in both conditions, and, though somewhat different from the malarial hue, the sallow, parchment-like color of the subject of a grave septic infection may readily be confused with the malarial tint. The examination of the blood will settle the question. Apart from the presence of parasites and pigment, there is a diminution in the number of leucocytes in malaria, while in the paroxysms due to other septic causes there is commonly a well-marked leucocytosis.

Chronic Malarial Cachexia.—The condition is chiefly to be distinguished from secondary or primary anæmia, or from leukæmia and pseudo-leukæmia. The presence of pigment or parasites in the blood is conclusive, but these may not be found, while the enlarged spleen, the grave anæmia, the tendency toward hæmorrhages or dropsical effusions—all symptoms common to these various conditions—may render the diagnosis extremely difficult. The history of the patient, however, and the progress of the case under treatment, will usually clear up the diagnosis. Malarial cachexia generally responds to treatment, though the improvement is often extremely slow. The examination of the blood will, of course, readily enable us to distinguish the case from one of leukæmia.

Post-malarial Anæmia.—It is by no means possible in many instances to determine from the examination of the blood alone that a given anæmia is post-malarial in nature. The diminution in the number of leucocytes which is common in post-malarial anæmias, with a relative increase in the large mononuclear forms, may, however, serve to suggest to us the nature of the process.

Malarial Nephritis.—There is nothing especially characteristic in the *nephritis* which follows or accompanies malarial fever. In case of nephritis associated with fever, especially if it occur in a malarious district, a careful examination of the blood should be made.

Complications and Mixed Infections.—A definite diagnosis in the combinations of malaria with many processes which we have mentioned, particularly with *typhoid fever*, is often only to be made after the administration of quinine. Following this the symptoms due to malaria will clear up, thus simplifying the clinical picture of the complicating disease.

Pneumonia is usually readily made out upon physical examination. The same is true of *pleurisy*. In the case of *pulmonary tuberculosis* we must depend, of course, upon the physical signs and the presence of tubercle bacilli in the sputum.

The occurrence of *diarrhœa* or *dysentery* during an acute infection may or may not depend upon the action of the parasites or their toxic products. The presence of the *amœba coli* in the stools is direct evidence of the existence of a complicating process, while in other instances of diarrhœa in acute malaria the results of the specific treatment must be awaited before one can form a definite diagnosis.

Parotitis, tonsillitis, acute rheumatism, and the *exanthemata* may be recognized by their usual symptoms.

Nervous Complications.—The true nature of some of the nervous complications of malaria is only to be appreciated after observation of the action of quinine, those symptoms due to the malarial infection clearing up under treatment by the specific drug.

PROGNOSIS.—(*a*) *Regularly Intermittent Fevers.*— The prognosis in tertian and quartan fevers is almost invariably good. This is at least true as far as relates to fatal results directly due to the malaria. I have never heard of a pernicious paroxysm occurring in tertian or quartan infection with the exception of the case of French, above referred to. On the other hand, very serious results not infrequently follow improperly treated or neglected infections. Thus tertian or quartan malaria may continue for months, indeed for years, constant relapses occurring every several weeks. The result in many instances is a grave chronic cachexia, through which the patient may become a ready prey to various secondary infections. With proper treatment, however, the disease need never be fatal of itself.

Æstivo-autumnal Fever.—The prognosis in the more irregular æstivo-autumnal infections is by no means as favorable. In the great majority of instances, unless pernicious manifestations have already appeared, vigorous treatment by quinine will be followed by a rapid disappearance of the symptoms, and in an ordinary case the prognosis is perfectly favorable.

Where, however, actual pernicious symptoms have appeared, the prognosis is always extremely grave; indeed, an entirely favorable prognosis can not be given until at least forty-eight hours after the initiation of treatment. Not infrequently the subsidence of one paroxysm may be rapidly followed by a second, which, despite all treatment, may have a fatal termination. If, however, this paroxysm be recovered from, a favorable prognosis may be given in almost all instances. Such cases, in the light of the extremely favorable results which have been reported by Baccelli, demand the intravenous administration of quinine.

Malarial Hæmoglobinuria.—The prognosis in malarial hæmoglobinuria is always grave. Those cases where the attack occurs with the malarial paroxysm are the most favorable in their course, while the post-malarial paroxysms are of particularly grave portent.

The prognosis in the hæmoglobinuria due to quinine is also grave, but less so, apparently, than in the last-mentioned form.

Complications.—The prognosis in the various complications of malarial fever is influenced only by the fact that the enfeebled organism of the patient affected by malaria may be somewhat less able to resist additional insults than that of the healthy individual. Thus a debilitated cachectic is less likely to recover from an acute pneumonia than a healthy, vigorous man.

Chronic Malarial Cachexia.—The prognosis in chronic malarial cachexia is usually good as far as life is concerned if the patient be in a position to wholly follow out the advice of the physician. Complete recovery usually occurs if the patient can be removed to a healthy, non-malarious district. Even in the most severely malarious regions judicious treatment will do much for most cases. Sometimes, however, without absolute removal from the malarious surroundings and a complete change in the manner of life, little can be done. In these cases the patient rarely dies from the chronic malarial cachexia itself, but falls a prey to some secondary infection. Secondary changes occurring in certain internal organs may lead to grave disturbances of function. Chronic nephritis, as has been said, may sometimes follow repeated or chronic malarial infections.

Malarial Nephritis.—As has been said above, there is little doubt that grave nephritis, both acute and chronic, may follow malaria. In the severe nephritis, particularly that following malarial hæmoglobinuria, the prognosis is always extremely grave. In most of the instances of mild nephritis occurring in connection with malarial infections of moderate severity the prognosis is perfectly good; with convalescence from the malarial infection the renal symptoms disappear.

In some instances, however, it is not impossible that the changes brought about by an acute infection may lead to a chronic nephritis with fatal termination.

Malarial Paralyses.—The prognosis in most malarial paralyses is apparently good, certainly in those occurring with acute pernicious paroxysms. In those cases which have suggested multiple sclerosis, and in the interesting instance reported by Bastianelli and Bignami which simulated Dubini's disease, complete recovery has followed under administration of quinine.

Post-malarial Psychoses.—The prognosis of the post-malarial psychoses is generally good.

TREATMENT.—The treatment of malarial fever may be divided into (*a*) General measures ; (*b*) Medicinal treatment.

(*a*) *General Measures—Rest in Bed.*—In any well-marked case of malarial fever it is prudent, if possible, to confine the patient to his bed at least until all febrile symptoms are past. This is unfortunately by no means always possible, as those who live in malarious districts often regard a chill as a relatively unimportant affair. The success, however, of treatment is considerably increased if we can keep the patient absolutely quiet for several days. There is a great difference, for instance, between the course which a mild tertian infection will pursue in an individual who keeps about his business and that in one who is willing to give from several days to a week to thorough treatment. Not infrequently the symptoms as well as the parasites disappear of themselves after a few days' rest in bed even without specific treatment. Generally, however, in such instances a relapse occurs.

Change of Surroundings.—If the patient's permanent place of residence or business be in a very malarious district, it is important, if possible, that he should be removed to more healthy surroundings. Treatment is usually considerably more efficacious if the sufferer can seek a high healthy region. This is, however, not an absolute necessity, and in a great majority of instances judicious treatment is followed by complete recovery wherever the patient be. It is important, however, if he be in a malarious district, that he should sleep in the upper part of the house, that he be warned against sitting out of doors at night during convalescence, and, further, that he be prevented, if possible, from fresh exposure to infection.

Exposure to the Air.—There are regions where experience has led the inhabitants to believe, and possibly justly, that exposure to the night air or sleeping with the windows open is liable to be followed by infection. In such regions the traveler may do well to follow the advice of the experienced residents. Under ordinary circumstances there is, however, no reason whatever why the malarial patient should be prevented from exposing himself in a normal manner to the fresh air by day or night. Certainly in the malarious districts in this country there is no reason to restrain an individual from sleeping with his windows open if he be used to it, provided he is in the upper part of the house. As I have observed in a recent article, there is no fever which we know to-day which is aggravated by fresh air and open windows, provided the individual be accustomed to them beforehand. There are facts which suggest that it may be important to protect one's self in a malarious district from the bites of mosquitoes or other suctorial insects. It is advisable to sleep under a mosquito netting.

Diet.—In the regularly intermittent fevers there is no reason to restrict the patient's diet. During the height of the paroxysm the invalid will naturally manifest little desire for food, and there is no reason why he should be compelled to take it.

In the more severe and continued æstivo-autumnal fevers a liquid diet may be given, or a soft diet consisting of broths, soups, milk, raw or soft-boiled eggs, etc.; and if there be no intestinal symptoms, more solid food may be administered, particularly if the patient desire it.

Where there are marked gastro-intestinal symptoms great care must, of course, be exercised with regard to the diet. Easily digested liquid foods, such as boiled or sterilized milk, albumen water made from the whites of eggs, broths, and soups should alone be administered.

(b) *Medicinal Treatment—Quinine.*—We are fortunate in possessing a true specific against infections with the malarial parasites. This remedy was introduced into Europe by Del Cinchon, in 1640. The wife of Cinchon, who was the Spanish governor of Peru, had recovered from a severe attack of intermittent fever after taking a powder prescribed by a *corregidor* of Loxa. The remedy had been used in this region by the Indians, who had discovered its value in the treatment of the malarial fevers. The powder introduced into Europe was first known as the " powder of the countess," and afterward as the "Jesuit's powder," as it had been brought into general use by the Jesuits in Rome in 1649.

It was prepared from the bark of a Peruvian tree, whence the name applied to it for years—*Peruvian bark*. Its officinal name—cinchona—is derived from that of Del Cinchon, who introduced it into the civilized world. It was first used in the form of pulverized bark, which contains a considerable quantity of tannin in addition to various other alkaloidal substances. The powdered bark has in great part fallen out of use, its place having been taken by various salts of its active alkaloidal principle, quinine.

Action of Quinine on the Malarial Parasite.—For centuries after the introduction of quinine and after its specific effect on malarial fever had been discovered the exact mode of action remained unknown. In 1867 Binz[*] correctly concluded that the efficacy of quinine in paludism depended upon its action as a protoplasmic poison upon some lower organism, which he assumed to be the cause of the process. The extremely toxic action of quinine upon the infusoria was at that time well known.

Since the discovery of the malarial parasite various attempts have been made to study the direct action of quinine upon the hæmatozoa. Laveran noted the immediate disappearance of the parasites following the administration of quinine, and in 1881 asserted that "it is because it destroys the parasite that quinine causes the disappearance of the manifestations of paludism." He showed that by allowing a 1-to-10,000 solution of quinine to run under the cover glass the movements of the parasite were immediately arrested, as they are upon subjecting the organism to any other protoplasmic poison.

Golgi[†] studied the action of quinine on the tertian and quartan parasites. He observed that after the administration of the drug the quartan organism in its endoglobular stage shows a coarser granulation with a metallic reflex, while the protoplasm is cloudy. Abortive segmenting forms sometimes occur, smaller than the normal sporulating body, with fewer and irregularly arranged segments. The pigment also may not collect as sharply in a clump in the middle of the parasite.

---

[*] Centralblatt f. d. med. Wiss., 1867, p. 308.
[†] Deutsch. med. Woch., 1892, 661, 695, 707, 729.

In the tertian organism the changes are more noticeable, owing to the greater normal activity of the parasite. The body becomes round and motionless, and shows a sharper outline than usual, while the pigment has a peculiar metallic reflex and tends to collect in clumps. Full-grown tertian forms may present a large transparent swollen appearance, with very active movements of the pigment granules. Sometimes the pigment may collect toward the periphery, leaving a hyaline space in the middle.

Mannaberg * observed that three hours after the administration of 0·5 gramme (gr. vijss.) of quinine the amœboid forms of the tertian parasite show a marked diminution in their activity. Several hours later the number has greatly diminished, while many of those present become fragmented, resulting in the presence of several separate spherules in the red corpuscle. In the full-grown forms the pigment loses its motility while the substance of the parasite takes on a somewhat refractive homogeneous appearance. Large hydropic forms with active pigment may also be seen. These two latter forms may occur normally during the paroxysm, as Golgi and Mannaberg have both noted; they are probably degenerate forms.

I have also observed in the case of the tertian parasite the somewhat greater refractiveness of the organism, the collection of the pigment into clumps, and the cessation of active movements, as well as the presence of a greater number of fragmenting forms.

Romanovsky † and Mannaberg ‡ studied the staining re-

---

* *Loc. cit.*
† Cent. für Bakt., 1892, xi, Nos. 6 and 7, 219; and St. Pet. med. Woch., 1891, Nos. 34, 35.
‡ *Loc. cit.*, and Cent. für klin. Med., 1891, No. 27.

actions of the parasite after treatment with quinine. Both observers describe a loss of affinity for coloring matters in the chromatin substance of the so-called nucleus. They also note that in the segmenting forms, after quinine has been given, the greater number of the segments show no nucleoli. These changes in the nucleus they believed to be evidence of a necrotic process. The segments without nucleolus Mannaberg terms "stillborn."

Baccelli* noted that in æstivo-autumnal fever, after the intravenous injection of quinine, there was at first an increase in the activity of the small amœboid forms, which, later, often inside of twenty-four hours, disappeared without showing any outward signs of degeneration.

Marchiafava and Bignami,† who also studied the æstivo-autumnal fevers, observed that the administration of quinine is followed by an increase in the number of shrunken, brassy-colored parasitiferous corpuscles. They believe that the included parasites are incapable of further development.

Experience has shown the correctness of Golgi's conclusion, that in tertian and quartan fever quinine acts most markedly on the free young segments and sporulating bodies, less upon the more advanced forms where the red corpuscle is in greater part destroyed, and least upon the young endoglobular forms. If quinine be administered several hours before the paroxysm, it will not prevent segmentation, but it will destroy the new group of parasites, the fresh segments. Segmentation takes place, toxic substances are produced and enter into the circulation, and the chill follows, being at most a little modified or retarded. The new group of organisms is,

---

* Deutsch. med. Woch., 1892, No. 32, 721.   † *Loc. cit.*

however, destroyed, and the parasites disappear from the circulation.

Marchiafava and Bignami* arrive at the same conclusion in the case of the æstivo-autumnal parasite. They state " that the maximum and most rapid action of the remedy is exercised on that phase of the extra-globular life of the parasite which follows the completed segmentation." They confirm Golgi's observation that, in the case of the tertian and quartan organisms, the segmentation can not be prevented if quinine be given after the parasite has reached the preparatory stages. "Quinine," they say, " acts on the amœba of malaria during those phases of its life in which it absorbs nourishment and develops; when the nutritive activity comes to an end, the transformation of hæmoglobin into black pigment having been accomplished, and the phase of reproduction begins, then quinine becomes inefficacious against this process."

To prevent the further development of a group of malarial organisms, quinine should be in solution in the blood at the time of setting free of the fresh parasites—i. e., during and several hours before the paroxysm. In tertian or quartan fever, moderate regular daily doses of quinine will result in the disappearance of the parasites from the peripheral circulation inside of three days. In æstivo-autumnal fever the time may be a little longer. The crescentic bodies are affected slowly, if at all, by the drug; they remain in the blood long after all other forms of the parasite have disappeared.

Effect of Quinine upon the Human Being.—Small therapeutic doses produce no subjective symptoms. Larger doses are, however, followed by ringing in the ears, roaring and tinkling noises, and, finally, by marked deafness. Still larger

---

* *Loc. cit.*

doses may result in dimming of vision, and, indeed, in complete blindness. Sometimes this may begin in one eye, and, indeed, it may remain unilateral for a considerable length of time. The pupils are usually dilated. There is an extensive literature on the amblyopias following quinine. The subject is well discussed by De Schweinitz.* Severe frontal headache, with giddiness and staggering gait, delirium, and great muscular weakness, may follow larger doses, and, finally, if still larger amounts be given, convulsions and death may occur.

A variety of cutaneous disturbances may follow large doses of quinine. Urticaria is not very infrequent. Sometimes this may assume a most striking morbiliform appearance, while in other instances a well-marked scarlatinoid rash occurs, followed, perhaps, even by desquamation.

Form in which Quinine should be given. Method and Time of Administration.—The exact form in which quinine is to be administered, the manner of administration, and the time at which it should be given are extremely important points. A neglect of proper consideration of these questions is responsible for many instances of relapse, of grave postmalarial phenomena, and of chronic malarial cachexia. There is scarcely another drug in the pharmacopœia, unless it be digitalis, which is more abused than quinine. The dictum of Laveran, " In a general way it may be said that in malarial districts far too much sulphate of quinine is given to patients who have no need of it, while a sufficient quantity is not given to patients suffering from paludism," is well justified. The lax way in which it is sometimes given is comparable with the manner in which two other equally valuable drugs—

---

* The Toxic Amblyopias, etc., 8vo, Phila., 1896.

mercury and iodide of potassium—are misused. Owing to its very efficacy, and to the fact that a few doses are often followed by complete disappearance of the symptoms, the patient and, unfortunately, sometimes the physician, fail to recognize the importance of continued treatment; the regular *régime* is abandoned, and relapses and cachexia follow.

The following tables, taken from Laveran, show the percentage of quinine in the different salts of the alkaloid, as well as their relative solubility.

SALTS OF QUININE CLASSIFIED ACCORDING TO THE PERCENTAGE OF THE ALKALOID WHICH THEY CONTAIN.

			Quinine, per cent.
100 parts of the basic muriate	of quinine contain	81·71
" " neutral muriate	" "	81·61
" " basic lactate	" "	78·26
" " basic hydrobromate	" "	76·60
" " basic sulphate	" "	74·31
" " basic sulphovinate	" "	72·16
" " neutral lactate	" "	62·30
" " neutral hydrobromate	" "	60·67
" " neutral sulphate	" "	59·12
" " neutral sulphovinate	" "	56·25

SALTS OF QUININE CLASSIFIED ACCORDING TO THEIR SOLUBILITY IN WATER (REGNAULD AND VILLEJEAN).

		Water, per cent.
1 part of the neutral hydrochlorate of quinine is soluble in	0·96
" " neutral sulphovinate " "	0·70
" " neutral lactate " "	2·00
" " basic sulphovinate " "	3·30
" " neutral hydrobromate " "	6·33
" " neutral sulphate " "	9·00
" " basic lactate " "	10·29
" " basic hydrochlorate " "	21·40
" " basic hydrobromate " "	45·02
" " basic sulphate " "	581·00

How and in what form shall we give quinine? The drug may be administered: 1, by the mouth; 2, hypodermically; 3, intravenously; 4, by the rectum.

1. *Administration of Quinine by the Mouth.*—Under ordinary circumstances quinine is given by the mouth, and, unless the symptoms be severe or the stomach very irritable, this is the simplest and best manner of administratration. For such purposes the basic sulphate of quinine is generally used. This is the most inexpensive preparation of the drug, and contains a good proportion of quinine. It is, however, extremely insoluble in water.

The best method of administering the sulphate of quinine is in water containing a sufficient quantity of dilute hydrochloric or sulphuric acid to hold the salt in solution. But little is required, the druggist ordinarily adding about a drop of the dilute acid to 0·065 gramme (gr. j) of the salt. The taste is very bitter and unpleasant; it may be somewhat masked by preparations of ginger.

Quinine may be given in the form of capsules or pills. The former are better than the latter, though, owing to the fact that they are so inexpensive, pills are very frequently administered. One should be very careful in prescribing pills, particularly in country districts, as quinine pills are very often so hard and insoluble as to be of little practical therapeutic value while their adulteration is, alas, only too common.

2. *The Hypodermic Use of Quinine.*—The hypodermic use of quinine is adapted to those cases where it is impossible to give the drug by mouth, or, more particularly, to cases of such marked severity that it is desirable to obtain immediate effect. De Beurmann and Villejean use the following formula:

R̃ Dihydrochlorate (bimuriate) of quinine................... 5·0
   Distilled water, q. s. ad.................................. 10·0

One cubic centimetre (♏ xv) of this solution contains 0·5 gramme (gr. vijss.) of quinine.

If the dihydrochlorate of quinine is inaccessible, the sulphate may be used as follows:

Sulphate of quinine	1·0
Tartaric acid	0·5
Distilled water	10·0

The officinal *bisulphate of quinine* is soluble in nine or ten parts of water, and may be used hypodermically if a more soluble salt can not be obtained.

An excellent salt for hypodermic use is the *bimuriate of quinine and urea*, which contains nearly eighty per cent of quinine, and is soluble in less than its own bulk of water.

The hypodermic use of quinine may be followed by a certain amount of pain, and there is always danger of subsequent abscess or necrosis. If the solution be prepared freshly, however, and the instruments be carefully sterilized, an abscess rarely results. The injection should always be made deeply, well into the subcutaneous tissue. If the needle be too superficially introduced, so that the solution is injected into the deeper part of the skin, extensive necrosis may follow.

3. *The Intravenous Administration of Quinine.*—Baccelli[*] emphasizes particularly the value of the intravenous administration of quinine in pernicious cases. He uses the following solution:

Dihydrochlorate of quinine	1·0
Chloride of sodium	0·075
Distilled water	10·0

The solution should be perfectly clear, and is to be injected lukewarm. Baccelli thus describes the procedure: "After the veins of the forearm have been made turgescent by means of a circular tourniquet, we introduce a **Pravaz**

---

[*] *Loc. cit.*

needle from below upward into the lumen of a vein. We select a small one, in order to avoid hæmorrhage afterward. Generally we are accustomed to select one situated upon the flexor side of the forearm. The syringe holds five cubic centimetres, and is filled according to the dose which is to be given and connected with the needle before its introduction." The most rigid antisepsis should be observed. The stab wound is closed with collodion after the needle has been withdrawn. I have used this method in several instances with excellent result.

4. *The Rectal Administration of Quinine.*—The rectal administration of quinine is unsatisfactory, and need rarely be resorted to. Sometimes, however, it may be attempted in the case of children. Easily soluble salts must be used.

Time at which Quinine should be given.—It may be remembered that Laveran, Golgi, Mannaberg, and others, have demonstrated that quinine acts with the greatest efficacy upon the parasite at the time when it is free in the blood as a segmenting body or a young spore, just before entering the red corpuscle. When we consider the close relation existing between the development of the parasites and the symptoms of the disease, we might, it would seem, be justified in concluding that the period just before and during the paroxysm would be that at which quinine should have its best effect. It has, in fact, been shown that this is the case. If in one of the regularly intermittent fevers quinine be given shortly before a paroxysm, the course of that individual paroxysm will be quite unaffected, and on examination of the blood sporulating bodies may be seen. On the following day, however, we fail to find any evidence of half-grown forms, while at the time when the paroxysm ought next to occur no symptoms follow.

Thus in the regularly intermittent fevers a single moderate dose of quinine given just before or during the paroxysm is often sufficient to completely terminate the manifestations due to that group of parasites. By a single dose of quinine we may, in double tertian infections, change a quotidian to a tertian chart, one group of the organisms having been removed (*vide* Chart No. V, page 118). The same is true in æstivo-autumnal infections, though the parasites are much less readily affected by quinine.

Treatment of the regularly Intermittent Fevers.—It is best, if possible, to confine the patient to bed during the first several days, and to begin immediately regular treatment with moderate doses of quinine, 0·13 to 0·325 gramme (gr. ij to v), every four hours. It is often wise to administer a single larger dose, 0·325 to 0·65 gramme (gr. v to x), just before an expected paroxysm, though, if the patient be kept in bed, a majority of cases will rapidly recover under doses as small as 0·13 gramme (gr. ij) every four hours.

The parasites of tertian and quartan fever disappear from the blood usually in from twenty-four to seventy-two hours after the beginning of the administration of regular doses of quinine. If it be impossible to keep the patient under systematic treatment for a few days, particularly if he insist upon keeping about his business, it may be necessary to give larger doses, and to be careful that the largest doses are administered just before or during the paroxysm. In such instances it is usually best to give as much as 0·325 gramme (gr. v) every four hours, and perhaps to administer 0·65 gramme (gr. x) before each of the first two expected paroxysms.

It is surprising how obstinate certain instances of tertian and quartan malaria may be in patients who keep on their feet and about, when the process is so rapidly controlled if they are kept quiet and in bed. After the treatment has been continued for several days or a week and the parasites have wholly disappeared from the blood, it is still important to continue small doses, 0·4 gramme (gr. vj) in twenty-four hours for at least three weeks. Many observers insist on the value of larger doses given on the seventh, fourteenth, and twenty-first days after the last paroxysm.

Treatment of the Æstivo-autumnal Fevers.—We should always endeavor to keep the patient in bed during the first days of treatment. In æstivo-autumnal fever larger doses of quinine must generally be administered. We are in the habit of beginning immediately with 0·325 gramme (gr. v) every four hours, and this may often be continued for as much as a week, unless it be followed by cinchonism. After this smaller doses, 0·4 gramme (gr. vj) in the twenty-four hours, may be given. It is prudent here, if a patient come under observation during a paroxysm, to begin treatment with a larger dose, 0·65 gramme (gr. x); and if after the beginning of treatment well-marked paroxysms occur, this dose may be repeated as soon as a distinct rise in temperature becomes evident. In cases where the symptoms are very severe it may be necessary to give larger doses, though more than one gramme (gr. xv) need rarely be administered. It may, however, be advisable to give several doses of this size at intervals of three or four hours during a long-continued paroxysm. Usually two or three doses at intervals of four hours are sufficient; afterward the quinine may be reduced to 0·325 gramme (gr. v) every four hours.

If there be grave nervous manifestations, or symptoms of collapse suggesting the possible development of a pernicious paroxysm, or in cases with marked gastro-intestinal disturbances, quinine should be given hypodermically or intravenously in doses of one gramme (gr. xv). Several such doses at intervals of four hours will usually prevent any further dangerous manifestations from this group of parasites, though it may be that a severe and perhaps fatal paroxysm may occur within forty-eight hours, due to another group of organisms which have been unaffected by the drug.

Marchiafava and Bignami* assert that in very rare instances they have seen a recurrence of the symptoms after four or five days of complete apyrexia despite the continued use of quinine. These recurrences they believe to be due to the awakening of some forms of the parasites which have been unaffected by treatment, forms which preserve the infection in a latent condition. These successive groups of parasites may, however, be destroyed in the ordinary way by quinine, and the infection eventually eradicated, by means of a sort of fractional sterilization, as it were.

In true pernicious paroxysms the dihydrochlorate should be given intravenously. Baccelli asserts that the results are materially better than those following the hypodermic use of the drug. Doses larger than one gramme (gr. xv) are rarely necessary.

Malarial Hæmoglobinuria. — Bastianelli's † conclusions with regard to the use of quinine in malarial hæmoglobinuria are so good that we shall trespass largely upon them. He very justly and emphatically says that "the rational specific treatment of hæmoglobinuria is impossible without an accurate examination of the blood."

If the attack occur spontaneously with a malarial paroxysm, the blood showing the presence of parasites, quinine should be freely administered hypodermically or intrave-

---

* *Op. cit.* † *Op. cit.*

nously. Vernazza,* who reports thirty cases, asserts that four grammes hypodermically, in doses of one gramme every six hours, is usually sufficient to overcome the manifestations, though he has given as much as from six to eight grammes in twenty-four hours.

If the parasites have disappeared, either as a result of the paroxysm itself or of doses of quinine already given, it may be as well to abstain, at least for a time, from the administration of the drug. It can not ameliorate the further course of the paroxysm, and the possibility, if it has been already given, that the symptoms may be in part due to quinine may be thought of.

If an attack arise in the middle of an ordinary malarial infection, after the taking of quinine, it is best to abstain for a time, at any rate, from the further use of the drug. That which has been given may have been enough to control the affection.

If, however, in an attack coming on after quinine, the parasites continue to develop, quinine should be again administered despite the slight possibility of its injurious action. The dangers from the further development of the parasite are probably the greater.

In post-malarial hæmoglobinuria quinine is, of course, useless.†

---

* Gaz. d. osp., 1895, xvi, 235.

† The differences of opinion which exist in different parts of this country with regard to the advisability of the use of quinine in malarial hæmoglobinuria are notorious. They probably depend upon the fact that the term "malarial hæmoglobinuria" covers a number of varying conditions. No one, I think, believes that quinine has any beneficial effect on hæmoglobinuria as such; it acts favorably only in so far as it removes the cause, which it does if that is an acute malarial infection. Quinine, probably, never shortens an attack of hæmoglobinuria once begun, but it prevents a recurrence. Some malarial hæmoglobinurias, as Plehn and others have shown,

Contra-indications to Quinine—Cinchonism.—Certain individuals are very susceptible to quinine, disagreeable symptoms being produced by surprisingly small doses. It is not infrequent for the physician to meet with persons who assert that they "can not take quinine." It must be stated, however, that the majority of these complaints are based upon the fact that the drug has been administered in injudiciously large doses. Many patients who experience very severe and annoying symptoms from ten grains of quinine may take smaller and sufficiently efficacious doses without any disagreeable effects. I have never observed but one case in which it was impossible to administer doses of quinine sufficient to control ordinary malarial infections. This instance occurred in a colleague, formerly one of the resident physicians in this hospital. Very small doses of quinine or other cinchona derivatives produced with him the most distressing symptoms. Thus 0·13 gramme (gr. ij) of the sulphate of quinine were followed in half an hour by a feeling of oppression in the epigastrium, nausea, and vomiting. This was rapidly succeeded by a hot, pricking sensation over the entire skin and an intense erythema. On one occasion there was a deep scar-

---

are followed by spontaneous recovery, some—the majority in some districts, perhaps—are truly post-malarial in nature, the immediate exciting cause being unknown. In both of these conditions quinine is unnecessary. But while in many of these instances quinine is of no use, there is little to prove that its judicious employment is harmful excepting in the very rare instances of true quinine hæmoglobinuria. The microscope will always give us the clew to proper treatment. But what are we to do when we are called to a case of hæmoglobinuria in a malarial patient under conditions such that we can not fall back upon the microscope? The safest answer would appear to be: If there be any reason to believe that there is still an active malarial infection, quinine should be administered.

A careful study of the hæmoglobinurias of the South in the light of the recent advances in our knowledge of the malarial fevers is urgently demanded.

latinoid rash, lasting for hours, and followed by desquamation. Again, after 0·2 gramme (gr. iij) of salicylate of cinchonidia there was a most intense general urticaria.

Cases of this nature are rare, and there are probably few individuals in whom the susceptibility to quinine is so marked that the drug can not be introduced in proper doses. It is sometimes necessary, however, on account of the prejudice in the mind of the patient, to introduce quinine in some unfamiliar form.

Other Cinchona Derivatives.—Other cinchona derivatives—cinchonin, cinchonidin, quinidia, and quinoidia—have been recommended. Their efficacy, however, is far below that of quinine, and the occasions for their use are limited.

Methylene Blue.—This drug has been of late years considerably used in the treatment of malarial fever. Its employment was suggested by Guttmann and Ehrlich in 1891.* These observers were led to their experiments by the observation of Celli and Guarnieri that the malarial parasites might be stained while yet alive by this substance. It was noted that the drug in moderate doses exercised a marked effect upon the malarial process, and subsequent observers have confirmed these results. In a considerable number of instances the fever disappears and the parasites are no longer to be found in the blood. Further observations have, however, shown that it is far less efficacious than quinine, while from our cases † it would appear that the parasite may acquire a tolerance of the drug.

In mild cases it may be given in capsules in doses of 0·13 gramme (gr. ij) every four hours. Larger doses have been

---

* Berl. klin. Woch., 1891.
† Johns Hopkins Hosp. Bull., 1892, 49.

given without ill effect, as much as three grammes (gr. xlv) in twenty-four hours.

Occasionally the administration of the drug may be followed by distressing symptoms of strangury. These may, however, be prevented by the administration of small quantities of powdered nutmeg. After ingestion of methylene blue the urine has a deep-blue color, while the fæces become blue after exposure to the air. The drug is far less efficacious than quinine, and the occasions for its use are probably very few.

Phenocoll.—In Italy the hydrochlorate or acetate of phenocoll, a derivative of phenacetine, has been used in the treatment of malarial fever with apparently some success. It has been particularly advised in the treatment of malaria in children; the dose for an adult is about one gramme (gr. xv).

Other Remedies.—Numerous other drugs have at one time or another been used in the treatment of paludism. *Cocaine, strychnine, sulphur, arsenic, alum,* preparations of *eucalyptus* and *helianthus,* have all been used. None are of any real value excepting arsenic, which will be spoken of later.

In conclusion, it may be wise to emphasize the fact that in quinine we have so efficacious a remedy that unless its administration be actually impossible it is quite unnecessary to search for other means of arresting the disease.

Further Treatment.—Besides the treatment by the specific drug, there are numerous manifestations, as in any infectious disease, which call for symptomatic treatment.

For a long time the value of purging has been insisted upon by many observers, and it is not impossible that the old method of initiating the treatment of malarial fever by a mercurial purge may be good practice. In cases where there are grave intestinal symptoms it should, however, be avoided.

310   LECTURES ON THE MALARIAL FEVERS.

Vomiting and *purging* during the paroxysm, if severe, should be controlled by morphine administered hypodermically.

Excitement and *active delirium* during the febrile period may also require the use of morphine.

In *collapse* occurring during a pernicious paroxysm active stimulation must be resorted to. Alcohol, strychnine, and ether may be freely administered hypodermically. In the *algid forms* external heat should be applied and subcutaneous or intravenous infusions of physiological salt solution may be given. Large enemata of warm water or salt solution may be of asistance.

Continued *high fever* calls for cool sponging or an actual cold tub bath.

The *anæmia*, one of the most serious post-malarial symptoms, often demands active treatment. In these cases iron and arsenic are our main-stays. In most cases iron alone is sufficient, and may be given in the form of Blaud's pills, or as the tincture of the chloride in full doses. In severe cases and in all obstinate post-malarial anæmias arsenic is often very efficacious. It is generally administered in the form of Fowler's solution. One may begin with doses of three drops three times a day, and increase the dose steadily one drop every other day until the physiological effects—suffusion and injection of the conjunctivæ, diarrhœa, or gastro-intestinal symptoms—are observed. The drug may then be omitted, and after a few days' rest begun again at a lower level, and increased slowly to the highest point at which it may be maintained. Some very grave anæmias which simulate pernicious anæmia yield under arsenic where iron has but little effect. The possibility, though the occurrence is rare, of inducing a peripheral neuritis by continued treatment with arsenic is not to be forgotten.

Chronic Malarial Cachexia.—The treatment of chronic malarial cachexia is often a very difficult matter. For acute malarial symptoms when parasites are present in the blood, vigorous treatment with quinine should be at once instituted. It is important, if possible, in all these cases to remove the patient to a healthy region. While, generally, prolonged and judicious treatment will result in recovery wherever the patient be, yet there are instances in which little headway is made without removal to more healthy regions, while in the meantime the patient is subject to all manner of secondary infections. The invalid should be kept quiet; all undue exercise should be forbidden; the diet should be nourishing and simple. The patient should be allowed to be as much as possible in the fresh air and in the sun, providing it be not too hot. Bitter tonics, particularly strychnine, are often of value.

The anæmia should be treated particularly by arsenic. Indeed, in cases of long-continued malarial cachexia more beneficial results are to be obtained through arsenical treatment than by any other steps, excepting the removal of the patient to healthy regions. A very considerable proportion of the cases of malarial cachexia owe their origin to the carelessness of the patient, who does not carry out proper treatment with quinine, and fails to observe ordinary prophylactic precautions.

Post-malarial Nephritis.—There is nothing special to be noted with regard to the treatment of nephritis following malaria.

Complications.—In the treatment of any process complicating malaria the first step should always be to put an end to the malarial infection by the proper use of quinine. The complicating process may then be treated according to the usual methods.

PROPHYLAXIS.—We can not enter here into general public prophylactic measures, which are well discussed in a recent article by Guttmann.* There are, however, certain steps which one can and should take if he expect to be exposed to infection. If it be necessary for one to visit notoriously malarious districts, let him, as far as possible, choose the season at which the fevers are less prevalent. Let him select his dwelling upon high and dry ground. Let him avoid exposure at night in damp or marshy districts. Let him choose sleeping apartments in an upper story of the house. Let him always sleep under a mosquito netting.

It may be wise to boil drinking water, despite the fact that all experimental evidence speaks against the possibility of infection by this method.

Repeated observations tend to show that small doses of quinine taken continually are very efficacious from a prophylactic point of view. Monti † has recently reported good results from the administration of the sulphate of quinine in doses of 0·4 gramme (gr. vj) every other day.

Sezary, ‡ in Algiers, believed that a smaller quantity, 0·13 gramme (gr. ij) daily, was sufficient protection.

---

* Vrtljhrschr. f. gerichtl. Med., 1895, 163. † *Op. cit.*
‡ Médecihe mod., 1892.

PLATE 1.
THE PARASITE OF TERTIAN FEVER.

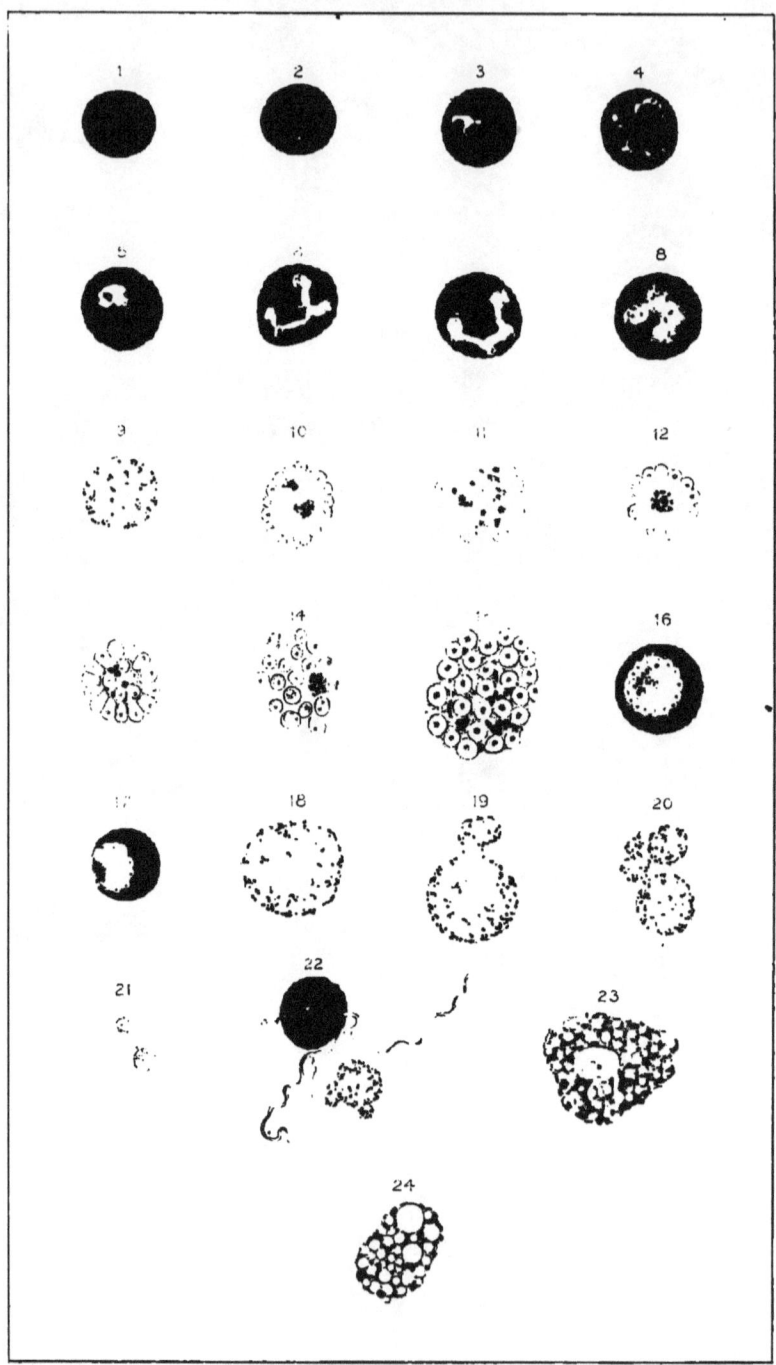

DESCRIPTION OF THE PLATES.

THE drawings * were made with the assistance of the camera lucida from specimens of fresh blood. A Winkel microscope, objective one fourteenth (oil immersion), ocular four, was used.

Figs. 4, 13, 23, and 24 of Plate I, and Fig. 18 of Plate II, were drawn from fresh blood, without the camera lucida.

PLATE I.
THE PARASITE OF TERTIAN FEVER.

1. Normal red corpuscle.
2, 3, 4. Young hyaline forms. In 4 a corpuscle contains three distinct parasites.
5, 21. Beginning of pigmentation. The parasite was observed to form a true ring by the confluence of two pseudopodia. During observation the body burst from the corpuscle, which became decolorized and disappeared from view. The parasite became almost immediately deformed and motionless, as shown in Fig. 21.
6, 7, 8. Partly developed pigmented bodies.
9. Full-grown body.
10–14. Segmenting bodies.
15. Form simulating a segmenting body. The significance of these bodies, several of which have been observed, is not clear to the writer, who has never met with similar bodies in stained specimens so as to be able to study the structure of the individual segments. They are possibly segmenting bodies which have undergone some changes in the preparation of the specimen.
16, 17. Precocious segmentation.
18, 19, 20. Large swollen and fragmenting extra-cellular bodies.
22. Flagellate body.
23, 24. Vacuolization.

---

* The writer desires here to express his gratitude to Mr. Broedel for his admirable work.

PLATE II.
The Parasite of Quartan Fever.

1. Normal red corpuscle.
2. Young hyaline form.
3–10. Gradual development of the intra-corpuscular bodies.
11. Full-grown body. The substance of the red corpuscle is no more visible in the fresh specimen.
12–15. Segmenting bodies.
16. Large swollen extra-cellular form.
17. Flagellate body.
18. Vacuolization.

PLATE III.
The Parasite of Æstivo-autumnal Fever.

1, 2. Small refractive ring-like bodies.
3–6. Larger disk-like and amœboid bodies.
7. Ring-like body with a few pigment granules in a brassy, shrunken corpuscle.
8, 9, 10, 12. Similar pigmented bodies.
11. Amœboid body with pigment.
13. Body with a central clump of pigment, in a corpuscle showing a retraction of the hæmoglobin-containing substance about the parasite.
14–19. Larger bodies with central pigment clumps or blocks.
20–24. Large bodies with central pigment blocks—presegmenting forms.
25–28. Segmenting bodies (from the spleen). Figs. 21–23 represent one body where the entire process of segmentation was observed. The segments, eighteen in number, were accurately counted before separation, as in Fig. 27. The sudden separation of the segments, occurring as though some retaining membrane were ruptured, was observed.
29–37. Crescents and ovoid bodies. Figs. 34 and 35 represent one body which was seen to extrude slowly, and later to withdraw two rounded protrusions.
38, 39. Round bodies.
40. Pseudo-gemmation, fragmentation.
41. Vacuolization of a crescent.
42–44. Flagellation. The figures represent one organism. The blood was taken from the ear at 4.15 P. M.; at 4.17 the body was as represented in Fig. 42; at 4.27 the flagella appeared; at 4.33 two of the flagella had already broken away from the mother body.

PLATE II.
The Parasite of Quartan Fever.

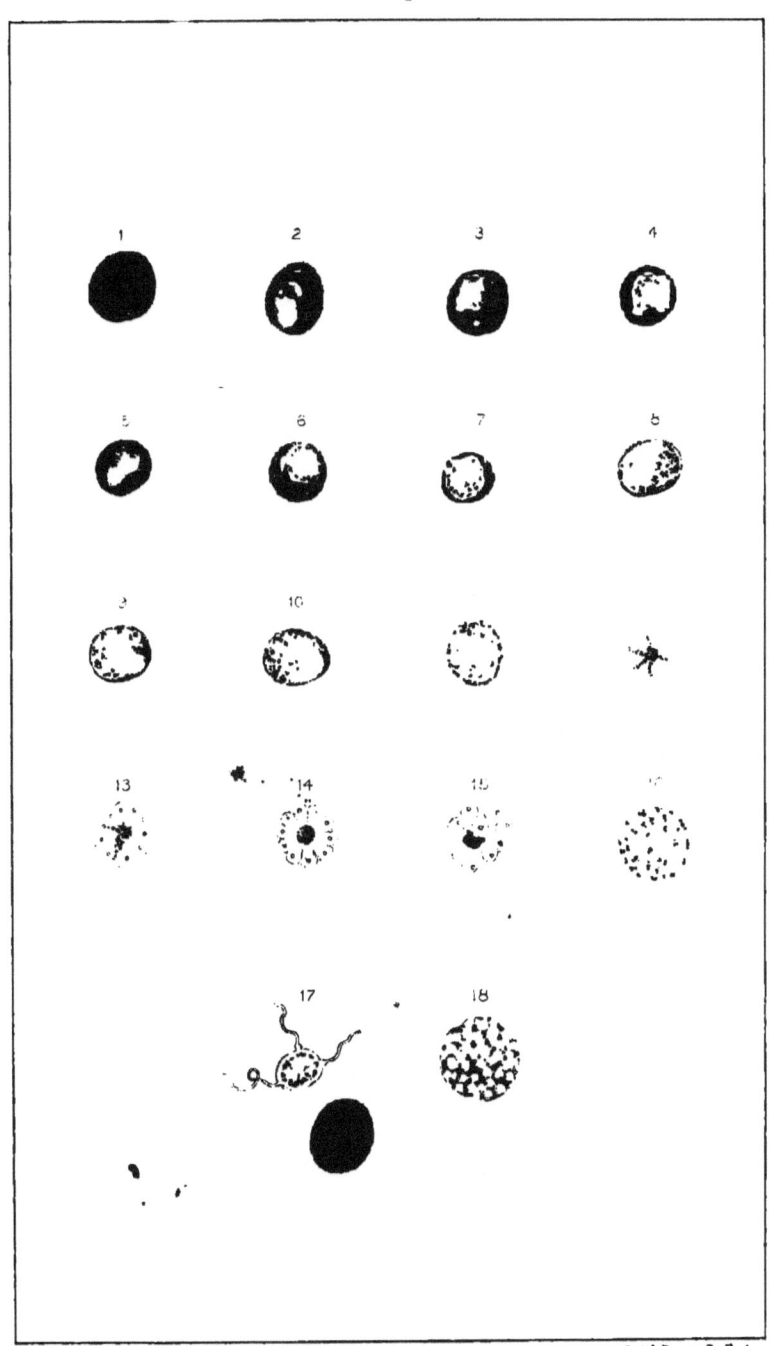

PLATE III.
The Parasite of Aestivo-Autumnal Fever.

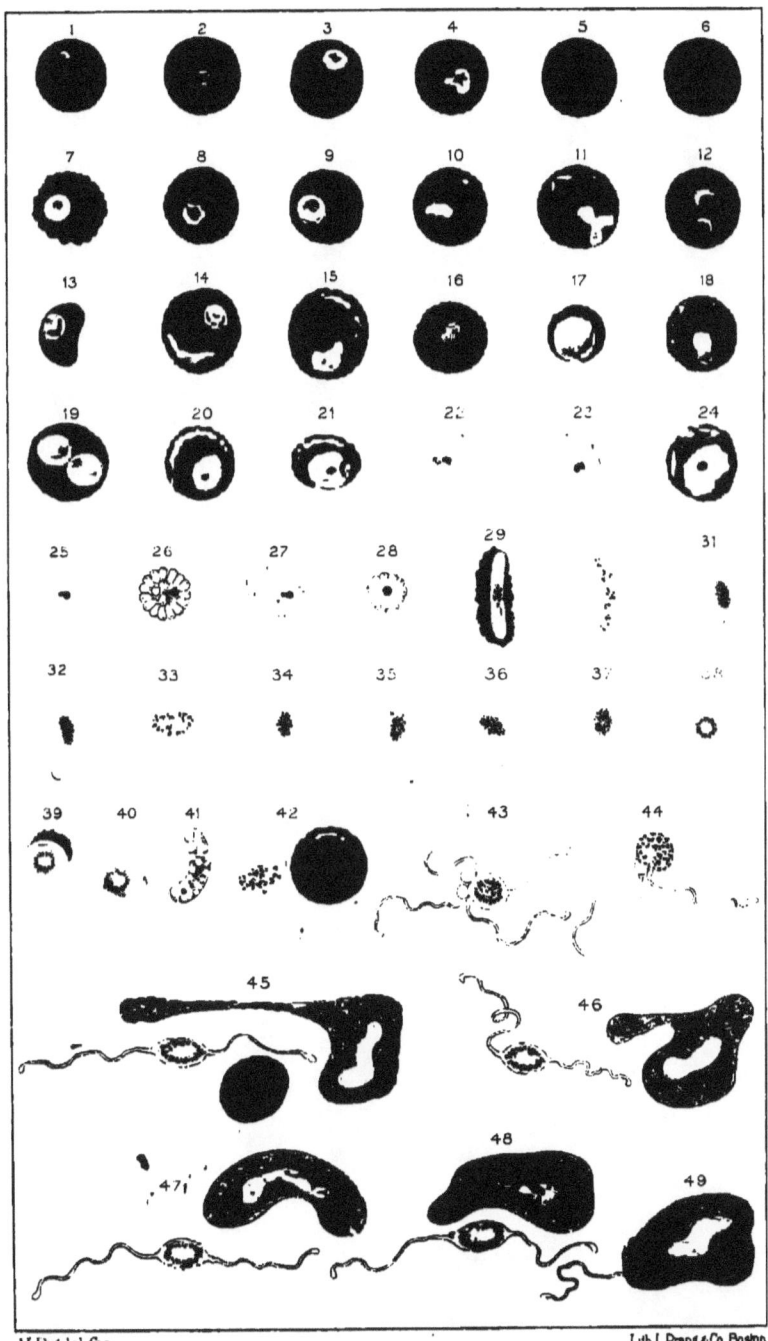

DESCRIPTION OF THE PLATES.   315

45–49. Phagocytosis.   Traced by Dr. Oppenheimer with the camera lucida.

NOTE.—These plates, produced here by permission, are essentially the same as those published in The Malarial Fevers of Baltimore, Thayer and Hewetson, Johns Hopkins Hospital Reports, vol. v, 1895, and in the article of Professor Welch in A System of Practical Medicine by American Authors, New York, Lea Brothers & Co., 1897. To the original plates, however, four drawings, Nos. 21–24 of Plate III, have been added, while other slight changes have been made in Plate I. The figures have been well reproduced by Prang from the original drawings in the shape of three plates, instead of two as previously.

INDEX OF AUTHORS.

Abbott (and Councilman), 12, 211.
Angelini (and Antolisei), 20, 29, 72, 73, 170.
Antolisei, 15, 79, 246, 247 ; (and Angelini), 20, 29, 72, 73, 170 ; (and Gualdi), 29.
Arnstein, 239.

Baccelli, 21, 29, 141, 154, 194, 247, 283, 289, 296, 301, 305.
Barker, 209, 211, 218, 221, 238, 242.
Bassi, 5.
Bastianelli, 74, 96, 158, 159, 162, 187, 188, 211, 221, 222, 224, 265, 268, 305 ; (and Bignami), 15, 20, 25, 29, 77, 78, 99, 147, 161, 165, 168, 196, 198, 209, 284, 291.
Bein, 27, 29.
Bernasconi (and Rem-Picci), 176.
Beurmann, de (and Villejean), 300.
Bignami, 74, 75, 94, 96, 102, 170, 171, 184, 195, 211, 219, 222, 225, 229, 236, 238, 242, 243, 270 ; (and Bastianelli), 15, 20, 25, 29, 77, 78, 99, 147, 161, 165, 168, 196, 198, 209, 284, 291 ; (and Dionisi), 95, 185, 188, 232 ; (and Marchiafava), 21, 23, 31, 62, 63, 68, 80, 134, 136, 145, 175, 193, 194, 220, 234, 268, 296, 297, 305.
Billings, 187.
Binz, 7, 294.
Blumer, 27, 28.
Boinet (and Salebert), 196.
Botazzi (and Pensuti), 177, 178, 181, 249.
Bouchard, 107.
Bouchardat, 6.
Boudin, 6, 205.
Brousse, 248.

Caccini (and Rem-Picci), 176.
Calandruccio, 29.
Canalis, 15, 17, 18, 21, 62, 72, 73, 169, 170.

Celli, 74, 82, 91, 147 ; (and Guarnieri), 24, 308 ; (and Marchiafava), 10, 11, 15, 16, 17, 18, 19, 21, 29, 32, 79, 197, 200, 239, 243 ; (and Sanfelice), 27 ; (and Santori), 100.
Childe, 237.
Ciarrochi (and Mariotti), 29.
Colosanti (and Iacoangeli), 181.
Coronado, 28, 31.
Councilman, 16 ; (and Abbott), 12, 211.

Da Costa, 196.
Danilevsky, 31, 73.
Del Cinchon, 293.
Dionisi, 185, 197 ; (and Bignami), 95, 185, 188, 232.
Dlauhy, 239.
Dock, 12, 15, 20, 31, 78, 211.
Dubini, 196.
Duchek, 95.

Ehrlich, 182, 189, 194, 282 ; (and Guttmann), 308.
Emin Pasha, 95.

Feletti (and Grassi), 15, 20, 22, 24, 25, 32, 47, 71, 72, 74, 79, 91.
Fischer, 26.
Flexner, 218, 238 ; (and Welch), 252.
French, 145, 289.
Frerichs, 193, 234, 235, 239.

Geppener (Heppener), 25, 26, 54, 202, 205.
Gerhardt, 28.
Giardina (and Terni), 15, 20, 73.
Golgi, 12, 13, 16, 17, 18, 21, 22, 55, 67, 69, 79, 112, 119, 169, 170, 214, 216, 245, 246, 248, 270, 294, 295, 296, 297, 302.
Gotye, 15, 20, 22, 25, 77.

Grassi, 42; (and Feletti), 15, 20, 22, 24, 25, 32, 47, 71, 72, 74, 79, 91.
Grawitz, 161, 198.
Griesinger, 95.
Gualdi (and Antolisci). 29.
Guarnieri, 26, 211, 218, 258; (and Celli), 24, 308.
Guttmann, 312; (and Ehrlich), 308.

Hamburger, 27, 28.
Heppener. See GEPPENER.
Hertz, 87.
Hewetson (and Thayer), 15, 20, 23, 202.
Hippocrates, 3.
Hischl, 239.

Iacoangeli (and Colosanti), 181.

James, 12.
Jancsó (and Rosenberger), 15.
Jones, 155.
Jourdan, 196.

Kahler (and Pick), 196.
Kalindero, 185.
Kamen, 15, 20.
Kelsch, 185, 186, 187, 197, 209; (and Kiéner), 163, 164, 224, 236.
Khetagurov, 188.
Kiéner, 233; (and Kelsch), 163, 164, 224, 236.
Kirkbride, 185.
Klebs (and Tomassi Crudeli), 7, 10.
Koplik, 15, 20.
Korolko, 15, 20.
Kruse, 38.

Labbé, 33.
Lancisi, 1, 5, 89.
Lanzi (and Terrigi), 7.
Laveran, 1, 2, 4, 8, 9, 10, 11, 16, 26, 31, 32, 78, 151, 152, 154, 211, 236, 239, 245, 251, 294, 302.
Lemaire, 6.
Lemoine (and Roque), 248, 249.
Lépine, 249.
Lodigiani, 237.

Macallum, 242.
Mannaberg, 15, 20, 23, 25, 31, 54, 63, 74, 75, 78, 295, 296, 302.

Manson, 31, 75, 80, 94, 95.
Marchiafava, 74, 147, 150, 152, 205, 214, 222, 241, 258, 259; (and Bignami), 21, 23, 31, 62, 63, 68, 80, 134, 136, 145, 175, 193, 194, 220, 234, 268, 296, 297, 305; (and Celli), 10, 11, 15, 16, 17, 18, 19, 21, 29, 32, 79, 197, 200, 239, 243.
Marino, 91.
Mariotti (and Ciarrochi), 29.
Massuriany, 107.
Mattei, di, 27, 29, 173.
Meckel, 8, 239.
Metschnikoff, 82.
Mingazzini, 32.
Mitchell, J. F., 27, 28.
Mitchell, J. K., 6.
Monti, 211, 214, 215, 216, 312.
Morton, 1, 5.
Muchry, 161.

Neumann, 240.
Nuñez y Palomino, 208.

Osler, 12, 14, 15, 32, 175.

Parkes, 87.
Patella, 15, 20.
Pensuti, 194; (and Botazzi), 177, 178, 181, 249.
Pes, 170, 263.
Planer, 239, 257.
Plehn, A., 155.
Plehn, F., 20, 31, 101, 155, 161, 164, 251, 306.
Pick (and Kahler), 196.
Poncet, 197.
Ponfick, 156.

Queirolo, 251.

Rasori, 5.
Reed, 252.
Regnauld (and Villejean), 299.
Remouchamps, 15.
Rem-Picci, 176, 177, 178, 179, 180.
Rho, 257, 281.
Richard, 10, 12, 26, 246.
Ringer, 178.
Romanovsky, 15, 24, 25, 26, 52, 54, 295.
Roque (and Lemoine), 248, 249.
Rosenbach, 27.

INDEX OF AUTHORS.

Rosenberger (and Jancsó), 15.
Ross, 80.
Rossoni, 186.
Russell, 207.

Sakharov, 15, 20, 23, 25, 27, 29, 54, 69, 74, 80.
Salebert (and Boinet), 196.
Salisbury, 6, 7.
Sanfelice, 20; (and Celli), 27.
Santori (and Celli), 100.
Schiavuzzi, 7.
Schmidt, 242.
Schweinitz, de, 298.
Sezary, 312.
Smith, F. R., 151.
Smith, Theobald, 94.
Sternberg, 12.
Sydenham, 1.

Terni, 72; (and Giardina), 15, 20, 73.
Terrigi (and Lanzi), 7.
Thayer, 188, 308; (and Hewetson), 15, 20, 23, 202.

Titov, 15, 20.
Tomaselli, 161.
Tomassi Crudeli (and Klebs), 7, 10.
Torti, A., 196.
Torti, F., 1, 2.
Trousseau, 122.

Uskov, 188.

Varro, 5.
Vernazza, 306.
Villejean (and De Beurmann), 300; (and Regnauld), 299.
Vincenzi, 170, 173.
Virchow, 8, 239.
Virey, 6.

Welch, 42, 61, 130, 166, 236, 243; (and Flexner), 252.
Wood, 7.

Zeri, 91.
Ziemann, 25, 26, 54.

GENERAL INDEX.

Age, relation of, to malarial infection, 92.
Algæ as causal elements of malarial fever, 7.
Altitude, influence of, on malarial fever, 87.
Alum, 309.
Amœba coli, 288.
Amyloid degeneration, 193, 234.
Anæmia, post-malarial, diagnosis of, 287.
   pathogenesis of, 255.
   treatment of, 310.
   types of, 188.
Animalcula as pathogenic agents of malarial fever, 5, 6.
Anticipation of paroxysms in tertian fever, 111.
   æstivo-autumnal fever, 136.
Arsenic, 309, 310.
Ataxia, 196.
Atrophy of gastro-intestinal mucosa, 194.
Auto-intoxications, post-malarial, 197, 198.

Bacillus malariæ, 7.
Bacteria as causes of malarial infection, 7.
Baltimore, deaths from malarial and typhoid fever in, 3.
Bark, Peruvian, 293.
Blood in æstivo-autumnal fever, 166.
   in amyloid degeneration, 194.
   changes in, 184.
   in chronic malarial cachexia, 192.
   methods of examination of, 34.
   platelets, confusion of, with segmenting bodies, 34.
   in post-malarial anæmia, 188, 189, 190.
   in quartan (double) infections, 127.
   (single) infections, 124.
   (triple) infections, 127.

Blood, stained specimens of, preparation of, 37.
   in tertian (single) infections, 111.
Blue, methylene, 308.
   Loeffler's, 39.
Bone marrow in malarial hæmoglobinuria, 222.
Brain in acute malarial infections, 212.
Brooklyn, deaths from malarial and typhoid fever in, 3.

Cachexia, chronic malarial, 190.
   diagnosis of, 287.
   prognosis in, 290.
   treatment of, 311.
Cerebral phenomena in æstivo-autumnal fever, 147.
   symptoms, pathogenesis of, 257.
Cheyne-Stokes respiration, 149.
Chill. See also PAROXYSMS.
   description of, 104.
   frequency of, in æstivo-autumnal fever, 132.
   in tertian infections, 105.
Chorea, electric, 196.
Cinchona, 293.
Cinchonidia, salicylate of, 308.
Cinchonidin, 308.
Cinchonin, 308.
Cinchonism, 307.
Cirrhosis and cirrhotic processes in malaria, 194, 235.
Climate, effect of, on malarial fevers, 83.
Cocaine, 309.
Coma in pernicious fever, 147, 148.
Combined infections, 172.
   diagnosis of, 278.
Complications, 200.
   diagnosis of, 288.

Complications, intestinal, 204.
  prognosis in, 290.
  pulmonary, 202.
  treatment of, 311.
Convulsions in pernicious fever, 150.
Corpuscles, red, areas of degeneration in, 11.
  changes in, 185.
  crenated, brassy colored, 18, 66, 67, 68, 267.
  destruction of, 156.
  colorless, 186.
Crescentic bodies. See PARASITES, ÆSTIVO-AUTUMNAL.
Cultivation, effects of, on malarial fever, 89.
Cutaneous manifestations during paroxysm, 107.

Delirium in pernicious fever, 150.
Diagnosis, 272.
Diarrhœa, 288.
Diet, 292.
Digestive tract as atrium of infection in malarial fever, 93.
Distribution of the malarial fevers, variations of, 92.
Drainage, effects of, on malarial fever, 89.
Dubini's disease, 196, 291.
Dysentery, 204, 288.
  amœbic, relation of, to malarial infection, 92.
  "malarial," 201.

Endocarditis, gonorrhœal, 273.
Eucalyptus globulus, 90, 309.
Exanthemata, 288.

Fever. See PAROXYSM.
Fever (febrile stage of paroxysm), 105.
  catheter, 276.
  Chagres, 83.
  malarial, æstivo-autumnal, 17, 130.
    blood in, 166.
    clinical picture of, 140.
    diagnosis of, 279.
    prognosis in, 289.
    similarity of, with typhoid fever, 140.
    tertian type of, 134.
    treatment of, 304.
    with longer intervals, 134.

Fever, malarial, anatomical changes following repeated or chronic infections, 224.
    occurring in acute malarial infections, 212.
    clinical description of, 97.
    complications of, 200.
    congenital, 95.
    continued, 136.
      due to tertian parasites, 116.
    cycles of severity of, 92.
    distribution, 82.
    endemic seats of, 82.
    general conditions of prevalence, 82.
    intermittent, pathogenesis of, 245.
    irregular, due to tertian parasites, 116.
    pathogenic agent of, 5.
    pernicious, 145.
      algid, 151.
      bilious, 153.
      cause of, 146.
      choleriform, 152.
      comatose, 148.
      diagnosis of, 284.
      gastralgic, 154.
      hæmoglobinuric, 154.
      hæmorrhagic, 152.
      pneumonic, 154.
      sudoriferous, 153.
      treatment of, 304.
    post-operative, 206.
      diagnosis of, 286
    post-partum, 206.
      diagnosis of, 286.
    pulmonary complications of, 202.
    quartan, 12, 119.
      diagnosis, 272.
      distribution of, 119.
      double infections, 125.
      parasites of. (See PARASITE, QUARTAN.)
      single infections, 119.
      triple infections, 127.
    quotidian, 113, 127, 132.
    regularly intermittent, 103.
      prognosis in, 288.
      treatment of, 303.
    relations of types of, to seasons, 84, 130.
    remittent, 136.
      diagnosis of, 279.

GENERAL INDEX. 323

Fever, malarial, tertian, 14, 103.
   clinical symptoms of, 103.
   diagnosis of, 272.
   double infections, 113.
   infections, with multiple groups of parasites, 116.
   parasites of. (See PARASITES, TERTIAN.)
   single infections, 103.
   types of, 97.
   with long intervals, 169.
   mountain, confusion of, with malarial fever, 87.
   Roman, 11.
   Texas cattle, 94.
   typhoid, 202, 276, 279, 288.
   "typho-malarial," 201, 203.
   typhus, 283.
Filaria sanguinis hominis, 94.
Forests, influence of, on malarial fever, 89.
Furunculosis, 209.

Gastro-intestinal symptoms, causes of, 258.
   tract in acute malarial infections, 219.
Gonorrhœa, 276.

Hæmamœba immaculata, 22.
Hæmamœba præcox, 22, 23.
Hæmamœba vivax, 42.
Hæmatomonas malariæ, 32.
Hæmatozoon falciparum, 130, 145.
   description of, 61.
Hæmocytozoa of malaria, description of, 42.
Hæmoglobin, 186.
Hæmoglobinæmia, 156.
Hæmoglobinuria, malarial, 154.
   anatomical changes in, 221.
   blood in, 168.
   clinical picture of, 162.
   diagnosis of, 285.
   distribution of, 155.
   prognosis in, 289.
   treatment of, 305.
   types of, 159.
   post-malarial, 160, 165, 198.
   predisposition to, 158.
   quinine, 162.
   prognosis in, 290.
   types of, 162.

Hæmosiderin, 240.
Hæmosporidia, 32.
Hallucinations in pernicious fever, 150.
Helianthus, 309.
Hemiplegia in pernicious fever, 150.
Hepatitis, malarial, 194.

Incubation, period of, 98.
   long, 101.
   variation of, 100.
Infection, malarial, acute, anatomical changes occurring in, 212.
   chronic or repeated, anatomical changes occurring in, 224.
   manner of, 93.
   mixed, 200, 208.
   diagnosis of, 288.
   septic, 209, 272, 283.
   with multiple groups of parasites, origin of, 259.
Influenza, 275.
Inoculation experiments, 26.
Insolation, 209.
Intermission between paroxysms, 109.
Intestinal phenomena in pernicious fever, 147.

Jaundice, pathogenesis of, 256.
Johns Hopkins Hospital, 69.
   deaths from malarial and typhoid fever in, 4.

Kidneys in acute malarial infections, 219.
   in chronic malarial affections, 233.
   in malarial hæmoglobinuria, 223.

Larvate malaria, 173.
Laverania malariæ, 23, 71.
Leucocytes. See CORPUSCLES, COLORLESS, also PHAGOCYTOSIS.
Leucocytosis, absence of, in malaria, 277.
   in pernicious malaria, 188.
Liver, cirrhosis of, 235.
   in acute malarial infections, 217, 218.
   in chronic malarial infections, 227.
   in malarial hæmoglobinuria, 221.

"Malaria," misuse of term, 1, 4.
Marrow, bone, in acute malarial infections, 220.
   in chronic malarial infections, 232.

Masked malaria, 173.
Mental diseases, 197.
Moisture, influence of, on malarial fever, 86.
Mosquito as agent in malarial infection, 94.
  as extra-corporeal host of malarial parasites, 94.
Murmur, splenic, 107.

Necroses, focal, 218, 238, 252.
Nephritis, malarial, 181, 192.
  diagnosis of, 287.
  prognosis in, 290.
Neuritis, peripheral, 196.
New York, deaths from malarial and typhoid fever in, 3.
Nutmeg, 309.

Occupation. relation of, to malarial infection, 93.
Orchitis, " malarial," 201, 206.
Oscillaria malariæ, 32.
Ovoid bodies. See PARASITES, ÆSTIVO-AUTUMNAL.

Pain in bones, pathogenesis of, 256.
Palmella as pathogenic agents of malarial fever, 6.
Paralyses, malarial, 195.
  prognosis in, 291.
Paralysis, bulbar, in malarial fever, 150.
Parasite, æstivo-autumnal, 16, 61.
  accumulation of, in internal organs, 18, 62, 146-148.
  aggregation of, in groups, 18, 61, 63.
  anticipation and retardation of, 64.
  crescentic and ovoid forms of, 19, 70.
  cycle of development of, 19, 63.
    length of, 19, 23, 62.
  description of, 61.
  development of, in internal organs, 21.
  flagellate forms of, 72.
  flagellation of, in stomach of mosquito, 80.
  fragmentation of, 73.
  inoculation of crescentic forms of, 75.
  multiple groups of, 64.
  pseudo-gemmation of, 73.
  reaction of, to quinine, 73.

Parasites, æstivo-autumnal, resistance of crescentic and ovoid forms of, to quinine, 20, 73.
  ring-shaped forms of, 18, 65.
  round bodies of, 72.
  segmentation of, 18, 67.
    crescentic forms of, 19.
    significance of crescentic and ovoid forms of, 20, 73.
  staining reactions of, 77.
    of crescentic forms of, 77.
  vacuolization of, 73.
  varieties of, 21.
of birds, 32.
malarial, classification of, 32.
  confusion of segmenting forms with blood platelets, 34.
  crescentic forms of, 9.
  cultivation of, 26.
  description of, 42.
  development of, within phagocytes, 270.
  discovery of, 8.
  finer structure of, 24.
  flagellate forms of, 10.
  flagellate bodies, attempts to stain, 54.
    nature of, 78.
  inoculation of, 28.
  karyokinesis in, 25.
  marguerite-like forms of, 12.
  non-pigmented forms of, 11.
  nucleolus of, 24, 25.
  nucleus of, 24, 25.
  nature of spores of, 31.
  ovoid forms of, 9.
  portal of entry of, into system, 93.
  preservation of, in leeches, 27.
  reproduction of, 31.
  ring-shaped forms of, 18, 43, 65.
  round forms of, 10.
  stability of types of, 30.
  unity or multiplicity of, 23, 24.
  variation in distribution of, 146, 212.
  varieties of, 22.
malignant tertian, 23, 63.
nature of extra-cellular form of, 50.
quartan, 12, 56.
  description of, 56.
  distinction of, from tertian parasites, 59, 278.

GENERAL INDEX. 325

Parasites, quartan, multiple groups of, 60.
  segmentation of, 58.
  quotidian, 21, 23, 63.
    pigmented, 23.
    unpigmented, 23.
  tertian, 14, 42.
    aggregation of, in groups, 42.
    description of, 42.
    distribution in the circulation of, 51.
    escape of, from corpuscle, 44.
    extra-cellular forms of, 48.
    flagellation of, 49.
    multiple groups of, 56.
    nature of flagellate bodies of, 50.
    fragmentation of, 48.
    infection with two groups of, 55.
    precocious sporulating forms of, 55.
    spores of, 47.
    sporulation of, 45.
    staining reactions of, 52.
    vacuolization of, 48.
Parotitis, 208.
Paroxysm, anticipation of, in æstivo-autumnal fever, 136.
  in tertian fever, 111.
  coincidence of, with sporulation of a group of parasites, 13.
  in children, 108.
  description of, in tertian and quartan fever, 104.
  in æstivo-autumnal fever, 132.
  duration of, in æstivo-autumnal fever, 132, 134.
  in quartan fever, 122.
  in tertian fever, 108.
  prolonged, in æstivo-autumnal fever, 136.
  retardation of, in æstivo-autumnal fever, 140.
  in tertian fever, 111.
Pernicious fever. See FEVER, PERNICIOUS.
Phagocytosis in æstivo-autumnal fever, 167, 265.
Phagocytosis in quartan fever, 125, 264.
  in tertian fever, 112, 264.
Phenocoll, 309.
Phenomena, post-malarial, 197.
Pigment, malarial, 8, 239.
"Plasmodium malariæ," 11, 32.
Pleurisy, 202, 288.
Pneumonia, 202, 288.

Pneumonia, "malarial," 201.
Polycholia, 157.
  cause of, 256.
Polyuria, post-malarial, 176.
Powder, Jesuit's, 293.
Prognosis, 288.
Prophylaxis, 312.
Psychoses, post-malarial, 197.
  prognosis in, 291.
Pyrosoma bigeminum, 94.

Quinidia, 308.
Quinine, 293.
  action of, on the human being, 297.
    on the malarial parasite, 294.
  administration of, hypodermically, 300.
    intravenously, 301.
    method of, 298.
    by mouth, 300.
    by rectum, 302.
    time for, 302.
  bimuriate of, 300.
  bisulphate of, 301.
  contra-indications to, 307.
  dihydrochlorate of, 300, 301.
  efficacy of, as protoplasmic poison, 7.
  sulphate of, 300, 301.
  time at which, is most efficacious in tertian fever, 116.
  and urea, bimuriate of, 301.
Quinoidia, 308.

Race, relation of, to malarial infection, 92.
Raynaud's disease, 197.
Relapses, 183.
  confusion of, with original attack, 88.
Remarks, introductory, 1.
Respiratory tract as atrium of infection in malarial fever, 93.
Rheumatism, acute, 209, 288.

Seasons, effect of, on malarial fever, 83.
Septicæmia—streptococcus infection, 209.
Sequelæ, 183.
"Scrafici," 5.
Severity, cycles of, in malarial fever, 92.
Sex, relation of, to malarial infection, 92.
Skin, infection through, in malarial fever, 94.
Soil, influence of, on malarial fever, 86.

Soil, interference with, effects of, on malarial fever, 89.
Spleen in acute malarial infections, 215.
  in chronic malarial infections, 224.
  in malarial hæmoglobinuria, 222.
Stain, Romanovsky's, 40.
  Geppener's modification of, 41.
Staining, methods of, 37.
Statistics, vital, 3.
Strychnine, 309.
Subcontinua biliosa, 153.
  typhoidea, 141.
Sulphur, 309.
Suprarenal capsules in acute malarial infections, 221.
Sweat, toxicity of, in malarial fever, 251.
Sweating stage of paroxysm, 108.

Table, parallel, of characteristic features of continued malarial and typhoid fever, 281.
  parallel, of characteristics of tertian and quartan parasites, 278.
  of percentage of quinine in different salts, 299.
  of solubility of different salts of quinine, 299.
Test, therapeutic, 2, 279, 281.
Tick, cattle, 94.
Time of day, effect of, on malarial fever, 83.
Tonsillitis, 209, 288.
Toxines of malaria, nature of, 253.
Treatment, 291.

Treatment, general, 291.
  medicinal, 293.
Tuberculosis, 205, 283.
  pulmonary, 274, 288.
Types of malarial fever, relations of, to the seasons of the year, 84.
Typhoid fever. See **Fever, Typhoid**.

Urine, 176.
  acidity of, 177.
  albumen in, 181.
  amount of, 176.
  bases in, 180.
  chlorides in, 179.
  color of, 177.
  diazo reaction in, 182.
  injection of, into animals, 248.
  iron in, 181.
  nitrogen in, 178.
  peptone in, 181.
  phosphates in, 179.
  potassium in, 180.
  sodium in, 180.
  solids of, 178.
  specific gravity of, 178.
  sulphates in, 179.
  toxicity of, in malarial fever, 248.
  urea in, 178.
  uric acid in, 179.
Urticaria, 107, 298.

Water, drinking, relation of, to malarial infection, 90.
Winds, influence of, on malarial fever, 89.

FINIS.

THE PRINCIPLES OF SURGERY AND SURGICAL PATHOLOGY.

General Rules governing Operations and the Application of Dressings.

By Dr. HERMANN TILLMANNS,
Professor at the University of Leipzig.

Translated from the third German edition by JOHN ROGERS, M. D., New York, and BENJAMIN TILTON, M. D., New York.

Edited by LEWIS A. STIMSON, M. D., Professor of Surgery in the University of the City of New York, Medical Department.

8vo. 800 pages. With 441 Illustrations.

Cloth, $5.00 ; sheep, $6.00.

"It was a wise combination of subjects in considering the principles of surgery and its pathology in the same treatise. It enables the surgeon to refer to both branches of the subject without loss of time, and each serves to accentuate the importance of the other. Not since Billroth's classic treatise on surgical pathology, that appeared some twenty-three years ago, has there been a more satisfactory exposition of surgical pathology than here given by Tillmanns. It is brought down to the immediate present under the light afforded by the most modern researches in bacteriology. A student should be taught pathology before he is instructed in surgical diseases and injuries. These latter he will then understand with a clearness that could not be possible if the method of teaching were reversed. The editor and the translators appreciating this fact have duly emphasized it in bringing out and making available as a text-book one of the best treatises on the principles of surgery and surgical pathology that has yet been written. It is impossible in the space now at our disposal for us to do more than express our opinion of this excellent work and to commend it to student and practitioner as a safe and scientific guide, which we do here and now."—*Buffalo Medical and Surgical Journal.*

"It is strange that this excellent work has been allowed to pass to a third edition in German without a translation into English until this time. The arrangement of the book is different from that of the average text-book on the subject. It is divided into three sections : First, General Principles governing Surgical Operations ; second, Methods of applying Surgical Dressings ; and third, Surgical Pathology and Therapy. The work of translators and editor has been excellently done. The book is printed and bound in the correct and elegant style for which the publishers are noted. The work is strictly modern, and none of the recent advances in surgical pathology have been left unconsidered."—*Chicago Medical Recorder.*

"It is just the book for surgeons who entered practice before surgical bacteriology had been developed so as to afford, as it now does, a firm foundation for the best clinical work. By its aid one's knowledge of the results of most recent investigations can be, so to speak, brought up to date. No surgeon, however experienced, can read it without having his *technique* consciously or unconsciously improved, and his grasp upon the fixed facts of surgical science made more secure. In illustrations, type, paper, and binding, Tillmanns's 'Surgical Pathology' is up to the Appleton standard, and that standard, as we all know, is unsurpassed."—*Canada Lancet.*

New York: D. APPLETON & CO., 72 Fifth Avenue.

A New, Thoroughly Revised, and Enlarged Edition of

QUAIN'S
DICTIONARY OF MEDICINE.

BY VARIOUS WRITERS.

Edited by Sir RICHARD QUAIN, Bart., M. D., LL. D., etc.,

Physician Extraordinary to Her Majesty the Queen; Consulting Physician to the Hospital
for Diseases of the Chest, Brompton, etc.

Assisted by FREDERICK THOMAS ROBERTS, M. D., B. Sc.,

Fellow of the Royal College of Physicians, etc.;

And J. MITCHELL BRUCE, M. A., M. D.,

Fellow of the Royal College of Physicians, etc.

With an American Appendix by SAMUEL TREAT ARMSTRONG, Ph. D., M. D.,

Visiting Physician to the Harlem, Willard Parker, and Riverside Hospitals, New York.

IN TWO VOLUMES.   Sold only by subscription.

This work is primarily a Dictionary of Medicine, in which the several diseases are fully discussed in alphabetical order. The description of each includes an account of its etiology and anatomical characters; its symptoms, course, duration, and termination; its diagnosis, prognosis, and, lastly, its treatment. General Pathology comprehends articles on the origin, characters, and nature of disease.

General Therapeutics includes articles on the several classes of remedies, their modes of action, and on the methods of their use. The articles devoted to the subject of Hygiene treat of the causes and prevention of disease, of the agencies and laws affecting public health, of the means of preserving the health of the individual, of the construction and management of hospitals, and of the nursing of the sick.

Lastly, the diseases peculiar to women and children are discussed under their respective headings, both in aggregate and in detail.

The American Appendix gives more definite information regarding American Mineral Springs, and adds one or two articles on particularly American topics, besides introducing some recent medical terms and a few cross-references.

The *British Medical Journal* says of the new edition:

"The original purpose which actuated the preparation of the original edition was, to quote the words of the preface which the editor has written for the new edition, 'a desire to place in the hands of the practitioner, the teacher, and the student a means of ready reference to the accumulated knowledge which we possessed of scientific and practical medicine, rapid as was its progress, and difficult of access as were its scattered records.' The scheme of the work was so comprehensive, the selection of writers so judicious, that this end was attained more completely than the most sanguine expectations of the able editor and his assistants could have anticipated. . . . In preparing a new edition the fact had to be faced that never in the history of medicine had progress been so rapid as in the last twelve years. New facts have been ascertained, and new ways of looking at old facts have come to be recognized as true. . . . The revision which the work has undergone has been of the most thorough and judicious character. . . . The list of new writers numbers fifty, and among them are to be found the names of those who are leading authorities upon the subjects which have been committed to their care."

New York: D. APPLETON & CO., Publishers, 72 Fifth Avenue.

August, 1897.

MEDICAL

AND

HYGIENIC WORKS

PUBLISHED BY

D. APPLETON & CO., 72 Fifth Avenue, New York.

AULDE (JOHN). The Pocket Pharmacy, with Therapeutic Index. A *résumé* of the Clinical Applications of Remedies adapted to the Pocket-case, for the Treatment of Emergencies and Acute Diseases. 12mo. Cloth, $2.00.

BARKER (FORDYCE). On Sea-Sickness. A Popular Treatise for Travelers and the General Reader. Small 12mo. Cloth, 75 cents.

BARKER (FORDYCE). On Puerperal Disease. Clinical Lectures delivered at Bellevue Hospital. A Course of Lectures valuable alike to the Student and the Practitioner. Third edition. 8vo. Cloth, $5.00; sheep, $6.00.

BARTHOLOW (ROBERTS). A Treatise on Materia Medica and Therapeutics. **Ninth edition.** Revised, enlarged, and adapted to "The New Pharmacopœia." 8vo. Cloth, $5.00; sheep, $6.00.

BARTHOLOW (ROBERTS). A Treatise on the Practice of Medicine, for the Use of Students and Practitioners. **Seventh edition,** revised and enlarged. 8vo. Cloth, $5.00; sheep, $6.00.

BARTHOLOW (ROBERTS). On the Antagonism between Medicines and between Remedies and Diseases. Being the Cartwright Lectures for the Year 1880. 8vo. Cloth, $1.25.

BASTIAN (H. CHARLTON). Paralyses: Cerebral, Bulbar, and Spinal. A Manual of Diagnosis for Students and Practitioners. With 136 Illustrations. Small 8vo, 671 pages. Cloth, $4.50.

BASTIAN (H. CHARLTON). Paralysis from Brain Disease in its Common Forms. With Illustrations. 12mo, 340 pages. Cloth, $1.75.

BILLINGS (F. S.). The Relation of Animal Diseases to the Public Health, and their Prevention. 8vo. Cloth, $4.00.

BILLROTH (THEODOR). General Surgical Pathology and Therapeutics. A Text-Book for Students and Physicians. Translated from the tenth German edition, by special permission of the author, by Charles E. Hackley, M. D. **Fifth American edition, revised and enlarged.** 8vo. Cloth, $5.00; sheep, $6.00.

BOYCE (RUBERT). A Text-Book of Morbid Histology. For Students and Practitioners. With 130 Colored Illustrations. Cloth, $7.50.

BRAMWELL (BYROM). Diseases of the Heart and Thoracic Aorta. Illustrated with 226 Wood-Engravings and 68 Lithograph Plates—showing 91 Figures—in all 317 Illustrations. 8vo. Cloth, $8.00; sheep, $9.00.

BRYANT (JOSEPH D.). A Manual of Operative Surgery. **New edition, revised and enlarged.** 793 Illustrations. 8vo. Cloth, $5.00; sheep, $6.00.

BURT (STEPHEN S.). Exploration of the Chest in Health and Disease. 8vo. 210 pages. With Illustrations. Cloth, $1.50.

CAMPBELL (F. R.). The Language of Medicine. A Manual giving the Origin, Etymology, Pronunciation, and Meaning of the Technical Terms found in Medical Literature. 8vo. Cloth, $3.00.

CARMICHAEL (JAMES). Disease in Children. A Manual for Students and Practitioners. Illustrated with Thirty-one Charts. 12mo, 591 pages. (STUDENTS' SERIES.) Cloth, $3.00.

CHAUVEAU (A.). The Comparative Anatomy of the Domesticated Animals. Revised and enlarged, with the co-operation of S. Arloing, Director of the Lyons Veterinary School. Second English edition. Translated and edited by George Fleming, C. B., LL. D., F. R. C. V. S., late Principal Veterinary Surgeon of the British Army; Foreign Corresponding Member of the Société Royale de Médecine, and of the Société Royale de Médecine Publique, of Belgium, etc. 8vo, 1084 pages, with 585 Illustrations. Cloth, $7.00.

CORNING (J. L.). Brain Exhaustion, with some Preliminary Considerations on Cerebral Dynamics. Crown 8vo. Cloth, $2.00.

CORNING (J. L.). Local Anæsthesia in General Medicine and Surgery. Being the Practical Application of the Author's Recent Discoveries. With Illustrations. Small 8vo. Cloth, $1.25.

DAVIDSON (ANDREW). Geographical Pathology: An Inquiry into the Geographical Distribution of Infective and Climatic Diseases. 2 vols. 8vo. Cloth, $7.00.

DENCH (E. B.). Diseases of the Ear. A Text-Book for Practitioners and Students of Medicine. With 8 Colored Plates and 152 Illustrations in the text. 8vo. Cloth, $5.00; sheep, $6.00.

DEXTER (FRANKLIN). The Anatomy of the Peritonæum. 12mo. With 39 colored Illustrations. Cloth, $1.50.

DOTY (ALVAH H.). A Manual of Instruction in the Principles of Prompt Aid to the Injured. Including a Chapter on Hygiene and the Drill Regulations for the Hospital Corps, U. S. A. Designed for Military and Civil Use. **Second edition, revised and enlarged.** 12mo. 121 Illustrations. Cloth, $1.50.

ELLIOT (GEORGE T.). Obstetric Clinic: A Practical Contribution to the Study of Obstetrics and the Diseases of Women and Children. 8vo. Cloth, $4.50.

EVANS (GEORGE A.). Hand-Book of Historical and Geographical Phthisiology. With Special Reference to the Distribution of Consumption in the United States. 8vo. Cloth, $2.00.

EWALD (C. A.). Lectures on the Diseases of the Stomach. By Dr. C. A. Ewald, Professor of Pathology and Therapeutics in the University of Berlin, etc. Translated from the German by special permission of the author, by Morris Manges, A. M., M. D. **Second edition, revised and rearranged.** Cloth, $5.00; sheep, $6.00.

FLINT (AUSTIN). Medical Ethics and Etiquette. Commentaries on the National Code of Ethics. 12mo. Cloth, 60 cents.

FLINT (AUSTIN). Medicine of the Future. An Address prepared for the Annual Meeting of the British Medical Association in 1886. With Portrait of Dr. Flint. 12mo. Cloth, $1.00.

FLINT (AUSTIN, JR.). Text-Book of Human Physiology; designed for the Use of Practitioners and Students of Medicine. Illustrated with three hundred and sixteen Woodcuts and Two Plates. **Fourth edition, revised.** Imperial 8vo. Cloth, $6.00; sheep, $7.00.

FLINT (AUSTIN, JR.). The Physiological Effects of Severe and Protracted Muscular Exercise; with Special Reference to its Influence upon the Excretion of Nitrogen. 12mo. Cloth, $1.00.

FLINT (AUSTIN, Jr.). The Source of Muscular Power. Arguments and Conclusions drawn from Observation upon the Human Subject under Conditions of Rest and of Muscular Exercise. 12mo. Cloth, $1.00.

FLINT (AUSTIN, Jr.). Physiology of Man. Designed to represent the Existing State of Physiological Science as applied to the Functions of the Human Body. Complete in 5 vols., 8vo. Per vol., cloth, $4.50; sheep, $5.50.
∗ Vols. I and II can be had in cloth and sheep binding; Vol. III in sheep only. Vol. IV is at present out of print.

FLINT (AUSTIN, Jr.). Manual of Chemical Examinations of the Urine in Disease; with Brief Directions for the Examination of the most Common Varieties of Urinary Calculi. Revised edition. 12mo. Cloth, $1.00.

FOSTER (FRANK P.). Illustrated Encyclopædic Medical Dictionary: Being a Dictionary of the Technical Terms used by Writers on Medicine and the Collateral Sciences in the Latin, English, French, and German Languages. The work consists of Four Volumes, and is sold in Parts; Three Parts to a Volume. (*Sold only by subscription.*)

FOSTER (FRANK P.). A Reference-Book of Practical Therapeutics, by various writers. In Two Volumes. Edited by Frank P. Foster, M. D., Editor of The New York Medical Journal. Vol. I. Cloth, $5.00; sheep, $6.00; half morocco, $6.50. (*Sold only by subscription.*)

FOURNIER (ALFRED). Syphilis and Marriage. Translated by P. Albert Morrow, M. D. 8vo. Cloth, $2.00; sheep, $3.00.

FREY (HEINRICH). The Histology and Histochemistry of Man. A Treatise on the Elements of Composition and Structure of the Human Body. Translated from the fourth German edition by Arthur E. J. Barker, M. D., and revised by the author. With 608 Engravings on Wood. 8vo. Cloth, $5.00; sheep, $6.00.

FRIEDLANDER (CARL). The Use of the Microscope in Clinical and Pathological Examinations. Second edition, enlarged and improved, with a Chromolithograph Plate. Translated, with the permission of the author, by Henry C. Coe, M. D. 8vo. Cloth, $1.00.

FUCHS (ERNEST). Text-Book of Ophthalmology. By Dr. Ernest Fuchs, Professor of Ophthalmology in the University of Vienna. With 178 Woodcuts. Authorized translation from the second enlarged and improved German edition, by A. Duane, M. D. Cloth, $5.00; sheep, $6.00.

GARMANY (JASPER J.). Operative Surgery on the Cadaver. With Two Colored Diagrams showing the Collateral Circulation after Ligatures of Arteries of Arm, Abdomen, and Lower Extremity. Small 8vo. Cloth, $2.00.

GERSTER (ARPAD G.). The Rules of Aseptic and Antiseptic Surgery. A Practical Treatise for the Use of Students and the General Practitioner. Illustrated with over two hundred fine Engravings. 8vo. Cloth, $5.00; sheep, $6.00.

GIBSON-RUSSELL. Physical Diagnosis: A Guide to Methods of Clinical Investigation. By G. A. Gibson, M. D., and William Russell, M. D. With 101 Illustrations. 12mo. (Student's Series.) Cloth, $2.50.

GOULEY (JOHN W. S.). Diseases of the Urinary Apparatus. Part I. Phlegmasic Affections. Being a Series of Twelve Lectures delivered during the autumn of 1891. With an Addendum on Retention of Urine from Prostatic Obstruction in Elderly Men. Cloth, $1.50.

GROSS (SAMUEL W.). A Practical Treatise on Tumors of the Mammary Gland. Illustrated. 8vo. Cloth, $2.50.

GRUBER (JOSEF). A Text-Book of the Diseases of the Ear. Translated from the second German edition by special permission of the author, and edited by Edward Law, M. D., and Coleman Jewell, M. D. With 165 Illustrations and 70 Colored Figures on Two Lithographic Plates. 8vo. Cloth, $6.50 sheep, $7.50.

GUTMANN (EDWARD). The Watering-Places and Mineral Springs of Germany, Austria, and Switzerland. Illustrated. 12mo. Cloth, $2.50.

HAMMOND (W. A.). A Treatise on Diseases of the Nervous System. With the Collaboration of Graeme M. Hammond, M. D. With One Hundred and Eighteen Illustrations. **Ninth edition**, with corrections and additions. 8vo. Cloth, $5.00; sheep, $6.00.

HAMMOND (W. A.). A Treatise on Insanity, in its Medical Relations. 8vo. Cloth, $5.00; sheep, $6.00.

HAMMOND (W. A.). Clinical Lectures on Diseases of the Nervous System. Delivered at Bellevue Hospital Medical College. Edited by T. M. B. Cross, M. D. 8vo. Cloth, $3.50.

HARVEY (A.). First Lines of Therapeutics. 12mo. Cloth, $1.50.

HIRT (LUDWIG). The Diseases of the Nervous System. A Text-Book for Physicians and Students. Translated, with permission of the Author, by August Hoch, M. D., assisted by Frank R. Smith, A. M. (Cantab.), M. D., Assistant Physicians to the Johns Hopkins Hospital. With an Introduction by William Osler, M. D., F. R. C. P., Professor of Medicine in the Johns Hopkins University, and Physician-in-Chief to the Johns Hopkins Hospital, Baltimore. 8vo, 671 pages. With 178 Illustrations. Cloth, $5.00; sheep, $6.00.

HOFFMANN–ULTZMANN. Analysis of the Urine, with Special Reference to Diseases of the Urinary Apparatus. By M. B. Hoffmann, Professor in the University of Grätz, and R. Ultzmann, Tutor in the University of Vienna. **Third edition, revised and enlarged.** 8vo. Cloth, $2.00.

HOLT (L. EMMETT). The Diseases of Infancy and Childhood. 8vo. Cloth, $6.00; sheep, $7.00; half morocco, $7.50. (*Sold only by subscription.*)

HOLT (L. EMMETT). The Care and Feeding of Children. A Catechism for the Use of Mothers and Children's Nurses. 16mo. Cloth, 50 cents.

HOWE (JOSEPH W.). Emergencies, and how to treat them. Fourth edition, revised. 8vo. Cloth, $2.50.

HOWE (JOSEPH W.). The Breath, and the Diseases which give it a Fetid Odor. With Directions for Treatment. **Second edition,** revised and corrected. 12mo. Cloth, $1.00.

HUEPPE (FERDINAND). The Methods of Bacteriological Investigation. Written at the request of Dr. Robert Koch. Translated by Hermann M. Biggs, M. D. Illustrated. 8vo. Cloth, $2.50.

JACCOUD (S.). The Curability and Treatment of Pulmonary Phthisis. Translated and edited by Montagu Lubbock, M. D. 8vo. Cloth, $4.00.

KEYES (E. L.). A Practical Treatise on Genito-Urinary Diseases, including Syphilis. Being a new edition of a work with the same title by Van Buren and Keyes. Almost entirely rewritten. 8vo. With Illustrations. Cloth, $5.00; sheep, $6.00.

KEYES (E. L.). The Tonic Treatment of Syphilis, including Local Treatment of Lesions. **Second edition.** 8vo. Cloth, $1.00.

KINGSLEY (N. W.). A Treatise on Oral Deformities as a Branch of Mechanical Surgery. With over 350 Illustrations. 8vo. Cloth, $5.00; sheep, $6.00.

LEGG (J. WICKHAM). On the Bile, Jaundice, and Bilious Diseases. With Illustrations in Chromolithography. 8vo. Cloth, $6.00; sheep, $7.00.

LITTLE (W. J.). Medical and Surgical Aspects of In-Knee (Genu-Valgum): Its Relation to Rickets, its Prevention, and its Treatment, with and without Surgical Operation. Illustrated by upward of Fifty Figures and Diagrams. 8vo. Cloth, $2.00.

LORING (EDWARD G.). A Text-Book of Ophthalmoscopy.
Part I. The Normal Eye, Determination of Refraction, and Diseases of the Media. With 131 Illustrations, and 4 Chromolithographs. 8vo. Buckram, $5.00.
Part II. Diseases of the Retina, Optic Nerve, and Choroid: their Varieties and Complications. The manuscript of this volume, which the author finished just prior to his death, has been thoroughly edited and revised by F. B. Loring, M. D., of Washington, D. C., and is now issued in the same style as the first volume. Profusely illustrated. Part II, buckram, $5.00. Two Parts, buckram, $10.00.

LUSK (WILLIAM T.). The Science and Art of Midwifery. With 246 Illustrations. **Fourth edition, revised and enlarged.** 8vo. Cloth, $5.00; sheep, $6.00.

MARCY (HENRY O.). The Anatomy and Surgical Treatment of Hernia. 4to, with about Sixty full-page Heliotype and Lithographic Reproductions from the Old Masters, and numerous Illustrations in the Text. *(Sold only by subscription.)*

MARKOE (T. M.). A Treatise on Diseases of the Bones. With Illustrations. 8vo. Cloth, $4.50.

MATHEWS (JOSEPH M.). A Treatise on Diseases of the Rectum, Anus, and Sigmoid Flexure. 8vo. With Six Chromolithographs, and Illustrations in the text. **Second edition.** *(Sold only by subscription.)*

MILLS (WESLEY). A Text-Book of Animal Physiology, with Introductory Chapters on General Biology and a full Treatment of Reproduction for Students of Human and Comparative Medicine. 8vo. With 505 Illustrations. Cloth, $5.00; sheep, $6.00.

MILLS (WESLEY). A Text-Book of Comparative Physiology. For Students and Practitioners of Veterinary Medicine. Small 8vo. Cloth, $3.00.

MORROW (PRINCE A.). A System of Genito-Urinary Diseases, Syphilology, and Dermatology. By various Authors. In Three Volumes, beautifully illustrated. Vol. I. Genito-urinary Diseases. Vol. II. Syphilography Vol. III. Dermatology. *(Sold only by subscription.)*

THE NEW YORK MEDICAL JOURNAL (Weekly). Edited by Frank P. Foster, M. D. Terms, $5.00 per annum.
Binding Cases, cloth, 50 cents each.
"Self-Binder" (this is used for temporary binding only), 90 cents.
GENERAL INDEX, from April, 1865, to June, 1876 (23 vols.). 8vo. Cloth, 75 cts.

NIEMEYER (FELIX VON). A Text-Book of Practical Medicine, with particular reference to Physiology and Pathological Anatomy. Containing all the author's Additions and Revisions in the eighth and last German edition. Translated by George H. Humphreys, M. D., and Charles E. Hackley, M. D. 2 vols., 8vo. Cloth, $9.00; sheep, $11.00.

NIGHTINGALE'S (FLORENCE) Notes on Nursing. 12mo. Cloth, 75 cents.

OSLER (WILLIAM). Lectures on Angina Pectoris and Allied States. Small 8vo. Illustrated. Cloth, $1.50.

OSLER (WILLIAM). Lectures on the Diagnosis of Abdominal Tumors. Small 8vo. Illustrated. Cloth, $1.50.

OSLER (WILLIAM). The Principles and Practice of Medicine. Designed for the Use of Practitioners and Students of Medicine. **Second edition, revised and enlarged.** Cloth, $5.50; sheep, $6.50; half morocco, $7.00. (*Sold only by subscription.*)

PELLEW (O. E.). A Manual of Practical Medical Chemistry. 12mo. With Illustrations. Cloth, $2.50.

PIFFARD (HENRY G.). A Practical Treatise on Diseases of the Skin. By Henry G. Piffard, A. M., M. D., assisted by Robert M. Fuller, M. D. With Fifty full-page Original Plates and Thirty-three Illustrations in the Text. 4to. (*Sold only by subscription.*)

POMEROY (OREN D.). The Diagnosis and Treatment of Diseases of the Ear. With One Hundred Illustrations. **Second edition,** revised and enlarged. 8vo. Cloth, $3.00.

POORE (C. T.). Osteotomy and Osteoclasis, for the Correction of Deformities of the Lower Limbs. 50 Illustrations. 8vo. Cloth, $2.50.

QUAIN (RICHARD). A Dictionary of Medicine, including General Pathology, General Therapeutics, Hygiene, and the Diseases peculiar to Women and Children. By Various Writers. Edited by Sir Richard Quain, Bart., M. D., LL. D., etc. Assisted by Frederick Thomas Roberts, M. D., B. Sc., and J. Mitchell Bruce, M. A., M. D. With an American Appendix by Samuel Treat Armstrong, Ph. D., M. D. In two volumes. (*Sold only by subscription.*)

RANNEY (AMBROSE L.). Applied Anatomy of the Nervous System, being a Study of this Portion of the Human Body from a Standpoint of its General Interest and Practical Utility, designed for Use as a Text-Book and as a Work of Reference. **Second edition, revised and enlarged.** Profusely illustrated. 8vo. Cloth, $5.00; sheep, $6.00.

ROBINSON (A. R.). A Manual of Dermatology. Revised and corrected. 8vo. Cloth, $5.00.

ROSCOE-SCHORLEMMER. Treatise on Chemistry.

Vol. 1. Non-Metallic Elements. 8vo. Cloth, $5.00.

Vol. 2. Part I. Metals. 8vo. Cloth, $3.00.

Vol. 2. Part II. Metals. 8vo. Cloth, $3.00.

Vol. 3. Part I. The Chemistry of the Hydrocarbons and their Derivatives. 8vo. Cloth, $5.00.

Vol. 3. Part II. The Chemistry of the Hydrocarbons and their Derivatives. 8vo. Cloth, $5.00.

Vol. 3. Part III. The Chemistry of the Hydrocarbons and their Derivatives. 8vo. Cloth, $3.00.

Vol. 3. Part IV. The Chemistry of the Hydrocarbons and their Derivatives. 8vo. Cloth, $3.00.

Vol. 3. Part V. The Chemistry of the Hydrocarbons and their Derivatives. 8vo. Cloth, $3.00.

ROSENTHAL (I.). General Physiology of Muscles and Nerves. With 75 Woodcuts. 12mo. Cloth, $1.50.

SAYRE (LEWIS A.). Practical Manual of the Treatment of Club-Foot. **Fourth edition, enlarged and corrected.** 12mo. Cloth, $1.25.

SAYRE (LEWIS A.). Lectures on Orthopedic Surgery and Diseases of the Joints, delivered at Bellevue Hospital Medical College. **New edition, illustrated** with 324 Engravings on Wood. 8vo. Cloth, $5.00; sheep, $6.00.

SCHULTZE (B. S.). The Pathology and Treatment of Displacements of the Uterus. Translated from the German by Jameson J. Macan, M. A., etc.; and edited by Arthur V. Macan, M. B., etc. With one hundred and twenty Illustrations. 8vo. Cloth, $3.50.

SHIELD (A. MARMADUKE). Surgical Anatomy for Students. 12mo. (STUDENT'S SERIES.) Cloth, $1.75.

SHOEMAKER (JOHN V.). A Text-Book of Diseases of the Skin. Six Chromolithographs and numerous Engravings. Second edition, revised and enlarged. 8vo. Cloth, $5.00; sheep, $6.00.

SIMPSON (JAMES Y.). Selected Works: Anæsthesia, Diseases of Women. 3 vols., 8vo. Per volume. Cloth, $3.00; sheep, $4.00.

SIMS (J. MARION). The Story of my Life. Edited by his Son, H. Marion-Sims, M. D. With Portrait. 12mo. Cloth, $1.50.

SKENE (ALEXANDER J. C.). A Text-Book on the Diseases of Women. Illustrated with two hundred and fifty-four Illustrations, of which one hundred and sixty-five are original, and nine chromolithographs. Second edition. 8vo. (*Sold only by subscription.*)

SKENE (ALEXANDER J. C.). Medical Gynecology. A Treatise on the Diseases of Women from the Standpoint of the Physician. 8vo. With Illustrations. Cloth, $5.00.

STEINER (JOHANN). Compendium of Children's Diseases: a Hand-Book for Practitioners and Students. Translated from the second German edition, by Lawson Tait. 8vo. Cloth, $3.50; sheep, $4.50.

STEVENS (GEORGE T.) Functional Nervous Diseases: their Causes and their Treatment. Memoir for the Concourse of 1881-1883, Académie Royal de Médecine de Belgique. With a Supplement, on the Anomalies of Refraction and Accommodation of the Eye, and of the Ocular Muscles. Small 8vo. With six Photographic Plates and twelve Illustrations. Cloth, $2.50.

STONE (R. FRENCH). Elements of Modern Medicine, including Principles of Pathology and of Therapeutics, with many Useful Memoranda and Valuable Tables of Reference. Accompanied by Pocket Fever Charts. Designed for the Use of Students and Practitioners of Medicine. In wallet-book form, with pockets on each cover for Memoranda, Temperature Charts, etc. Roan, tuck, $2.50.

STRECKER (ADOLPH). Short Text-Book of Organic Chemistry. By Dr. Johannes Wislicenus. Translated and edited, with Extensive Additions, by W. H. Hodgkinson and A. J. Greenaway. 8vo. Cloth, $5.00.

STRÜMPELL (ADOLPH). A Text-Book of Medicine, for Students and Practitioners. Translated, by permission, from the sixth German edition by Herman F. Vickery, A. B., M. D., Instructor in Clinical Medicine, Harvard Medical School, etc., and Philip Coombs Knapp, Physician to Out-patients with Diseases of the Nervous System, Boston City Hospital, etc. With Editorial Notes by Frederick C. Shattuck, A. M., M. D., Jackson Professor of Clinical Medicine, Harvard Medical School, etc. Second American edition. With 111 Illustrations. 8vo. 981 pages. Cloth, $6.00; sheep, $7.00.

THOMAS (T. GAILLARD). Abortion and its Treatment, from the Standpoint of Practical Experience. A Special Course of Lectures delivered before the College of Physicians and Surgeons, New York, Session of 1889-'90. From Notes by P. Brynberg Porter, M.D. Revised by the Author. 12mo. Cloth, $1.00.

THOMPSON (W. GILMAN). Practical Dietetics, with Special Reference to Diet in Disease. 8vo. Cloth, $5.00.

THOMSON (J. ARTHUR). Outlines of Zoölogy. With thirty-two full page Illustrations. 12mo. (STUDENTS' SERIES.) Cloth, $3.00.

TILLMANNS (HERMANN). The Principles of Surgery and Surgical Pathology. Translated by John Rogers, M.D., and Benjamin Tilton, M.D., New York. 8vo. With 441 Illustrations. Cloth, $5.00; sheep, $6.00.

ULTZMANN (ROBERT). Pyuria, or Pus in the Urine, and its Treatment. Translated by permission, by Dr. Walter B. Platt. 12mo. Cloth, $1.00.

VAN BUREN (W. H.). Lectures upon Diseases of the Rectum, and the Surgery of the Lower Bowel, delivered at Bellevue Hospital Medical College. **Second edition, revised and enlarged.** 8vo. Cloth, $3.00; sheep, $4.00.

VAN BUREN (W. H.). Lectures on the Principles and Practice of Surgery. Delivered at Bellevue Hospital Medical College. Edited by Lewis A. Stimson, M.D. 8vo. Cloth, $4.00; sheep, $5.00.

VOGEL (A.). A Practical Treatise on the Diseases of Children. Translated and edited by H. Raphael, M.D. **Third American from the eighth German edition, revised and enlarged.** Illustrated by six Lithographic Plates. 8vo. Cloth, $4.50; sheep, $5.50.

VON ZEISSL (HERMANN). Outlines of the Pathology and Treatment of Syphilis and Allied Venereal Diseases. **Second edition,** revised by Maximilian von Zeissl. Authorized edition. Translated, with Notes, by H. Raphael, M.D. 8vo. Cloth, $4.00; sheep, $5.00.

WAGNER (RUDOLF). Hand-Book of Chemical Technology. Translated and edited from the eighth German edition, with extensive Additions. by William Crookes. With 336 Illustrations. 8vo. Cloth, $5.00.

WALTON (GEORGE E.). Mineral Springs of the United States and Canadas. Containing the latest Analyses, with full Description of Localities, Routes, etc. **Second edition, revised and enlarged.** 12mo. Cloth, $2.00.

WEBBER (S. G.). A Treatise on Nervous Diseases: Their Symptoms and Treatment. A Text-Book for Students and Practitioners. 8vo. Cloth, $3.00.

WEEKS-SHAW (CLARA S.). A Text-Book of Nursing. For the Use of Training-Schools, Families, and Private Students. Second edition, revised and enlarged. 12mo. With Illustrations, Questions for Review and Examination, and Vocabulary of Medical Terms. 12mo. Cloth, $1.75.

WELLS (T. SPENCER). Diseases of the Ovaries. 8vo. Cloth, $4.50.

WORCESTER (A.). Monthly Nursing. **Second edition, revised.** Cloth, $1.25.

WYETH (JOHN A.). A Text-Book on Surgery: General, Operative, and Mechanical. Profusely illustrated. **Second edition. revised and enlarged.** 8vo. *(Sold only by subscription.)*

www.ingramcontent.com/pod-product-compliance
Lightning Source LLC
Chambersburg PA
CBHW020243240426
43672CB00006B/626